Coaching

Basketball

FOR

DUMMIES®

by National Alliance For Youth Sports
with Greg Bach

BICENTENNIAL
1807
WILEY
2007
BICENTENNIAL

Wiley Publishing, Inc.

Coaching Basketball For Dummies®

Published by
Wiley Publishing, Inc.
111 River St.
Hoboken, NJ 07030-5774
www.wiley.com

Copyright © 2007 by Wiley Publishing, Inc., Indianapolis, Indiana

Published by Wiley Publishing, Inc., Indianapolis, Indiana
Published simultaneously in Canada

For general information on our other products and services, please contact our Customer Care Department within the U.S. at 800-762-2974, outside the U.S. at 317-572-3993, or fax 317-572-4002.

For technical support, please visit www.wiley.com/techsupport.

Wiley also publishes its books in a variety of electronic formats. Some content that appears in print may not be available in electronic books.

Library of Congress Catalog Number: 2007935018

ISBN: 978-0-470-14976-8

Manufactured in the United States of America

10 9 8 7 6 5 4 3 2 1

WILEY

Coaching Basketball For Dummies®

Cheat Sheet

What to Bring to Practice

- ❑ A practice plan with drills broken down by time segments.
- ❑ A list of reserve drills in case any of your scheduled drills are ineffective.
- ❑ Extra basketballs and any pylons or markers you need for specific drills.
- ❑ A whistle.

- ❑ A properly stocked first-aid kit. (See Chapter 6 for a rundown of the items that should be in the kit.) Here's a quick glimpse at some of the items:
  - Sterile gauze and athletic tape
  - Bandages
  - Bags of ice
  - Latex gloves

Tips for Making Practice Fun

- ✔ Give each child plenty of repetitions.
- ✔ Keep the kids active; don't force them to stand in lines.
- ✔ Involve the parents in drills to rev up the excitement.
- ✔ Sprinkle your practices with new drills throughout the season to keep the kids' interest.
- ✔ If drills turn out to be boring or ineffective, discard them and switch to new ones.
- ✔ Give the kids the chance to select their favorite drills to use during practice.
- ✔ Solicit feedback and ideas from older kids on drills you should use.
- ✔ Stop practice briefly to point out when players do things well — not when they make mistakes.
- ✔ Applaud the slightest improvements to maintain your kids' efforts.
- ✔ Conclude practice with the most popular drill to end the session on a high note.

Tips for Keeping Players Motivated

- ✔ Continually encourage players to do their best on both ends of the floor — regardless of the score.
- ✔ Stay in control of your emotions, and refrain from yelling instructions all the time.
- ✔ Allow kids the freedom to make mistakes, and coach effort over skills.
- ✔ Always exude confidence in your players' abilities.
- ✔ When correcting errors, use words that inspire confidence and reinforce positive thoughts. For example, instead of saying, "Don't turn the ball over," say, "Control the ball just like you did so well in practice this week."
- ✔ Use timeouts to relay positive information to your players.

For Dummies: Bestselling Book Series for Beginners

Coaching Basketball For Dummies®

How to Deliver the Pre-Game Talk

- Speak in a calm and relaxed manner with a smile on your face.
- Be brief.
- Conduct the talk away from any potential distractions.
- Stress the importance of having fun and displaying good sportsmanship at all times during the game.
- Avoid using pressure phrases, like "Let's score 20 points today." Kids *can* give you their best effort, but they *can't* control the outcome of games.
- Build the kids' confidence by letting them know that you're looking forward to watching them perform.

How to Give the Post-Game Chat

- Keep the focus on the fun you had and the fun you will have.
- Don't let the scoreboard influence what you say to the kids — or how you say it.
- Recognize the good sportsmanship your players displayed.
- Accentuate the positive.
- Conclude on a high note with a team cheer and send 'em home with a smile.

How to Speak to the Team at Halftime

- Highlight the positives of the first half, regardless of the score, and stay upbeat. Don't dwell on any mistakes, because they're part of the learning process.
- Zero in on a couple main points that you want to get across. Giving the kids too much information to digest isn't productive.
- Pile on the praise for their hard work in the first half.
- At the more advanced levels, solicit feedback and suggestions on strategy from your players.
- Tell them to drink water to rehydrate!

Building Your Players' Confidence

- When providing feedback, use the "sandwich" method: Place a critical remark between two encouraging comments.
- Reinforce that making mistakes is part of the learning process. Even the pros make mistakes every game.
- Give kids high-fives and pats on the back so they know that their efforts are appreciated.
- Set realistic goals so the kids can gain a real sense of satisfaction upon reaching them.
- Maintain positive body language. Never allow your tone or body language to reveal disappointment in a child's performance or ability.

For Dummies: Bestselling Book Series for Beginners

About the Author

Greg Bach is the communications director for the National Alliance For Youth Sports (NAYS), a position he has held since 1993. Before joining NAYS, he worked as the sports editor of the *Huron Daily Tribune* in Bad Axe, Michigan, where he captured numerous writing awards from the Associated Press, Michigan Press Association, and the Hearst Corporation. He has a journalism degree from Michigan State University, which he earned in 1989. He's an avid sports fan — particularly of his beloved Spartan basketball team — and has coached a variety of youth sports. He's also the author of *Coaching Soccer For Dummies, Coaching Football For Dummies,* and *Coaching Baseball For Dummies.*

The National Alliance For Youth Sports has been America's leading advocate for positive and safe sports for children for the past 25 years. It serves volunteer coaches, parents with children involved in organized sports, game officials, youth sports administrators, league directors, and the youngsters who participate in organized sports. The Alliance's programs are utilized in more than 3,000 communities nationwide by parks and recreation departments, Boys & Girls Clubs, Police Athletic Leagues, YMCAs/YWCAs, and various independent youth service groups, as well as on military installations worldwide. For more information on the Alliance's programs, which appear in the following list, visit www.nays.org.

National Youth Sports Coaches Association — More than 2 million volunteer coaches have been trained through NYSCA, which provides training, support, and continuing education.

Parents Association for Youth Sports — Parents gain a clear understanding of their roles and responsibilities in youth sports through this sportsmanship training program, which is utilized in more than 500 communities nationwide.

Academy for Youth Sports Administrators — More than 2,000 administrators worldwide have gone through the Academy, which is a 20-hour certification program that raises the professionalism of those delivering youth sport services. A professional faculty presents the information, and participants earn Continuing Education Units (CEUs).

National Youth Sports Administrators Association — This program provides training, information, and resources for volunteer administrators responsible for the planning and implementation of out-of-school sports programs.

National Youth Sports Officials Association — Officials who go through this certification program gain valuable knowledge on skills, fundamentals, and the characteristics that every good official must possess.

Start Smart Sports Development Program — This proven instructional program prepares children for the world of organized sports (without the threat of competition or the fear of getting hurt) through an innovative approach that promotes parent-child bonding.

Hook A Kid On Golf — Thousands of children of all ages and skill levels tee it up every year in the nation's most comprehensive junior golf development program, which features an array of instructional clinics and tournaments.

Game On! Youth Sports — This worldwide effort introduces children to actual game experience by giving them the freedom to create and play on their own.

Dedication

From the National Alliance For Youth Sports: This book is dedicated to all the volunteer basketball coaches who devote countless hours of their free time to work with children and ensure that they have positive, safe, and rewarding experiences. We applaud your efforts and commend you for making a difference in the lives of youngsters everywhere.

From Greg Bach: This one's for Sandra, with all my love, for all the special times we've shared.

Author's Acknowledgments

A successful youth basketball program doesn't just happen. It takes a real commitment not only from dedicated volunteer coaches, but also from parents who understand their roles and responsibilities and league directors and administrators who know what it takes to ensure that all children who step on the basketball courts in their communities have safe, fun, and rewarding experiences. Basketball plays an important role in the lives of millions of children and provides them with the opportunity to learn the skills of the game and the chance to develop both emotionally and physically as individuals. The National Alliance For Youth Sports extends a heartfelt thank-you to every person who makes a positive difference through basketball in the life of a child.

This book is the result of a lot of hours of hard work from a lot of talented people at Wiley. Thanks to Stacy Kennedy, the acquisitions editor, whose efforts behind the scenes in working with the National Alliance For Youth Sports have resulted in this being the fourth book in a series for youth coaches, with more to come; to Chad Sievers, the project editor, and Josh Dials, the copy editor, whose insight on the sport, eye for detail, and never-ending reservoir of great ideas made a tremendous difference in every chapter of this book; to the wonderful illustrations put together by Rashell Smith and Jake Mansfield to supplement many of the techniques covered; and to Curt Bell, varsity girls' basketball coach in New Castle, Indiana, who was a terrific asset with all of his in-depth knowledge about every aspect of the game.

Publisher's Acknowledgments

We're proud of this book; please send us your comments through our Dummies online registration form located at www.dummies.com/register/.

Some of the people who helped bring this book to market include the following:

Acquisitions, Editorial, and Media Development

Project Editor: Chad R. Sievers

Acquisitions Editor: Stacy Kennedy

Copy Editor: Josh Dials

Technical Editor: Curt Bell

Editorial Manager: Michelle Hacker

Editorial Assistants: Erin Calligan Mooney, Joe Niesen, Leeann Harney

Cover Photos: © Tom and Dee Ann McCarthy/CORBIS

Cartoons: Rich Tennant (www.the5thwave.com)

Composition Services

Project Coordinator: Adrienne Martinez

Layout and Graphics: Shane Johnson, Stephanie D. Jumper, Jake Mansfield, Rashell Smith, Alicia B. South, Ronald Terry

Anniversary Logo Design: Richard Pacifico

Proofreaders: John Greenough, Sossity R. Smith

Indexer: Glassman Indexing Services

Special Help: Pam Ruble

Publishing and Editorial for Consumer Dummies

Diane Graves Steele, Vice President and Publisher, Consumer Dummies

Joyce Pepple, Acquisitions Director, Consumer Dummies

Kristin A. Cocks, Product Development Director, Consumer Dummies

Michael Spring, Vice President and Publisher, Travel

Kelly Regan, Editorial Director, Travel

Publishing for Technology Dummies

Andy Cummings, Vice President and Publisher, Dummies Technology/General User

Composition Services

Gerry Fahey, Vice President of Production Services

Debbie Stailey, Director of Composition Services

Contents at a Glance

Drills at a Glance

Table of Contents

Introduction

· ·

*W*elcome to *Coaching Basketball For Dummies,* a book dedicated to helping all the volunteer coaches everywhere enrich the lives of young men and women and grow the sport of basketball. These people — and hopefully you — dedicate their valuable time and energy in order to teach and encourage children in this sport. Youth basketball is enormously popular, as millions of children annually flock to facilities throughout the United States and Canada to loft jump shots, grab rebounds, and run up and down courts. The game features so many qualities — from the thrill of having a shot drop through the net to the pure enjoyment of dribbling a ball — that grab kids' interest.

We hope you find this book informative, entertaining, and — most important of all — useful in your quest to ensure that every child on your team has a fun, safe, and rewarding experience. After all, that's what coaching youth basketball is all about.

About This Book

We wrote this book for many types of youth volunteer coaches. For first-time coaches looking for some guidance before they step on the court to conduct practices and oversee games. For coaches who've been on the sidelines for a season or two and want to gain some more insight on specific areas of the game. For coaches looking to transition from working with younger kids to coaching older, more advanced kids. For veterans of the postseason pizza parties who have spent countless hours at the local basketball courts. And even for coaches who want to manage all star or travel teams.

No matter your situation, it's perfectly understandable if you're somewhat nervous about what you've gotten yourself into. Don't reach for the antacid tablets, though. You can take comfort in knowing that this book will be at your side as you prepare for the season. It will be your handy companion as you guide the kids to a fun-filled season. And it will be there when your season ends and you prepare to coach another team next season!

Each chapter is packed with useful and straightforward info. The more chapters you read, the more knowledgeable you'll become about coaching this great game. The smiles on the kids' faces — and all the learning and skill development that will take place — will be a nice payoff. We cover everything from drills you can use to raise your players' skills to details on different offensive and defensive strategies you can employ, among many other topics.

Conventions Used in This Book

To help you navigate this book, we use the following conventions:

- ✔ *Italics* emphasize certain words and highlight new words and terms that we define in the text.

- ✔ **Boldface** text indicates keywords in bulleted lists or the action parts of numbered steps.

- ✔ `Monofont` sets apart Web addresses. If you find that a specific address in this book has changed (and they seem to evolve all the time), try scaling it back by going to the main site — the part of the address that ends in .com, .org, or .edu.

We also pack this book full of diagrams of practice drills that you can work on with your team. The following chart is the key to understanding all the squiggly lines, arrows, and dashes in these diagrams:

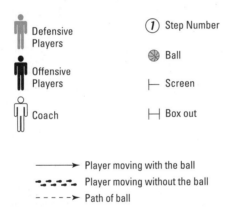

Defensive Players	① Step Number
Offensive Players	Ball
Coach	├─ Screen
	┤├─ Box out

⟶ Player moving with the ball
▪▪▪▪▪➤ Player moving without the ball
- - - - ➤ Path of ball

What You're Not to Read

Hey, if we were in your position, we'd read this book from cover to cover. That's how good — and informative — we think it is. If you're short on time, though, we'll let you in on a little secret: You don't have to read every single word, because this is a reference book.

To get through the book a little more quickly, you can skip over the sidebars — the shaded gray boxes. They contain interesting info, but nothing critical to your understanding of the chapter or topic. So sit back, relax, and dig into these chapters at your own pace. And if you have time — between your soon-to-be busy schedule of practices and games — we'd love to know what you think of the book!

Foolish Assumptions

Here are some things that we assume about you, our dear reader. Some of these assumptions may be right on target; others may not apply to you at all:

- ✔ You know that basketball is played on a court and requires little equipment.

- ✔ You may have a child who wants to take up the game this year, but you're not sure how to teach the basics.

- ✔ You're a novice youth basketball coach, and you need to get your coaching skills up to speed.

- ✔ You don't have any aspirations of climbing the coaching ladder and pacing the sidelines as a high school basketball coach.

- ✔ You just want the basics — for instance, what skills to focus on early in the season, how to determine who plays where, and how to make sure the kids have a fun time playing for you.

- ✔ You're coaching an older and more advanced team for the first time and you need some good drills to challenge the kids and keep their interest levels high.

- ✔ The kids on your team have plenty of basketball experience, and you're not sure how to upgrade their level of play at the offensive and defensive ends of the court.

- ✔ You want some good information on keeping the kids safe and reducing the risk of injury.

- ✔ You're looking for tips on how to run a quality practice that the kids look forward to participating in all week long.

If any of these descriptions hits the mark, you've come to the right place!

How This Book Is Organized

This book is divided into parts, with each one pertaining to a specific aspect of coaching a youth basketball team. Here's a quick rundown of what you can expect to find in each part of this book.

Part I: Getting Started Coaching Youth Basketball

What you do before you and your team ever step on the court can make the difference between a fun-drenched, stress-free season and a chaotic and confusing debacle. In this part, you get the lowdown on how to prepare for the season. We explain how to put together a coaching philosophy that fits your kids' needs and that you'll feel comfortable executing. You also find out what all the markings mean on the court and get a crash course on all the violations and rules of the game (and your league). Finally, we include valuable information on how to conduct a preseason meeting for parents, which is crucial for opening the lines of communication, reducing the chances of misunderstandings, and keeping your sanity.

Part II: Building Your Basketball Coaching Skills

This part is where the real fun — and actual coaching — begins. Here we serve up answers to those challenging questions swirling around in your head:

- How do I figure out who plays where?
- How do I conduct practices that the kids will look forward to?
- How do I work with the uncoordinated, shy, and talented kids all at once?
- How do I assess my team at midseason to ensure that we're headed in the right direction?

Plus, we show you the game-day ropes. We touch on everything from giving your pre-game and post-game talks to conducting efficient warm-ups to making critical halftime adjustments.

Part III: Working with Beginning and Intermediate Players

Helping kids get a handle on the basics of the game — from dribbling and shooting to rebounding and defending — is crucial for their long-term enjoyment of the sport. This part shares how you can relay the basics by providing a variety of lessons you can teach. It has chapters for offense and defense, for beginners and intermediate players. We include fun-filled drills that are highly effective for teaching skills to beginning players. And when your team has the basics down, this part also has a chapter devoted to intermediate skills to raise your players' abilities another notch or two.

Part IV: Moving On to Advanced Basketball Strategies

As players progress in the sport, they'll crave opportunities to practice some more advanced skills to increase their effectiveness on game day. You can utilize the chapters in this part to help spur their development. The pages are filled with in-depth techniques for raising the level of play on offense and defense. Plus, you can find set plays to run on offense and specific defenses to employ to make your team even more competitive. We also provide an assortment of drills you can use to help your players maximize their development.

Part V: Shooting for the Extra Points

This part is a smorgasbord of information on several topics — some we hope you won't face this season, and others that may be the crowning achievement of your youth coaching career. Here we help you recognize and handle player injuries, confront problem parents, and deal with discipline problems on your team. You also find valuable info on pre- and post-game nutrition to help maximize your players' performance. And, for those of you with your eye on coaching a travel team, you find all the information you need to help make your transition to this more competitive level a smooth one.

Part VI: The Part of Tens

A *For Dummies* book just wouldn't be complete without the Part of Tens. Here you find all sorts of quick-hitting, valuable information that you can put to use to boost the fun and enjoyment levels this season. We include some great tips for helping the kids relax before a game, and we present ways to stay realistic when coaching young kids.

Icons Used in This Book

To help you navigate this book and to make it easier to read the extra-valuable information, we include some icons, or little graphics, in the margins. These beacons point out some key ideas you need to consider. We use the following icons in this book:

The tip icon signals valuable info that can save you time and frustration and that can really enhance your experience. If you're scanning a chapter, take a moment to read these tips when you come across them, and then put them to work. You — and your players — will be glad you did.

A lot goes into coaching youth basketball. The remember icon alerts you to key information that's worth revisiting. You want to remember this info long after you close the book.

Sometimes you'll encounter issues during a practice or game that you need an extra hand with. Consider these paragraphs your troubleshooters that can help you on the court.

Watch out! The warning icon lets you know about situations that can be dangerous — perhaps to your players' health, to the safety of spectators, or to your sanity.

Where to Go from Here

One of the really cool things about this book is that you can jump in anywhere. Just check out the table of contents or the index for the topic you want to explore and then flip right there to get the scoop. Each chapter is divided into sections, and each section contains information on a specific topic concerning youth basketball.

If this season is your first on the sidelines, you probably have several questions about everything from what to do with the kids at the first practice to how to teach them the fundamentals of the game. You may be most comfortable digging in with Chapter 1 and moving forward from there. Or, perhaps what's causing you the most concern is being an effective coach on game day; if that's the case, head to Chapter 7 to get the scoop on how to handle your game-day responsibilities. Wherever you go, though, you can be confident that the info you gather along the way will ensure that your youth basketball team has a fun, safe, and memorable season.

Part I
Getting Started Coaching Youth Basketball

The 5th Wave
By Rich Tennant

"I switched out regular glassware for dribble glasses. It should help you on the court."

In this part . . .

*B*efore stepping on the court with your players, you need to take care of some behind-the-scenes tasks to ensure that your season starts on a positive note. Specifically, you need to define your coaching philosophy, get a handle on how your league runs, familiarize yourself with the terms and rules of the game, and prepare to meet with your players' parents. We cover all this — and more — in this first part.

Chapter 1

Teaching Basketball to Children

· ·

In This Chapter

▶ Preparing before you take the coaching reins

▶ Performing your duties on the floor

▶ Handling the dual role of coach and parent

· ·

Congratulations on your decision to volunteer to coach a youth basketball team. Your season-long journey — beginning when you meet the kids and parents, continuing at the first practice, and ending with the final game and awards ceremony — will be packed with special moments. The job you do will bring a smile to your face, and you and your players — regardless of their age, skill levels, or experience — will remember this season for the rest of your lives.

And if you're picking up this book because you haven't decided if you want the job yet, we hope the information can convince you that your job as a coach will be one of the most rewarding experiences of your life — as long as you do it for the right reasons. Heading into the season, your goals should be zeroed in on fun, skill development, and safety, as well as making it all happen in a stress-free environment.

Please be aware that if you volunteer to coach youth basketball, you're taking on a very important role. How you approach the season and how you interact with the kids will affect how they feel about themselves, the sport of basketball, and you. Your coaching style can either help them develop an unquenchable passion for the game or sweep away all their interest in playing organized sports.

To start and finish your job, you need some quality information on all the different aspects of the game. Consider this chapter your jumping-off point to this book and to the world of coaching youth basketball. Using this chapter and the rest of this book as a guide, you can find everything you need to navigate your players to a safe, fun-filled, rewarding, and memorable season.

Before You Grab the Clipboard: Preparing for Your Season

People get involved with coaching youth basketball for all sorts of reasons. Perhaps you volunteered this season because spending extra time with your child while introducing him to the game sounded like a fun experience. Maybe the league has a shortage of coaches, and you chose to step forward and help out the kids. Or perhaps you simply love working with kids, and the thought of coaching a youth basketball team sounded pretty appealing.

Whatever your reason, you must recognize that you're accepting an enormous responsibility that you can't take lightly. Hopefully, you've stepped forward for all the right reasons, rather than for many of the wrong reasons some get involved in the game, such as hoping to win a shiny first-place trophy to show off to friends and neighbors, or to guide their children to future athletic scholarships. Before any youngster begins dribbling or shooting a ball, you have plenty of behind-the-scenes work to do to ensure that the season gets off to a smooth start and stays smooth throughout. This section gives you a preview. Check out Chapter 2 for the complete lowdown.

Gaining mom and dad's support

The vast majority of the moms and dads you'll meet while coaching youth basketball will be wonderful, supportive, and caring people — as long as you do your part to make and keep them this way. When working with your players, you'll stress the importance of teamwork. When it comes to working with parents, it's really no different. When coaches and parents commit to working together — the adult form of teamwork — they create a special formula that produces tremendous benefits for the youngsters. When coaches and parents clash over everything from playing time to strategy, it can spoil the experience for everyone involved.

You can make an immediate connection with the parents and sidestep many potential problems by gathering them for a special meeting before you begin the season. You can lay the ground rules on what you expect in terms of behavior during games, and you can outline their roles and responsibilities. (Check out Chapter 4 for tips on how to run this preseason meeting.)

No matter what, never forget that parents play important roles in youth basketball programs. Keep the following points in mind to help make your dealings with the parents go smoothly:

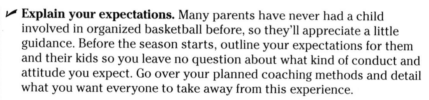

✔ **Explain your expectations.** Many parents have never had a child involved in organized basketball before, so they'll appreciate a little guidance. Before the season starts, outline your expectations for them and their kids so you leave no question about what kind of conduct and attitude you expect. Go over your planned coaching methods and detail what you want everyone to take away from this experience.

Telling parents firsthand that you're committed to skill development and fun over winning, and that you'll distribute playing time equally — regardless of skill level — squashes any chance of petty squabbles surfacing. Chapter 2 helps you develop your all-important coaching philosophy and become knowledgeable with all your league's policies and rules regarding playing time and other considerations.

✔ **Include parents whenever possible.** Parents invest a lot of time and money into their child's basketball experience. The season will be much more enjoyable for them and their youngster if you can find ways to include them on your season-long journey. Parents can do so much more than bring snacks and drinks to games. You can involve them in your practices and recruit the right ones to assist on game day (see Chapter 4). Plus, it's a great gesture on your part. (Chapter 6 covers planning your practices.)

✔ **Communicate with them.** Besides conducting a preseason parents meeting, you need to keep the communication lines open all season long. Regularly talk to the parents about their kids' progress; share your thoughts on areas of the game where the kids are really improving; offer suggestions for ways they can help their youngsters develop; and check in to make sure their kids are still having fun. (Chapter 8 details how you can talk with parents during the season.)

We'd be remiss if we didn't warn you that some parents will take their kids' participation more seriously than necessary. They think they're doing what's best for their children, but they can end up being sources of season-long aggravation. No matter what, there's always a chance that problems will materialize. If a problem pops up, you should remain calm and in control of your emotions, and never allow situations to escalate. Chapter 19 gives the rundown on some of the more common problems that you may need to address and presents the best approaches for solving them before they disrupt your season.

Getting a handle on the rules and terms

Just like any good auto mechanic understands how all the different parts of a vehicle work, a good basketball coach knows all the rules of the game and how they're applied. A good coach also knows how to teach the rules — along with the various terms and strategies associated with the game — to players. That isn't as complicated as it may seem, but it does take some time and effort on your part to learn all the rules that comprise this great game.

In Chapter 3, we dig into basketball's rulebook to help you cover key basketball terms. We also explain the many violations that refs often whistle. The information there serves as a basis for the skills, techniques, and strategies you need to pass along to your players (which we cover throughout Parts II, III, and IV of this book).

Make sure you know any special rules that your league has in place. Quite often, leagues utilize different rules depending on the age and experience level of the players. Everything from the size of the court to what types of rules are enforced change from community to community. Knowing these rules — and being able to share them with your players — makes a tremendous difference in your coaching and how you can motivate your players to have the most fun possible.

Hitting the Court

The most fun you'll have during the season will occur on the court — both during practices and on game days — when you're working closely with the kids in all different areas of the game. During your practice sessions with the kids, you'll instruct them both one-on-one and in group settings, and you'll teach, motivate, and applaud them every step of the way. When game days roll around, you'll have a front row seat as you watch them transfer those skills to a more competitive setting against other teams. During these moments, you can forge special bonds with your players and help them improve in the game.

Always keep in mind that coaching youth basketball is much more than helping a youngster deliver passes, make shots, and protect the ball. Coaching during practice and games also is about putting a smile on a youngster's face when she's on the court and seeing the excitement in her eyes as she has fun learning how to perform a variety of skills. While you're teaching and coaching, always keep the focus on fun. It could mean the difference between a child playing one season or forever. This section touches on what to do during court time, including practices and games.

Mapping out your practices

When you plan your practices, you'll create sessions that kids look forward to because they set the tone for all sorts of learning and skill development. If your practices aren't carefully planned — perhaps you put them together while sitting in your car, five minutes before the players arrive — you minimize the sessions' productivity and smother a lot of the fun that could've taken place. Planning is important. But how you design your practices and choose drills also has a direct impact on the kids' enjoyment. (To help you prepare for and run a great practice, check out the info in Chapter 6.)

Keep the following thoughts in mind to help squeeze the most fun and productivity out of every practice you run:

✔ **Be more than a coach.** Your position as coach gives you a special opportunity to make a difference in a lot of other areas of the kids' lives. Sure, you'll teach kids the basics of the game, but your impact can extend far beyond how to set a screen or take a jump shot.

For example, while your kids are warming up for practice (see Chapter 18), take the time to talk to them about the importance of doing well in school. You also can speak about the importance of staying away from tobacco and drugs and leading a healthy lifestyle. The words you deliver may stick with a child for the rest of his life.

✔ **Set a relaxed atmosphere.** Let the kids know during the first practice of the season (see Chapter 6) that mistakes are part of the game, and that all you ask is that they listen to your instructions and give their best effort — with a smile on their face, of course. Make your practices stress-free sessions where youngsters can make mistakes without the fear of criticism or embarrassment. In this environment, your kids will play much more relaxed, which clears the way for them to have more fun, learn skills quicker, and perform better.

Focusing on fundamentals first

Although you may be enthusiastic about teaching kids all facets of the game, temper your enthusiasm so that you don't overwhelm them by throwing too much at them. When taking the court with a beginning-level team, you must focus on the most basic of skills, such as dribbling the basketball. After youngsters have a decent understanding of that skill, you can progress to other areas, such as shooting and passing. Gradually, after spending several practice sessions with them, you'll find that some kids will become more proficient at executing certain skills, and others will probably have some difficulty that, as the coach, you have to find ways to help them overcome.

Ultimately, your long-range goal is to help kids become all-around players who can perform a variety of skills at both the offensive and defensive ends of the court. But remember, that won't occur during a one-hour practice with you. It's going to take a lot of time — and plenty of patience on your part — to help kids get there. So relax, build on the fundamentals of the game, and enjoy your season-long journey helping the kids enjoy learning and embracing the game.

When choosing practice drills for your sessions, your best bet is to opt for drills that keep the kids moving and are challenging enough to hold their interest. Standing-around time drastically reduces the amount of learning that can take place. The array of drills we present for both offense and defense in Chapters 11, 14, and 17 will challenge and excite beginning, intermediate, and advanced players.

Surviving game day

One of the challenges of coaching basketball is constantly adapting to ever-changing conditions. This challenge is especially prevalent on game day, when you have to make all sorts of decisions with little time to sort through your options, all while distractions are grabbing for your attention. For instance, you have playing time to monitor, plays to call, strategies to adjust, and pre-game, halftime, and post-game talks to deliver. (That's why it's so helpful to have assistants! Chapter 4 goes through the process of choosing the right assistants.) Yes, game day brings with it a lengthy list of responsibilities, but don't go reaching for the antacid tablets just yet. Chapter 7 gives you all you need to help game day go smoothly. (Also, Chapters 12, 13, 15, and 16 go through many strategies on both sides of the ball and present many plays that you can call during a game.)

We also have you covered with more detailed information if you're coaching a more basketball-savvy, older squad. Part IV of this book covers strategies for offense and defense, and Chapter 20 covers coaching a travel team.

Besides giving kids the chance to use all their skills against a real opponent, game day provides you with some great teachable moments, too. Reinforce what you brought up during practice that week, such as the importance of teamwork, displaying good sportsmanship, abiding by the rules, doing your best at all times, and having fun regardless of what the scoreboard reads.

Juggling Your Parenting and Coaching Responsibilities

Parenting presents an endless list of challenges and responsibilities; tacking on the role of coaching your child can be doubly difficult. As soon as you step on the court with your child, all sorts of issues can appear out of nowhere. Don't worry, we help prepare you as best we can in this section. If you can handle the issues, you'll create an experience that will be enormously rewarding and memorable for both you and your child.

Making the decision and navigating the season from the sidelines

Before you decide to grab the whistle and clipboard and assume the role of basketball coach, sit down with your child and gauge how he feels about you running the team. If you don't ask, you'll never know. Many youngsters are thrilled to have their dads or moms as coaches, and if you see that sparkle in his eyes when you bring up the subject, that makes all the time and effort you'll have to put into the season well worth it. On the other hand, some children — for whatever reason — don't feel comfortable with the idea and would prefer that their parents don't coach their teams. Take your child's wishes into account before making the decision. After considering all the issues, your family must decide if you should indeed coach your child this season.

If you and your child agree that it's okay for you to coach the team, keep the following "don'ts" in mind as you navigate through the season:

- ✔ **Don't overlook your parenting duties.** Whether the team wins or loses, you have to put down your playbook and remember that you're a parent first. Ask your child whether he had fun, and pile on the praise for doing his best and displaying good sportsmanship.

- ✔ **Don't close the lines of communication.** You want your child to know that he can come to you to talk about a concern at any time during the season. Open communication helps ensure that you'll be able to monitor how the season is going.

- ✔ **Don't carry over practice sessions to home.** If your child has some difficulty performing a specific skill during practice, avoid the urge to insist on working on the skill as soon as you get home. You can ask in casual conversation if he'd like to spend some time working on a certain skill, *if* you sense that he's really interested. If he is, great, but if not, let it go. Pushing your child can drain his interest in the sport.

- ✔ **Don't compare your child to siblings.** Let your child develop at her own rate. Children should never feel burdened by expectations to match the skills or abilities of older or younger siblings. Such comparisons can crush self-esteem and chase away the desire to play basketball.

- ✔ **Don't mislead your child.** You shouldn't heap on the praise when actual honesty about his skill level or work ethic needs to be addressed. Act as you would if he wasn't focusing on his school work or needed some extra help in a particular subject.

- ✔ **Don't shortchange the praise.** Be sure to praise your child's willingness, understanding, and cooperation in this special venture. Coaching your child can be one of the most rewarding experiences you'll ever have, but it isn't always easy.

Sidestepping problems with your child

To derive maximum benefits from coaching your child, you have to find the proper balance between providing preferential treatment and overcompensating. It's a tricky proposition — sort of like balancing on a high wire, minus the safety net — but we have you covered with some pointers in the following list. Ideally, your behavior should fit somewhere between these two extremes, which each carry negative consequences:

- ✔ **Providing preferential treatment:** It isn't uncommon for coaches to show preferential treatment to their own children, whether they realize it or not. For instance, they may provide their children with extra playing time, more attention, and special team duties (such as captain). Be aware that showing favoritism pushes your child into an uncomfortable position with his teammates, weakening your team camaraderie and his chances to have fun with his peers.

- ✔ **Overcompensating to steer clear of preferential treatment:** Don't go too far in trying to ensure that no one thinks you're giving preferential treatment to your child. For instance, don't reduce your child's playing time, give him less attention or instruction during practices, or constantly criticize him and have expectations that are too high. Taking these measures creates a negative atmosphere for your child, because it detracts from his enjoyment of the game for reasons that he doesn't understand.

As a parent, you want your child to excel in any activity he undertakes. Just don't view your coaching position as an opportunity to control your child's destiny and steer him toward stardom. You don't want to compromise his experience by pushing him harder than the other kids, demanding more from him, and criticizing him when he doesn't fulfill your unfair expectations. If you lose sight of what youth basketball is all about — fun, skill development, and relationship building — you'll negatively impact your child's emotional well-being and his interest in learning and playing in the future.

Chapter 2

Preparing for a Successful Season

• •

In This Chapter

▶ Defining your coaching philosophy

▶ Running down the rules and setup of your league

▶ Making sure your players are equipped

• •

Coaching a successful youth basketball season — meaning the kids learn the key fundamentals, have fun, and want to play again next season — takes a lot of preparation. A bag of basketballs, a clipboard, and a notebook overflowing with drills is a good start, but you have to go the extra mile to ensure a memorable season.

This chapter covers the all-important areas that can propel your season along a fun-filled path. Specifically, we talk about how to motivate your players, how to create a team atmosphere, what you hope to accomplish with the kids, and how you can help them reach their goals. We also discuss sportsmanship, getting to know the rules of your league, and covering all your bases in terms of equipment. Take a close look at this chapter. Whether your team wins the league championship or doesn't win a game, the info here can help you deliver a slam dunk of a season for you and your players.

Crafting Your Coaching Philosophy

When you signed up to be a basketball coach, you probably first thought about putting together your starting lineups and creating practice drills. An equally important but easily overlooked part of preparation is crafting your coaching philosophy. A coaching philosophy is pretty easy to put together but challenging to live up to all season long.

A *coaching philosophy* reflects the standards you set for yourself and your team. It's the foundation of your values and beliefs when you take the court. It allows you to lead your players in the direction you know is right as you strive to instill in them the values that you want your own kids to exhibit in their lives — the true goal of youth sports. Entering the season without a coaching philosophy is like going to a tropical island without sunscreen — you're setting yourself up to get burned. A sound coaching philosophy keeps you on the right track as you navigate your way through the season. This section introduces the various components when developing a philosophy that stresses respect, sportsmanship, skill development, safety, and fun.

Setting your philosophy: Where to start

When figuring out your coaching philosophy, you don't have to look far. Many recreation departments have mission statements and policies that explain their stances on sportsmanship, skill development, parental behavior, and so on. These documents can serve as great starting points for your coaching philosophy. If you don't have a copy of your league's policy manual, check with your recreation director or league supervisor about obtaining one.

If you need to seek additional advice, you may want to ask other coaches about their philosophies to get a feel for where yours should be. You can also turn to your old coaches who you have great respect for to gain some perspective.

Even a carefully planned coaching philosophy can be tough to adhere to at times. At some point, Ken's mom will confront you about why the team isn't in first place, or Jenny's dad will question why his daughter isn't playing point guard. You have to be prepared to deal with all sorts of situations. Explain your coaching philosophy to the parents before the season gets underway to minimize these potential headaches (see Chapter 4). (For more on dealing with problem kids and parents, see Chapter 19.)

Gearing your philosophy to a specific age group

Although each child has his own unique strengths and weaknesses when it comes to basketball-related skills, all youngsters possess general characteristics dictated by age. Children are continually growing and evolving, and part of your coaching responsibility is knowing what to expect from them both physically and emotionally.

No matter the age or skill level of your players, always be supportive and enthusiastic. Pile on the praise and never stop encouraging them. You want to build their confidence and self-esteem, whether they're 6 or 16. Self confidence is a gift that lasts for years and impacts how the kids approach life away from the basketball court. The following sections present some general characteristics that apply to specific age ranges.

Ages 6 and under

Children ages 6 and under probably haven't played basketball before, and this season may be their first experience in any type of organized team setting. Your job is to introduce them to basketball's most basic elements and whet their appetite for future participation in the sport. (For a look at teaching the offensive and defensive basics of the game, check out Chapters 9 and 10.)

Children at this age are primarily interested in being with friends and having fun playing the sport. Competition takes a backseat with this group; your kids will be more interested in the post-game snack than in who won the game. Many programs for the youngest kids don't even bother turning on the scoreboard because of its irrelevance to the experience.

Ages 7–9

Youngsters in the 7–9 age group are interested in mastering some of the basics of the sport. They crave feedback from coaches and parents on how they're performing certain skills and how they're progressing with new ones. They begin noticing their teammates' abilities and skill levels, and when you verbally recognize one of their peers for properly executing a skill, they'll want to earn that same feedback. Your coaching philosophy should focus on fun, of course, but also helping the kids increase their skill development and knowledge of the game.

Ages 10–12

More than likely, children in the 10–12 age group have had some experience playing organized basketball and are continuing with it because they enjoy the sport and the competition. Your job as coach is to keep the positive momentum going by adding to their foundation of skills and fueling their desire to continue playing. Many of these kids become more competitive, and winning and losing take on more importance in their lives. They want to put their skills to the test and enjoy competing against peers. When they can help the team prevail, these players feel immense satisfaction and a sense of accomplishment unique to the sport of basketball. (Chapters 12 and 13 cover some intermediate skills you can focus on with these types of players.)

Ages 12 and up

Welcome to the challenging and ever-changing world of the teenager! Kids ages 12 and up have probably developed many of the basic skills needed to play basketball and now want to focus on improving them. (In Chapters 15–17, we cover more advanced techniques you can teach older kids and provide an assortment of challenging drills.)

If you volunteer or get recruited into coaching at this age group, don't panic! Instead, welcome the chance to enhance your coaching abilities and embrace the opportunity to coach kids who have a deep-rooted love for the game. Be sure to let them know that you value their opinions, suggestions, and input. A youngster's passion for basketball at this age is wonderful, and that enthusiasm can make your job easier if you let it.

Gaining the respect of your players is always important to your coaching success — particularly when coaching kids in this age range. These kids have probably developed a real passion for the sport. They may have attended basketball camps, may play on travel teams (see Chapter 20), and, in some cases, may be more knowledgeable in some areas of the sport than you are. If you neglect your homework and don't come to practice with session plans that have been prepared in advance (see Chapter 6), the kids will notice, and learning and skill development will grind to a halt.

Promoting teamwork

Basketball is a team game. Although the sport allows individuals to create plays on their own (when they drive to the basket, for instance), you and your team will be much better off if you can get everyone to work together as a cohesive unit. Teamwork translates into more quality scoring opportunities on offense and better defensive play. Of course, promoting teamwork with youngsters is easier said than done.

There are no clear-cut methods for teaching the essence of teamwork to your players. However, if you continue to work on team play during your practices and through the drills you choose, your players will (hopefully) begin to see the enormous benefits gained by working together as a team. Keep in mind the following pointers when coaching during practices and when on the sidelines for games:

> ✔ **Applaud team efforts.** Be sure to recognize the efforts of your entire team when possible. For example, if you're conducting a 3-on-2 fast-break drill and the offense scores a basket, your natural tendency may be to applaud the end result and the youngster who converted the basket (see Chapter 11 for more on offensive drills). Don't neglect the other players involved, though, because without their accurate passes, your offense wouldn't have been in position to score a basket. Acknowledge all the components that go into making a play work.

When you spread your praise equally among all the players involved in making a basket, you convince your youngsters that they each play a significant role on the team and that good rebounding, good passing, and good ball-handling skills are just as important as the ability to score.

✔ **Encourage players to congratulate teammates on the floor.** You want your players to acknowledge the efforts of their teammates. A player who receives a pass and scores during a 3-on-2 fast-break drill should holler "great pass" to his teammate after the play. Get your kids in the habit of giving high-fives or verbal praise so you can strengthen team unity.

✔ **Promote sideline support.** Encourage players on the bench to stay involved by supporting their teammates. Doing so keeps them focused on the action on the court so they aren't glancing into the stands to see what their parents are doing. Hearing teammates' cheers also provides extra encouragement for the players on the court.

✔ **Rotate your captains.** Don't stick with the same two or three players to serve as team captains throughout the season, because this elevates them above everyone else. Give all your kids the chance to lead warm-ups (see Chapter 18) or to lead the team out onto the court on game day.

✔ **Create a team cheer.** Work with your players to come up with a clever team cheer that you can shout before games. The cheer helps to remind players that they're taking the court as a team. You can use something as basic as "one . . . two . . . three . . . together!" as a positive reminder to play together and support one another.

Motivating players

Some of your players will respond in a positive manner to your challenges — such as seeing whether they can sink five free throws in a row (see Chapter 9). For other players, that task may put too much pressure on them and actually detract from their motivation to participate. You have to discover for yourself what type of motivational tactics work for each player to get the best out of him. (For more on evaluating your players, see Chapter 5.)

Here are some general cues you can employ to help motivate your players to become the best they can be:

✔ **Embrace your position.** If you display a sincere passion for basketball and teaching it to children, your excitement and enthusiasm will rub off on your players, and they'll respond accordingly.

✔ **Set attainable goals for players.** Forget about trying to win every game or having the league's most prolific offense. Those aren't helpful goals for kids in a youth basketball program. Setting goals that are within reach stimulates and encourages players to keep working. (For details on setting individual and team goals, check out Chapter 8.)

If a child senses that your expectations are impossibly far-fetched, he'll question the point of even trying, and his play will suffer. Convey to the players that the essence of participating is always putting forth their best effort. Instilling this habit in kids carries over to how they approach everyday life. A winner is someone who always gives his best effort, regardless of the situation.

✔ **Point out the positives at practice.** Being positive is simply one of the best motivational tools around. Think about it: If your boss publicly tells you that you did a great job on a presentation, the praise will make you feel pretty good, and you'll give even more effort on your next project. The same goes for kids playing basketball.

Stay away from using threats as motivation. Making a child run laps around the court for failing to meet your expectations has no place in youth basketball. Kids are there to play and learn from their mistakes, not be punished for them. You don't want to make a youngster afraid of making another mistake that will translate into additional punishment. Nothing saps the fun out of the game faster. Instead, take a closer look at how you're teaching the child. If he's giving it his all with no success, you have to take a different approach to teaching the skill. (For proper disciplinary actions for misbehavior, see Chapter 19.)

Opening the lines of communication

Establishing open lines of communication with your players is important. You want them to feel comfortable coming to you with any questions, problems, or concerns at any point during the season. Besides being their coach, you can do your part to be their friend and confidant.

At different points during the season, talk with all your players about topics other than basketball to forge special bonds that will last all season and beyond. While they're stretching, for example, go around and ask your players how they're doing in school and what their favorite subjects are. On practice days when some kids show up early, you can find out whether they have any brothers or sisters, ask about the names of their pets, or discover what hobbies they enjoy. Getting to know the kids on a non-basketball level lets them know that you care about them as individuals and makes it easier for them to open up to you if they need to come to you with a problem.

Making every kid count

As the coach, your job is to work with all the youngsters on your team, regardless of how talented they are. Every player on your team should feel prized and respected. Sometimes, this evenhandedness is a lot more difficult than it sounds. It takes real focus and effort to make sure that each child feels valued and appreciated for her efforts. After all, it's easy to become enamored with kids who are more athletically gifted, and you may end up showering them with all your attention, accolades, and praise. Just remember: Making every kid count is the cornerstone of good coaching.

Providing immediate positive feedback and continually recognizing all players for their various contributions are the most effective ways to make every player on your roster count (and feel like they count). Consider these points that will aid in your efforts:

- ✔ **Applaud positive attitudes and strong work ethics as much as you do basketball skills.** Work to inflate all your kids' self-esteem and maintain their interest in playing the game. You can applaud a child's hustle when she's chasing down a loose ball; acknowledge a player's enthusiasm and the way she encourages her teammates from the bench; and point out to the rest of the squad the good sportsmanship a player displayed during the game. If you applaud all positive contributions, you convey to the rest of the team that they should follow the examples set by these players.

- ✔ **Provide awards for all players.** If you choose to hand out awards to your players during or after the season, make sure you come up with something for everyone on the team. In other words, don't settle for just the old "Most Valuable Player" route. Using a little imagination, you can recognize all the kids on the team. Some examples of awards you can give out include the following:

   • Most Likely to Dive for a Loose Ball

   • Best Passer

   • Most Improved Player

   • Hardest Worker in Practice

Keep a roster handy at all times on a clipboard or with your practice plan for the day (see Chapter 6), and put a check mark next to a child's name whenever you give her positive feedback. You can easily monitor how you're distributing praise so you can make sure that all players get a nice confidence boost. You never want players to leave the court without hearing a single word of praise for their efforts that day.

Emphasizing fun and skill development

Don't let the vision of what's best for your players become blurred by a quest to win every game so you can line your mantel with shiny first-place trophies. Your team's win-loss record at the end of the season (if your league keeps such standings) doesn't define how successful you are as a coach; the true measure of your coaching is whether your kids safely learn skills and have a great time doing so. Use every practice and game as a building block in your players' development, and never forget that having fun must be a major component of the sport. If you stick with this approach, your team will surely enjoy the journey with you.

The younger and more inexperienced your players are, the less you should focus on wins and losses. Concentrate on teaching skills and having fun playing the game. Certainly, at the more advanced levels of play (see Chapter 20 for examples), winning takes on a more prominent role. At these stages, you shouldn't brush off the concept because it's a part of playing basketball. Indeed, winning is something everyone strives for in order to achieve some level of success in everyday life. Doing well on a test is a form of winning. So is beating out a dozen other people for a job you really want.

But when coaching youth basketball, you must exercise great caution, because children are highly impressionable. If they think that winning is all that really matters to you, they'll forget the importance of having fun and developing skills. If you allow this to happen, altering your season's course and getting everything back on track becomes really difficult.

And here's another point to consider: Just because your team won the game doesn't necessarily mean that your players turned in a good performance. A team can put forth a lackluster effort and still win because the other team simply didn't have the talent or desire to compete. You have more room to maneuver after a win, because you can emphasize improving and the kids doing their best. The players will be more receptive to these comments after a victory; plus, it reinforces that winning games isn't your only goal and that doing their best and striving to improve mean just as much in your eyes. Conversely, your team can play its best game of the season and still lose. Following setbacks, kids need to hear plenty of positives from you to boost their confidence and self-esteem. Never turn to the scoreboard for feedback on judging how your team played, and don't let wins and losses control how much fun you have on the court.

Modeling good sportsmanship

Teaching kids the importance of good sportsmanship can be challenging. What makes teaching (and modeling) good sportsmanship particularly tricky is that youngsters are bombarded with images of older basketball players trash talking, showboating, and disrespecting opponents and officials. However, keep in mind that you're fighting the good fight: Good sportsmanship is one of the healthiest ideals you can instill in your players.

Incorporate the following suggestions into your coaching philosophy. They can help make your team one of the most liked and respected teams in the league (and your players the envy of all parents in the stands):

✔ **Talk about sportsmanship outside your team.** While your players are going through warm-ups, you can discuss a game they watched on television and ask whether they saw any displays of good sportsmanship. Praising these displays and subtly reinforcing their importance goes a long way toward instilling the right qualities in your players.

✔ **Set a positive tone on game day by shaking hands with the opposing coach.** The players, fans, and opposing coaches will notice your gesture of sportsmanship. Plus, it will remind everyone that basketball is just a game and you're all there for the kids.

✔ **Always be a model of good sportsmanship.** Don't yell at officials or question their judgment. If you aren't a model of good sportsmanship, you can't expect your players (or their parents) to be good sports. Your players will take their cue from you, so if you rant and rave about a call, expect your players to show disrespect toward the refs as well.

✔ **Shake hands after the game.** Regardless of the outcome, have your players line up and shake hands with the opposing team and its coaches. If your team won, your players should tell their opponents that they played a good game, and if your squad lost, your players should congratulate the opponents on their victory. Another classy move is for your players to shake the officials' hands following the contest.

✔ **Recognize good sports during your post-game talk.** Perhaps one of your players went out of his way after the game to congratulate an opponent who played a strong game. Recognizing such displays reinforces to your players that how they behave during and after games really does matter to you and to all the spectators. (Chapter 7 discusses the post-game talk in more detail.)

Understanding the Rules and Purpose of Your League

Youth basketball programs are as different as the millions of kids who step on courts to play in them. Along with this diversity comes a wide range of rules and policies that leagues can apply at their discretion. Some leagues adhere strictly to the official rules of basketball and allow for no modifications; the majority of youth programs, however, alter their rules and set policies to fit the age and experience level of the kids. This section looks at the possible rules differences and policies you may encounter and helps you to understand what type of league you'll be coaching in this season.

What are my league's rules?

To be successful as a coach this season, you have to know the rules of basketball as well as the specific rules your league is enforcing. Plus, you have to be able to teach the rules to your players. If you don't know and understand the rules, you can't expect your team to, either.

Even if you have an extensive knowledge of basketball and can remember the glory days when you starred on the court, do yourself and your team a big favor and take a look at your league's rulebook as a refresher. (When you agree to coach a team, the league supervisor typically gives you a rule book. If not, be sure to ask how you can get your hands on one.) Chances are good that your league uses some rules that weren't applied in the same way when you played. Even though you probably prefer a bestseller or an entertainment magazine, your league's rulebook should be bedside reading for you — and we don't mean as a sleeping aid!

Don't dive in and attempt to memorize all your league's rules in a single sitting. Instead, review a few pages every night prior to the season's start until you become pretty comfortable with them. (For a primer on the rules — and some common league modifications — check out Chapter 3.)

Likewise, don't assume that older kids have a firm grasp on the league rules simply because they've played basketball for awhile. If past coaches haven't taken the time to explain certain confusing rules, players may not have learned them. They may have moved from season to season without really understanding them. You can make a difference by clearly spelling out all the rules and how referees enforce them.

If you can arrange it, have one of the league officials come to one of your preseason practices and officiate a team scrimmage or a series of drills. This gives the kids — especially those new to the sport — a feel for what types of fouls and violations will be whistled on game day.

Do we play makeup games?

In many parts of the country, Mother Nature can wreak havoc on game day. Yes, basketball is played indoors, but unless your league plays its games on your home court, you'll have some travel issues. When inclement weather, such as a snowstorm or flash flood, makes it unsafe to drive kids to the game, your league will either cancel games or postpone them until a later date.

At the start of the season, some leagues reserve certain dates to be used for makeup games. Knowing your league's policy on makeup games allows you to alleviate a lot of the confusion parents and team members will have when bad weather arrives. (You can share your league's policy with parents during your preseason meeting; check out Chapter 4 for more info.)

What are the scheduling policies for practice time?

The ages of your players generally dictates how much time you can spend conducting practices during the season. Many leagues restrict the number of practices a coach can hold, so be aware of this rule before you put together your practice plans (see Chapter 6). In most beginner leagues, coaches get a single one-hour practice per week, along with a game on a Saturday morning, for example. In more advanced leagues, the scheduling often is left in your hands.

Some leagues will set the teams' practice schedules for the entire season based on the number of available courts and what other programs require the space. During the season, your team may practice every Wednesday from 6:30 to 7:30 p.m., for example. This league control helps eliminate a lot of your scheduling headaches, though you must be able to adapt to whatever time slot the league gives to your team.

Is the league for fun or first place?

The two distinct classifications that exist for youth basketball programs are *recreational* and *competitive*. Each type requires vastly different coaching approaches, so you need to know what type of league you're coaching in so you can plan accordingly. If it's a competitive league for advanced players, the issue of equal playing time for each youngster doesn't carry the importance it would in a recreational league for beginning-level players. Prior to agreeing to volunteer for the coaching post, you can check with the league's recreation director to learn more about the nature of the league. Make sure it's the right fit for you!

Recreation leagues

If this will be your first season carrying a clipboard and whistle as coach, chances are you'll be involved in a recreational league — at least you should be, anyway. Rec programs are for the younger age levels and for inexperienced kids, and they focus on fun and teaching kids the basic skills.

In a recreation league, you may encounter any of the following types of rule modifications that can affect your coaching style:

- ✔ **Playing time requirements:** Generally, rec programs have rules in place regarding equal playing time for all the kids, which makes your job easier. All your kids should get a fair chance to play, regardless of how well they pick up skills.

- ✔ **Mini-games:** Some rec leagues scale down teams to four-on-four, or even three-on-three, and have the kids play on shorter courts with lower baskets (see Chapter 3 for more on the layout of the court). Setting up mini-games gives the kids more chances to touch the ball and sink shots instead of spending most of their time running back and forth on a regulation court with limited opportunities to dribble, shoot, or pass.

- ✔ **Teaching rather than rule enforcement:** Rec leagues often alter the rules of basketball to meet the needs of the kids. In the younger divisions, for instance, refs may not call three-second lane violations.

- ✔ **Hands-on coaching:** Some rec programs allow coaches to roam the court during games. This gives you a chance to provide immediate instruction, feedback, and help during the course of play, which is crucial when young kids are unsure of themselves and are still learning the basics.

In recreational leagues, the focus is all on helping the kids learn and develop and have fun doing it. When you meet with the opposing coach before a game, encourage him or her to provide positive feedback to your players, and let him or her know that you'll do the same with all the youngsters.

Competitive leagues

Some children will develop a thirst for competition that a local recreational program simply can't satisfy. These youngsters search out a more competitive environment to participate in, and many competitive youth leagues provide this environment.

Some competitive leagues are referred to as *all-star* or *travel teams* (check out Chapter 20). These programs are for youngsters who have demonstrated high skill levels and a deep interest in playing the game. These elite programs give kids the chance to compete against peers with similar ability in their community or in surrounding cities. Many communities also offer programs with a level of play that's a notch above recreational to give kids, at all different ages, the chance to compete against others in a more competitive setting.

Coaches usually only sign up to head a competitive team if they have a strong coaching background and have proven to be well-versed in the techniques of the game. If you have a few seasons under your belt and are confident and enthusiastic about stepping up to the next level, contact your local recreation department and explore what opportunities are available. Even if there are no head coaching positions open, look into getting the contact information for the head coaches and see if they would be interested in having you join as an assistant coach. This is a great way to gain some valuable experience and can help make your transition to this level go more smoothly when you do take over a team in the future.

If, on the other hand, you've volunteered for a competitive league that you don't think you're ready for — perhaps your son convinced you to coach or the parents took a vote and want you in — notify the league director immediately. Tell him or her that you're keeping the best interests of the kids at heart, and you'd prefer to coach a less-experienced team in a less-competitive league. Down the road, if you choose to go the competitive coaching route because you have an interest in working with kids at this level, you'll be better prepared to do so.

Covering Equipment Responsibilities

One of the many great things about basketball — one reason it's so popular in so many places all over the world — is that it requires little equipment (just a ball and a hoop). As a youth league coach, though, you need to know what your league provides for your team and what your players are responsible for bringing so you can alert the parents. This section addresses your equipment needs and who's responsible for these items.

What the league is responsible for

Many leagues provide a set number of basketballs for each coach to use at his or her practices. The balls will be distributed at the start of the season, and the coaches must turn them back in after their last practices. As always, check with your league to make sure. If your league doesn't have the financial resources to provide enough basketballs, you may need to ask your players to bring balls to practice so you can run through all your drills without sacrificing valuable time (see Chapters 11, 14, and 17).

Many programs also give coaches pylons or other markers, or access to them, for use in practices, along with whistles, clipboards, and, of course, access to the facility's courts. Others leave it up to you to purchase any extra items that will help with your practices.

What the child is responsible for

Find out what your league doesn't provide in advance so you can let the parents know what the kids will need to bring. A good time to share this information is during your preseason parents meeting (covered in Chapter 4). Players typically are responsible for several items, such as the following:

- **Shoes:** A player should have a pair of comfortable shoes that provide good traction on the court so she isn't slipping and sliding around. At the more advanced levels of play, kids may want to opt for shoes made specifically for basketball; these shoes provide extra support for the ankles.

- **Mouthpiece:** Many leagues require that players wear mouthpieces when involved in action on the floor. Even if your league doesn't have this policy in place, you should encourage your players to wear mouthpieces to protect their teeth.

- **Water bottle:** Make sure all the kids bring their own water bottles to every practice and game.

- **Uniforms:** The cost of your team uniform often is built into the registration fee parents pay for the league. At the youngest levels, kids typically receive only a shirt; at the older and more advanced levels, kids may receive a shirt and shorts. Here are a couple more uniform considerations for players:

    - **Socks:** Kids should wear a comfortable pair of athletic socks.

    - **Athletic cups and sports bras:** At the older levels of play, kids need to use these supportive undergarments.

Make sure you check on your league's policies regarding accessories. A lot of kids enjoy wearing sweatbands or headbands to emulate their favorite college or professional players, but your league may not allow them. Also, most programs don't allow any type of jewelry to be worn because of the injury risk. Even if the league does allow jewelry, make it a team rule with your players not to wear any.

Chapter 3

Covering the Basketball Basics

In This Chapter

▶ Taking the basketball court's measurements

▶ Mastering the terms, signals, and rules of the game

▶ Analyzing the required skills and responsibilities

Chances are you played basketball as a youngster — either in organized leagues or in pickup games on the playground. As an adult, you may enjoy watching college and professional basketball games on television; and if you're a hardcore fan (or a hardcore fantasy player), you may even be able to recite the stats of your favorite players. Perhaps, though, you never played much basketball, and the only time you get geared up to watch is when you pick your brackets for the college tournament. Regardless of your playing background or passion for the game, being a coach who kids love playing for and learning from requires more than fandom and shooting skills.

As coach of a youth team, you have many responsibilities. First off, you need to know all the rules — both general and league-specific guidelines — and you have to be able to explain them to your players. You must be able to identify every area on the court. You should have a grasp on all the skills your kids need to acquire — on the offensive *and* defensive ends of the floor. Plus, you can enhance your players' experiences by introducing them to commonly used basketball terms and phrases. All that valuable information and more is at your fingertips right here in this chapter.

Measuring the Court

Most sports have marked-off areas where the games take place, and knowing the layout of these areas is vital for playing the games. If you're new to the sport of basketball or haven't played since short shorts were in, teaching your kids about all the lines and markings on the basketball court may seem a little intimidating — but no need to worry. In this section, we give you a quick rundown of what you'll find when you step on the court with your players, from the baseline to the mid-court circle down to the free-throw line.

The markings of a true basketball court

One of the neat characteristics of a basketball court is that every marking — from lines to circles to semicircles — serves a distinct purpose that's integral to the game. To play the sport properly, your kids need to be able to identify these markings and know their contexts within the game. So, your tour of the floor begins here (see Figure 3-1).

A basketball court features the following markings:

- **Baselines:** The lines that run underneath the baskets at both ends of the court. Also known as the *end lines,* the baselines separate the playing court from the out-of-bounds area. Players who step on a baseline while in possession of the ball are considered out of bounds; this action turns the ball over to the other team. After an opponent makes a basket, a player *inbounds* the ball by moving behind the baseline and passing to a teammate standing in the court of play.

- **Sidelines:** The lines that run the court's length of the court. The sidelines define the playing area from the out-of-bounds area. Players who touch these lines while handling the ball are considered out of bounds. Depending on where the ball gets knocked out of play, players often inbound the ball from behind the sidelines. The benches for both teams also are located along one sideline, as well as the *scoring table* (where score is kept and where players go to substitute into the game).

- **Mid-court line:** This line, also called the *division line,* bisects the court vertically. When a team inbounds the ball under its basket, its players must get the ball across this line in less than ten seconds. After crossing this line, the team in possession of the ball can't pass it back over the line to the other side of the court (called a *backcourt violation*).

- **Center circle:** The circle in the middle of the court! This is where the game begins with a jump ball between a player from each team. A ref tosses the ball into the air, and the players jump and try to tip it to their teams.

- **Lanes:** The rectangular (often colored) areas in front of each basket — also known as the *paint.* Offensive players can't stand in this area for more than three seconds at a time (known as a *three-second violation*). Also, during free throws, players aren't allowed to step into the lane until the ball has been released by the shooter; otherwise, it's a *lane violation.*

- **Free-throw lines:** The lines at the top of the lanes at each end of the court. The free-throw line is where players stand to attempt free throws.

- **Blocks:** The squares (often colored) on both sides of the lanes near the baskets. When a player attempts a free throw, players from the opposing team stand next to these blocks. Usually, the tallest players occupy these spots because they're in the best position to grab rebounds.

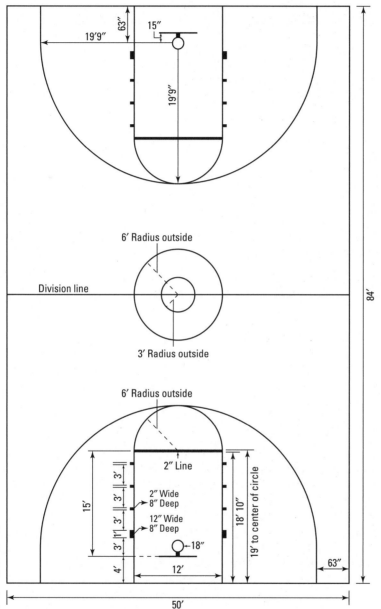

Figure 3-1:
Perusing the
court of
play.

The figure includes the following labels: 63", 15", 19'9", 19'9", 6' Radius outside, Division line, 3' Radius outside, 6' Radius outside, 2" Line, 2" Wide 8" Deep, 12" Wide 8" Deep, 15', 3', 3', 3', 3', 1', 18', 4', 12', 18' 10", 19' to center of circle, 63", 84', 50'

✔ **Tabs:** The short lines that extend from both sides of the lanes. The tabs mark where players stand while attempting free throws.

✔ **Top of the key:** The half circle that arcs above the free-throw line.

✔ **Wing:** The area outside the three-point line where players take long shots.

Sweeping the court's dimensions

You can put away your tape measure, because this section provides all the measurements for every significant marking on the court. After all, you can't be a quality coach if you're not familiar with your surroundings. The following list displays the measurements for what you'll find on the court:

- **The court:** Court sizes at the youth level vary, based on the program. Generally, they're 84 feet long and 50 feet wide. Usually, the smaller the kids, the smaller the court so that they don't get overwhelmed by the size of the playing surface.

- **Baskets:** The top of the rim is 10 feet off the ground; the rim itself is 18 inches in diameter. Again, depending on the age of the participants and the particular program, basket heights vary. Popular heights that are used for some of the younger kids are 8 and 9 feet.

- **Backboard:** The piece of equipment the basket attaches to is 6 feet wide and 3½ feet high. The front of the rim is 24 inches from the backboard, and the backboard extends 4 feet from the baseline. The painted rectangle above the rim is there for kids to aim their shots when banking them off the backboard.

- **Free-throw line:** The distance from the free-throw line to the front of the rim is 13 feet (15 feet to the backboard).

- **Key:** The *key* (the area from the baseline to the free-throw line) is 19 feet to the center of the circle and 12 feet wide.

- **Half circle above the key:** The radius of the half circle above the key is 6 feet.

- **Blocks:** The blocks are 12 inches wide and 8 inches deep.

- **Three-point line:** The three-point line begins with a straight line extending from the baseline and curves around the perimeter; the distance is 19 feet, 9 inches.

Grasping the Rules of the Game

Basketball is a complex game, and it involves many rules. Some of the rules are basic and easy to grasp; others may leave you scratching your head. If you're not familiar with the rules, becoming overwhelmed by them (and all the little nuances of the game) is easy. The problem is, if you're overwhelmed by the rules, you won't be able to teach them properly, and your kids will suffer. That's where we come in! The following sections break down the rules of the game, from the basics to your specific league considerations.

First of all, don't panic. You shouldn't try to learn every single rule in one sitting. In the weeks leading up to the season, focus on learning two or three rules each night. Concentrate on how they're applied and build from there. You can't expect your youngsters to learn every rule during the first practice, so don't put that kind of pressure on yourself either.

The basics of how to play basketball

Basketball, in simple terms, is the offensive team, consisting of five players, moving the ball down the court by dribbling and passing in order to make baskets, all while the defensive team (also five players) does its best to stop the offense. Each team tries to score the most points within the time limit of the game. Most youth league basketball games feature four 6-minute quarters, with a halftime separating the first two quarters from the second two. If the game is tied at the end of regulation, an overtime period is played. Usually, this is a 3-minute session that's played to determine the winner.

A game begins with a jump ball in the center circle at midcourt. The team that gains possession is the offensive team; it can score points in a number of ways. It can score *field goals,* which are baskets worth two or three points (depending on where the shot is taken). Teams also can score single points via free throws, which you take when the defensive team commits a foul on a player in the act of shooting. If the player makes a basket *and* gets fouled, he gets to attempt one free throw to complete a three-point play (or a four-point play if he's fouled while making a three-point shot). Your team can also attempt free throws after the defensive team commits a set number of fouls in a quarter or half (putting it *over the limit*).

Digesting the important terms

When vacationing in a foreign country, your chances of communicating with everyone from waiters to hotel staff are enhanced if you know some of the native language. The same applies to your coaching. The better handle you have on the terms associated with the game, the better you can teach them to your players, and the better the experience will be for everyone. This section helps you with the basic terms of the game.

Offensive terms

When your team gets the ball and goes on offense, your main goal is to try to score. Your players can notch points for the team with bank shots, jump shots, free throws, and lay-ups, among others. The following list presents some basic terms and phrases associated with the offensive end of the court:

- **Assist:** A pass (to a teammate) that leads directly to a basket. (See Chapter 9 for more on passing fundamentals.)
- **Ball handler:** The player dribbling or trying to pass the ball.
- **Bank shot:** A shot that bounces off the backboard and goes into the basket.
- **Beat the defender:** When an offensive player, with or without the ball, gets past the player guarding him in order to take a shot or receive a pass.
- **Charging:** When an offensive player runs into a defensive player who has already established set position.
- **Crossover dribble:** A player dribbling the ball from one hand to the other in front of his body.
- **Double bonus:** After a team has committed a set number of fouls in a quarter or half, the opponent receives two free throws for every foul during that quarter or half.
- **Dribbling:** A ball-movement method carried out by repeatedly bouncing the ball on the floor. You bounce the ball by using the fingertips of one hand to push or tap it toward the floor. (See Chapter 9 for more on dribbling fundamentals.)
- **Drive:** When a player with the ball advances toward the basket by trying to beat his defender.
- **Fake (or feint):** When an offensive player tries to put the player guarding him off-balance with a deceptive move. This creates an advantage for getting an open shot, dribbling past the defender, or delivering a pass to a teammate. Offensive players can execute fakes with the head, body, or by movement of the basketball.
- **Fast break:** When a team gains possession of the ball and immediately tries to advance it down the floor as quickly as possible to outnumber the defense and generate a good scoring opportunity.
- **Field goal:** A basket that's made during regular play. A field goal is worth two points within (or when standing on) the three-point line and three points beyond it.
- **Free throw:** An unguarded shot taken from behind the free-throw line by a player whose opponent committed a foul on him. A made free throw is worth one point.
- **Jump ball:** Games begin at midcourt, where the referee tosses the ball into the air between two opposing players, who jump up and try to tap the ball to teammates who are lined up outside the center circle.

✔ **Lay-up:** A shot that occurs when a player drives to the basket (or gets a rebound) and attempts a close-range shot, usually by banking the ball off the backboard (see Chapter 9 for more).

✔ **Offensive rebound:** When an offensive player secures the ball after a teammate's missed shot.

✔ **One and one:** A free-throw attempt awarded to the offense when the opposing team commits a foul that puts it over the limit. The shooter gets a second free-throw attempt only if he makes the first one.

✔ **Pivot:** When a ball handler has stopped dribbling, the *pivot* is the foot that must remain touching the floor until he shoots or passes. He can rotate on whichever foot he establishes as his pivot; he can spin completely around, if needed.

✔ **Posting up:** When an offensive player goes into the lane, with the defensive player behind him, and establishes an advantageous position to receive a pass and score a basket.

✔ **Release:** The moment the ball leaves a shooter's hands.

✔ **Screen:** A play in which an offensive player stands between a teammate and his defender in order to obstruct the opponent and allow his teammate to get open for a shot, a pass, or a drive to the basket; also called a *pick*. (See Chapter 12 for more on setting screens.)

✔ **Set offense:** A team with a set offense (also known as the *half-court offense*) brings the ball down court slowly and runs specific plays to create scoring opportunities. (Chapters 12 and 15 introduce some offensive plays you can run.)

✔ **Shooting range:** The distance from which a player has a legitimate chance of making shots.

✔ **Squaring up:** When a player sets his shoulders to face the basket as he releases the ball for a shot.

✔ **Turnover:** When the offensive team loses possession of the ball to the opponent prior to taking a shot.

Defensive terms

When your team is swarming the court on defense, your players must work together to prevent the offense from scoring. The following list presents some basic terms associated with the defensive end of the court:

✔ **Blocked shot:** Deflecting an attempted shot by an opponent by swapping the ball with a hand.

✔ **Boxing out:** When a player positions his body between an offensive player and the basket (with his back toward the player) in an attempt to grab a rebound. This position prevents the other player from getting the ball. Boxing out is also called *blocking out* or *checking out*. (For the basics on boxing out, see Chapter 10.)

- **Defensive rebound:** A rebound of an offensive player's missed shot by a defender

- **Deflection:** When a defensive player gets his hand on the ball just enough to knock it off its intended course, whether it's a pass, shot, or dribble.

- **Double team:** When two defenders guard an offensive player.

- **Fouling out:** Refers to a player using his maximum number of fouls allowed (usually five), at which point he can't play the remainder of the game.

- **Held ball:** When a defensive player grabs the ball while an offensive player is holding it; both players possess the basketball, but neither has sole possession. Most leagues use an alternating possession rule, in which the refs award the ball to the team that didn't get it after the last held ball, at the beginning of the game, or at the last break.

- **Help defense:** When a defensive player assists a teammate with guarding an offensive player who poses a scoring threat.

- **Loose ball:** When neither team has possession of the ball and it's up for grabs.

- **Over the limit:** Also known as *in the penalty,* this situation occurs when a team commits a specific number of fouls in a quarter or half, determined by the league you're in. The penalty results in the opposing team receiving free-throw opportunities when subsequent fouls are committed.

- **Steal:** When the defensive team takes the ball from the offense.

- **Trap:** When two defenders converge on a ball handler to catch him by surprise, usually near the sidelines or baselines.

Violations

Many violations don't result in fouls or free-throw attempts, but they still cost your team because you lose possession of the ball (called a *turnover*). Basically, you give your opponent an extra opportunity to score. The following list presents the basketball violations you need to know and teach:

- **Double dribble:** When a player dribbles the ball, stops her dribble, and then dribbles again. A ref can also call double dribble if a player dribbles with both hands at the same time.

- **Illegal defense:** Some leagues have specific rules in place regarding what types of defenses a team can play. If man-to-man is the only defense allowed (see Chapter 13), and a team gets caught playing a zone, the official calls this violation. It usually results in a free throw for the offensive team, which retains possession afterward by inbounding the ball.

✔ **Lane violation:** During a free throw, players can't step into the lane until the ball hits the rim.

✔ **Line violation:** When a player is inbounding the ball, she can't step on or over the boundary line until the ball leaves her hands.

✔ **Over and back:** After the ball and both of the ball handler's feet cross the half-court line on offense, no part of the ball or the dribbler can go back over the line (also called a *backcourt violation*).

If the defensive team deflects the ball into the backcourt, an offensive player can retrieve it without being whistled for a violation as long as she wasn't the last person to touch the ball before it went into the backcourt.

✔ **Palming:** When an offensive player puts her hand underneath the ball and rotates it over to dribble. (Head to Chapter 9 for the scoop on teaching proper dribbling techniques.)

✔ **Traveling:** When a ball handler takes more than 1½ steps without dribbling the ball. A player also can travel, or *walk,* when she picks up her dribble and then moves or changes her pivot foot, or when she secures a loose ball on the ground and stands up with it. A player on the ground must look to pass to a teammate or call a timeout.

In beginning-level programs, many violations aren't called simply because the focal point for youngsters is learning the basics of the game. Make sure you check with your league before the season starts so you know which violations the refs will enforce; with this knowledge, you can spend time teaching the proper rules to your players.

Time-related terms

The clock plays an important role in the game of basketball, to both offenses that want to keep the ball and defenses that want to take possession. As a coach, you have the responsibility of making your players aware of the clock rules. Teach them during practices and reinforce your teachings during games.

Here's a list of time violations that your players must avoid if they want to keep the ball or take advantage of if they want to take it away (make sure you check with your league to see if these rules are in place — especially if you coach very young players):

✔ **Ten seconds in the backcourt:** When a team has possession of the ball in the backcourt (after a made basket or an opponent's violation), its players must get the ball across the mid-court line in less than ten seconds.

✔ **Five seconds to inbound:** A team has five seconds to inbound the ball from the sidelines or the baseline. If a player can't spot an open teammate, he can call a timeout and his team can try again.

✔ **Closely guarded for five seconds:** When an offensive player catches the ball and a defender jumps in to guard him within six feet, the referee starts a five-second count. If the ball handler starts to dribble and the defender maintains his guarding position, a new five-second count starts. When the offensive player ends his dribble and the defender again maintains his guarding position, a new five-second count starts.If at any time during these counts the referee reaches five, she calls a violation.

✔ **Three seconds in the lane:** When your team has the ball, your players can't be in the lane for more than three seconds at a time.

Identifying common fouls

When kids commit no-nos on the basketball court, they get whistled for fouls by the referees. A *personal foul* is the most common and minor type of foul in basketball; it consists of making illegal contact with an opposing player. An example of a personal foul is a defensive player slapping down on an offensive player's arm when she's shooting. (For more info, check out the nearby sidebar "The more serious fouls".)

In the game of basketball, refs call six types of basic fouls: blocking, hand checking, holding, illegal use of hands, offensive fouls (either player control or team control), and pushing. Here's a quick glance at them:

✔ **Blocking:** When a defender illegally prevents an opposing player from moving forward by sliding in front of her without being in the legal guarding position or after the offensive player has already committed herself in the air.

✔ **Hand checking:** When a defender uses one or both hands on an opposing player to keep her in front.

✔ **Holding:** A player grabbing with her hands to disrupt or stop an opponent from moving.

✔ **Illegal use of hands:** When a player reaches in to steal a ball and makes contact with any part of the opponent's body.

✔ **Offensive fouls:** These are control fouls, such as charging, where an offensive player runs into a defensive player who has established position.

✔ **Pushing:** When a player shoves an opponent to gain an advantage in positioning. Refs often call this near the basket when players are vying for rebounding position.

The more serious fouls

As youngsters get bigger and stronger — and gain more experience playing the game — the intensity level picks up. That can lead to some more serious fouls that generally aren't found at the beginning levels of play. The following is a quick glance at these fouls:

✔ **Intentional:** A hard foul deliberately committed by a defensive player to stop the clock. Teams that are trailing late in games intentionally foul the offense in the hopes that an opposing player will miss the free throws and give them a chance at a rebound. When a team gets called for an intentional foul, though, its players were a bit overzealous in the foul attempt. Now the opponent gets two free throws with the lane cleared and then possession of the ball at the site of the foul.

✔ **Technical:** Fouls whistled for unsportsman-like behavior. For example, a player may be arguing with the referee over a call, or a coach or player may be using inappropriate language. The opponent gets to shoot one or two free throws, depending on your league's rules, and gets to keep possession of the ball.

✔ **Flagrant:** Unnecessary or excessive contact against an opposing player. Flagrant fouls usually get called if the defender isn't making a play on the basketball when he commits the foul. For example, if an offensive player is driving toward the basket for a lay-up and a defender shoves him hard from behind, a ref will call a flagrant foul. The opposition gets to shoot two free throws and retain possession of the ball.

Knowing the referee's responsibilities and common hand signals

Referees are important parts of every basketball game. They run around the court monitoring the action, protecting the players, and enforcing the rules. Without them, the game would quickly deteriorate into total chaos, like every playground game where the players must regulate themselves. Professional, college, and most high school games feature three officials. Youth basketball games, on the other hand, typically use one (in beginner leagues) or two (at the more advanced levels).

Having a ref is great, but his game management won't make much sense if you and your players don't know his signals. In some cases, a referee will be striking some strange poses! You can check out the most commonly used ref signals in Figure 3-2. (See the previous section and the "Violations" section to connect these signals with their specific rules.)

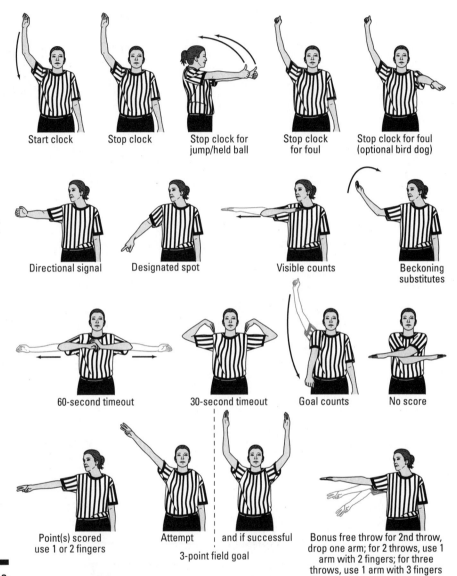

Start clock

Stop clock

Stop clock for jump/held ball

Stop clock for foul

Stop clock for foul (optional bird dog)

Directional signal

Designated spot

Visible counts

Beckoning substitutes

60-second timeout

30-second timeout

Goal counts

No score

Point(s) scored use 1 or 2 fingers

Attempt and if successful

3-point field goal

Bonus free throw for 2nd throw, drop one arm; for 2 throws, use 1 arm with 2 fingers; for three throws, use 1 arm with 3 fingers

Figure 3-2:
You and your players should know these referee signals.

Delayed lane violation

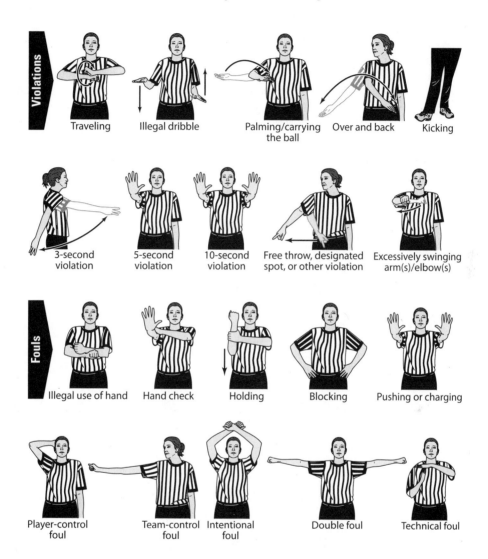

Traveling	Illegal dribble	Palming/carrying the ball	Over and back	Kicking
3-second violation	5-second violation	10-second violation	Free throw, designated spot, or other violation	Excessively swinging arm(s)/elbow(s)
Illegal use of hand	Hand check	Holding	Blocking	Pushing or charging
Player-control foul	Team-control foul	Intentional foul	Double foul	Technical foul

Considering special league rules

One of the many great things about basketball is that you can easily modify the game and its rules to fit the age, experience, and skill levels of the people who play it — in this case, your youngsters. The beginning levels of youth basketball are all about teaching kids the basics; you don't have to adhere to the rule book that the college and pro players use. The following sections show how many youth leagues tweak the rules to benefit youngsters. These adjustments help ensure that the kids get the most out of their participation and have more fun.

Honey, I shrunk the game: Making everything smaller

With youth basketball, the younger the kids in your league, the higher the chance that your league will make some adjustments to the rules. You can't expect youngsters in their size-4 shoes to be able to run up and down a regulation court without becoming exhausted and frustrated. Some of the basic adjustments deal with the size of the court and the things on it. Check with your league right away, because it may make the following changes:

- ✔ **Shorter court:** Confining young players to a small playing area allows them to stay involved in the action instead of constantly running. Quite often, one regulation basketball court can accommodate several youth games at the same time. Many league facilities have the capability to divide a court into sections, with the kids running the width of the court rather than the length.

- ✔ **Lower baskets:** It makes little sense to expect a 6-year-old to launch a ball all the way up to a regulation rim with the proper shooting techniques. Baskets in the 6- to 7-foot range are common.

- ✔ **Smaller balls:** Youngsters have little chance of maintaining control of a regulation basketball with their small hands; trying to do so and constantly failing may lead to disenchantment with the sport. Balls come in a variety of sizes, and youth leagues often use smaller ones for their players.

- ✔ **Faster games:** Because beginning players, with their short attention spans, become bored easily, games are typically shortened so that kids don't lose interest while on the court. The number of breaks and time-outs a team receives often are cut down, too, to speed along the pace of play.

- ✔ **Fewer kids on the court:** The idea at the younger age levels is to introduce the kids to the game by giving them plenty of chances to dribble, take shots, and guard opposing players. With fewer players on the court, kids get to experience more of these facets of the game. Scaled-down youth games, such as four-on-four and three-on-three, are quite common around the country.

Designing plays and positioning players takes a backseat when you're coaching at the younger age levels. You just want the kids to learn some of the game's basics before you introduce them to the more advanced aspects of the sport. (See Chapter 2 for more on forming your coaching philosophy.)

Not the NBA: Enforcing technical rules modifications

Many leagues go to great efforts to ensure that all the kids involved in their basketball programs have a memorable experience and will rush to sign up again next season. You need to be aware of any rule modifications your league makes that can enhance your impact with the kids. The following list outlines some ways that many youth leagues modify the rules of the game to meet the needs of the kids:

✔ **Allowing on-the-court coaching:** In beginning-level leagues, coaches often are allowed on the court so they can talk to their teams and provide helpful instruction and positive feedback during play.

✔ **Permitting only basic defenses:** Coaches can be tempted to introduce different defensive styles of play as soon as the season gets underway — especially after observing college or pro teams on television. This can be pretty confusing to youngsters who are just starting out.

✔ **Banning full-court pressure:** Programs often stipulate that coaches can't use full-court, or even half-court, defensive pressure (see Chapter 16). Leagues want all youngsters to have a chance to get the ball up the court and set up the offense.

✔ **Ignoring three-second violations:** Because many young kids won't pay attention to their position around the lane, leagues often allow kids on offense to stand in the lane as long as they want.

Preparing Your Kids to Step on the Court

In a regulation basketball game, your team will have five players on the floor at a time — two guards (point guard and shooting guard), two forwards (small forward and power forward), and one center. Basketball uses a numbering system to identify the positions on the floor. The point guard is referred to as the 1; the shooting guard is the 2; the small forward is the 3; the power forward is the 4; and the center is the 5.

Each position on the basketball court carries its own unique set of responsibilities and calls for a specific skill set — the older the kids become, the more true this statement rings. (At the younger levels of play, you're likely to see all ten players hovering wherever the ball is; positioning is the furthest thing from their minds!) In the following sections, we take a closer look at what's required at each position in terms of responsibilities and skills.

During the season, you can modify your lineup and use all sorts of different combinations in terms of positions. For example, you may decide that your team is best suited to use three guards and two forwards (maybe you have shorter, younger players); or perhaps you want to go with just one guard teamed with three forwards and a center (depending on your skills, height, and athleticism). After your season gets going and you have a chance to evaluate your kids' skills, you can formulate lineups that fit the strengths of your team. (For more details on evaluating players, flip to Chapters 5.)

Reviewing responsibilities of the positions

Each position on the court, at both the offensive and defensive ends, carries specific responsibilities — especially at the more advanced levels of play. When assigning players to positions (see Chapter 5), you must understand what's expected of each position and be able to share that information with your kids. The more knowledgeable you are regarding the positions, the better chance you have of matching the right players to the most appropriate positions. For a quick glance at the many responsibilities and desired characteristics for each specific position, check out Table 3-1.

Table 3-1	Breakdown of Desired Characteristics by Position	
Position	*Offense*	*Defense*
Point guard (the 1 position)	Best dribbler and ball handler; best passer; good outside shooter; good leadership abilities; ability to run set offense	Quickness; ability to shut down drives to the basket and pressure outside shots; willingness to be the first line of defense against breaks; quick hands to create turnovers
Shooting guard (the 2 position)	Best shooter; ability to manufacture own shot; good ball handler and passer; good shooting range	Good perimeter defender; ability to deny penetration; quickness to get back on defense
Small forward (the 3 position)	Good dribbler; able to create own shot; comfortable moving around the lane to receive passes; ability to penetrate the defense; good inside and outside shooter	Most versatile defender; athletic; can defend both post players and outside shooters; ability to prevent penetration
Power forward (the 4 position)	Comfort level dribbling in traffic; ability to move around the lane and get open; good scoring moves in the post; good passer after rebounds and when double teamed; good hands for catching passes; ability to set screens	Very good post defender; very good rebounder; willingness to provide help defense on open players; ability to take charges; ability to block shots

Position	Offense	Defense
Center **(the 5 position)**	Biggest threat to score from close range; good close-range scoring moves; good hands; decent passer; good screen setter; willingness to work to get open; works to get offensive rebounds	Best shot blocker; willingness to take many charges; very good rebounder; works to alter inside shots; prevents inside scoring and offensive rebounds

Specific skills required to play

One of the many unique characteristics of basketball — and one of the most challenging aspects of coaching it — is that players need an assortment of different skills to enjoy success. Within just one minute, a player could use all the main skills: dribble, shoot, pass, rebound, and defend. Adding to the sport's complexity is that players must constantly transition from offense to defense — often in the blink of an eye.

The more skills your players develop, and the more they grasp the fundamentals, the more enjoyment they'll get from the game. In the following sections, we dissect the basic and essential components of the game. Chapter 5 allows you to assess your players to see how well they execute these skills.

Dribbling

More so than any other skill, *dribbling* the basketball — the act of using either hand to bounce the ball on the court — is a skill that all players, regardless of position, must be able to perform. Dribbling is essential because every time a player gets his hands on the ball, he'll be much easier to defend if he can't dribble well. Also, he won't have many opportunities to shoot because the ball will always be swiped by the defense. Your players can utilize different types of dribbles based on the game's circumstances. (For more details on the types of dribbles and teaching your kids sound dribbling techniques, flip to Chapters 9 and 12.)

Being an effective dribbler is important at all positions for a number of reasons. The following list is a quick glance at why the players on your team should be proficient dribblers:

  ✔ **Guards:** A guard who can't dribble is like a chef who doesn't have any cooking utensils. Guards must be able to handle the ball efficiently (without looking at it at the more advanced levels) to help their teams get set on offense, to maneuver out of double teams and traps, to drive to the hoop against defenders, and to find openings to pass to teammates.

✔ **Forwards:** The most effective forwards are the ones who can use the dribble to create shots from the outside and to drive to the basket. A good dribble is vital for power forwards to get close to the basket. These players often rely on the dribble when they're defended tightly in the post and need to be able to maneuver.

✔ **Center:** Although centers dribble less often than their teammates, their dribbling in the paint makes them strong inside forces. For example, when a guard feeds the ball into the post area, the center's ability to make a quick dribble to the left or right determines his scoring opportunities. Occasionally, after pulling down a defensive rebound, the center may have to dribble the ball up the floor — especially if his teammates are closely guarded.

Passing around some basketball lingo

Understanding the terms and rules of basketball — and teaching them to your players — is one of your top priorities. To that end, gaining insight on some basketball jargon is as much a part of the game as high-top shoes and tank tops. One of the many interesting aspects of this great game is the off-the-wall phrases and words people use to describe play at the offensive and defensive ends of the court. Introduce your kids to some of the following phrases, which really add a lot of flavor to the game; they'll get a kick out of it:

✔ While possessing the ball, a player has many options. He can shoot from *downtown* (shooting the ball from long range) or dribble *coast-to-coast* (dribbling from one end of the court to the other). You can shoot an air ball, take the air out of the ball, or even have a dead ball. An *air ball* is a shot that doesn't hit the rim. *Taking the air out of*

the ball refers to a team that constantly dribbles around and passes to run out the clock.

✔ An offensive player can *drain a shot* (make a basket), *take a rainbow jumper* (a high-arcing shot), or *make a living from behind the three-point line* (rely on making a lot of three-pointers). He can also take the ball *to the hole* (drive toward the basket), *dish the rock* (deliver a pass to a teammate), or *convert from the charity stripe* (make a free throw).

✔ On defense, players can *get in an opponent's jersey* (guard him really closely), *rub out a player* (box him out to grab a rebound), and get called for *goaltending* (interfering with a shot while it's on its downward flight toward the basket or making contact with the ball while it's directly above the basket or on the rim).

Shooting

Shooting the ball (when a player releases the ball from his hands in an effort to drop it through the basket) is the universal symbol for basketball and is, without question, what your kids will enjoy doing the most. After all, seeing the ball drop through the net is one of the most thrilling aspects of the game. Teaching your kids the proper shooting techniques can be equally enjoyable for you. At the youngest age levels, you should zero in on building good shooting fundamentals (see Chapter 9). If you're working with older kids who have more experience with the game, your focus should shift to executing more difficult shots that may be required in games (see Chapters 12 and 15).

Passing

The most difficult offenses to defend feature players who embrace passing the ball all over the court. *Passing* is when one player delivers the ball to a teammate by throwing, tossing, or bouncing it to him. When you force defenses to work hard covering every player because of your ball movement, you increase your chances of generating quality shots. Plus, if your players rely on one-on-one moves and throw up haphazard shots, they won't have nearly as much fun as teams that willingly distribute the ball to open team-mates. This is especially important for younger players. (Chapter 9 covers how to teach your players the basics of passing.)

Rebounding

Your team's ability to create scoring opportunities for your offense while lim-iting your opponent's offense hinges on rebounding. *Rebounding* is when a player grabs a shot that misses its mark and doesn't go in the basket. It's an area of the game that emphasizes hustle and makes a significant difference in a team's effectiveness at both ends of the court:

- ✔ A good offensive rebounding team can reap a number of benefits. After rebounding a teammate's missed shot, a player may be in great position to attack the basket and score. Or, after securing the rebound, a player may spot an open teammate to pass to for a scoring opportunity, or he can send the ball back to the perimeter so a teammate can reset the offense. These are all good things. After all, when you keep the ball away from your opponents, they can't score (see Chapter 9)!

- ✔ A strong defensive rebounding team really limits what the opposition can accomplish on offense. For example, when your team grabs most of the rebounds off your opponent's missed shots, you really put the pres-sure on the other team to get quality shots — and make them — because its players won't get many second-chance opportunities (see Chapter 10).

Defending

Playing defense may not be as fun or exciting for younger kids, but it's a major part of the sport because roughly half of every game is spent on defense. *Defending* is when a player guards an opponent on the offensive team and tries to prevent him from executing skills such as shooting, passing, and dribbling. Playing good defense requires quickness, footwork, and, above all, a passion for denying opposing players chances to generate offensive production.

When teaching defense to youngsters (see Chapters 10, 13, and 16), stress that being a good defender is a great way to excel in the sport for years to come. You don't have to be tall to be a good defender, and you don't have to be blessed with tons of natural ability. The most important ingredients to becoming a defender who drives opposing players crazy are tenacity and hard work. Any youngster with drive can utilize those qualities.

Chapter 4

Getting to Know the Parents

*B*eing a successful youth basketball coach involves not only teaching your kids assorted skills, but also connecting with their parents. Communicating with the moms and dads is essential for establishing a positive and fun-filled environment; how well you do it makes a big difference in whether the season is problem-free or filled with hurdles.

This chapter takes a look at when you get your first chance to meet the parents: the preseason parents meeting. Here, we run down all the key topics you have to cover with the parents — ranging from explaining your coaching philosophy to outlining the type of behavior you expect in the stands — before you take the court with the kids. We also sort through the paperwork maze you have to navigate — covering the consent, medical evaluation, and emergency treatment authorization forms — and we share the best ways to recruit parents for the assistance they can provide. With a little help, you can keep your focus zeroed in on the kids. So, are you ready to meet the parents?

Working with the parents, rather than against them, makes for an enjoyable season for everyone involved. Establishing this mantra from the outset with open communication and by demonstrating your willingness to do everything possible to help their children is a positive step in the right direction.

Setting the Tone with Mom and Dad

Gathering the parents before you hit the hardwood gives you the chance to first introduce yourself and then review what will happen and what you expect this season so they aren't surprised by any moves you make at any point. During your introduction, establish that you want to work with the parents — not against them — to ensure that their youngsters have a fun-filled, safe, and rewarding season.

During your introductory meeting, you get your only chance to make a good first impression. Approach the preseason meeting with the same focus, effort, and enthusiasm you'd give during a job interview — or when meeting a future in-law you really want to impress! Don't worry, no one expects you to be a professional speaker. You just need to clearly explain your thoughts on the topics you cover to demonstrate how deeply you care about the upcoming season and about each child on the team. Listening to your thoughts on the upcoming season should put the parents at ease and make them feel comfortable turning their children over to you.

The more comfortable your kids' parents are with you, the stronger your relationship will be with both them and their children. Keep the following points in mind to make your introduction to your parents a successful one:

- ✔ **Make the meeting convenient.** You're busy and so are the parents of your players, so try to make the meeting easily accessible for all. Your best bet is to hold it at the recreation department that runs your league. Because the parents had to go to the league headquarters to sign up their children for the league, it's the most obvious meeting spot. Let your league director know that you want to use the space so he or she can make arrangements to reserve a room. If space is a problem, local libraries often have meeting rooms available.

- ✔ **Choose a convenient time.** Go with a time that promotes maximum participation. If you choose a mid-week afternoon or a Friday night, you'll likely be speaking to an empty room. If your recreation department has an open gym on Saturday mornings, schedule a meeting then. The children can shoot baskets and get to know each other while you meet with the parents. If that isn't possible, a 7:30 p.m. starting time during the week is a wise choice; this time gives most families a chance to have dinner before coming to your meeting.

- ✔ **Set it up as soon as possible.** As soon as you get your hands on your team roster, contact each child's parents to introduce yourself as the coach and to let them know the date, time, and location you've chosen for your meeting. During your calls, stress the importance of attendance at the meeting. Giving parents as much notice as possible gives them time to arrange their schedules.

- ✔ **Keep it structured.** Plan on spending at least a half hour, and no more than an hour, to cover all your topics during the meeting.

- ✔ **Outline your thoughts.** Begin by jotting down the main points you want to cover and then fill in the minor points under each of the appropriate categories.

A great starting point is to ask yourself what you'd want to know if you were handing over your child to a new coach. You'd probably want to know what type of coaching experience the individual has had, how often the team will practice (see Chapter 2), and how the coach plans to determine positions (see Chapter 5), among other things.

- ✔ **Rehearse your presentation.** During the season, you'll tell your players that the only way they can become better shooters or ball handlers is by practicing; use the same mindset to prepare for your meeting. After you outline your points and put them in order, rehearse what you're going to say to become familiar with the material. Being prepared is the best antidote for conquering speaking nerves. During your preparation, practice taking plenty of deep breaths! If you think that speaking in front of a small group will be a bit nerve-racking, practice in front of your spouse, a family member, or some friends.

- ✔ **Use notes.** Bring a notepad that features your main points outlined and refer to it during the meeting. Having notes indicates that you want to make sure you cover all the important points for the parents' benefit.

Don't write out every point you want to make and read them word for word at the meeting. That technique will bore the parents and make them wonder just how much fun their children will have with you this season.

- ✔ **Include time for parent introductions.** The parents will be seeing quite a bit of each other during the season, so the preseason meeting is a good time for them to break the ice and form bonds right away. At the end of the meeting, have the parents introduce themselves and their children.

- ✔ **Open up the floor.** Don't forget to include time for a question-and-answer session at the end. (Check out the "Concluding the Meeting with Q & A" section later in this chapter.)

- ✔ **Save the paperwork for the end of the meeting.** Distribute the necessary paperwork for parents to fill out at the conclusion of your meeting to avoid distractions. (For info on the specific paperwork you want to hand out, check out the section "Putting Together the Paperwork" later in this chapter.)

- ✔ **Have a backup plan.** Ideally, your meeting will feature a flawless presentation and 100-percent attendance. Unfortunately you can't control the attendance of others. If a parent simply can't attend, arrange a time when you can cover everything over the phone, or meet with the parent at a time that's convenient for all parties.

In addition to making initial contact with your players' parents and covering the upcoming season, the preseason meeting serves other purposes, for both the parents and you:

- ✔ **Your players' parents get a chance to know who their children will be spending time with this season.** This helps put them at ease and sets the tone for a positive experience for everyone.

- ✔ **You get some valuable insight on the kids by meeting their parents.** Knowing if a child has a hearing problem, for example, makes you aware that when working with the youngster you must make some adjustments to ensure that he has a positive experience.

- ✔ **You explain how you'll handle the team, which can reduce the likelihood of problems arising.** When parents know the ground rules in advance, it cuts down on the chances of them questioning how you run the team throughout the season (to deal with problems, head to Chapter 19).

More John Wooden than Plato: Explaining Your Coaching Philosophy

Parents may come to the preseason meeting armed with more questions than Alex Trebek. By detailing your coaching philosophy — how you'll handle everything from delegating playing time and assigning positions to emphasizing good sportsmanship and defining the role winning plays — you can answer many of their questions and minimize the chances of misunderstandings occurring during the season. (Check out Chapter 2 for more details on crafting a coaching philosophy.)

This section explains how you can convey your coaching style and philosophy to the parents. If they don't like your philosophy or don't think the league is a good fit, this heads-up at the preseason meeting provides ample time for them to find a more appropriate league or level of competitiveness for their children.

Relaying your stance on wins and losses

You won't have any trouble getting the parents' full attention if you bring up the topic of winning and losing. Because of the nature and sensitivity of the subject, your stance on winning and losing will be one of the most important discussions you have during the preseason meeting. The following sections detail how you should handle this conversation.

Coaching younger children

If you're coaching young kids — 5–10 years old — you want the parents to understand that your goal isn't winning. You'll aim to introduce the kids to the basic concepts of basketball — like dribbling, shooting, and rebounding — and to make the process enjoyable so that they can't wait to work on their skills at practice and to pull on their colorful jerseys on game day. For young children involved in the sport, what the scoreboard says at the end of the game isn't nearly as important as whether they had fun with their teammates, got to run back and forth down the court, and improved on some basics of the game.

Countless studies indicate that children are far less concerned about winning and losing — especially at the younger levels — than their parents. Share this information with your parents, and let them know that your main job is to build a strong fundamental foundation and pique the kids' interest in basketball so that they'll want to keep playing and learning. Many leagues at the beginning levels don't even turn on the scoreboard during games *or* keep standings — it serves no useful purpose.

Coaching older children

If you're coaching a team of experienced ballers — around ages 11 and above — let your parents know that along with teaching the fundamentals of the game and basic strategy, your goal will be to encourage the kids to compete hard and do their best to try to win games. However, also stress that winning only matters if you do it within the rules of the game while displaying good sportsmanship.

As youngsters become older and more advanced in the game, winning and personal performance play more prominent roles in their attitudes. These kids want to devote more time to training and practicing to improve their skills and win totals, and their parents will expect you to take your coaching skills up a notch with respect to game-day strategy and those tricky mid-game adjustments. (For more details on these aspects of coaching, flip to Chapter 7.) Regardless of the level of play, though, winning isn't everything; having fun and striving to improve is what it's really all about.

Emphasizing good sportsmanship

Although your kids' parents will assume that you'll be teaching basketball fundamentals, they may not be aware, going into the preseason meeting, of your commitment to teaching good sportsmanship. Parents will appreciate that you plan to teach their youngsters this important trait, because sportsmanship is a valuable lesson that can be applied to many areas of life.

During the preseason meeting, go over your plan for stressing good sportsmanship. Share with the parents that you'll have their kids do the following:

✔ Shake hands with their opponents following games

✔ Refrain from excessive celebration that opponents could misinterpret as gloating

✔ Congratulate their opponents for playing well after losses

✔ Follow your lead when it comes to good sportsmanship

✔ Discuss both good and bad examples of sportsmanship from the professional and collegiate ranks that they see on television

Being a good sport is especially tough on days when the shots don't fall and the calls go in the other team's favor; however, playing fairly, showing respect toward refs, and accepting the game's results graciously are important lessons for young players to learn.

Stressing the importance of model behavior in the stands

The kids aren't the only ones you should expect model behavior out of; your expectations of good sportsmanship should carry over into the stands where the parents roam. Stress during the preseason meeting that your coaching philosophy on sportsmanship includes both players and parents.

During your meeting, you can explain to the parents how you expect them to behave in certain situations. Leave no room for misinterpretation. Be sure to cover the following points:

✔ **Emphasize the importance of good sportsmanship before, during, *and* after games by *all* parties.** If parents show poor sportsmanship at any point during a contest, their kids are more likely to copy their behavior, no matter what the coach stresses. Let them know that mixed signals do no good. Actions speak much louder than any words spoken about being a good sport, and you need parents working *with* you as you teach your players proper behavior.

✔ **Explain that you won't hesitate to have people removed from the stands if they're being negative influences.** Don't be condescending or adversarial in your tone; just hammer home the point that the game is about the kids and making sure their memories are of having fun and developing skills, not of listening to out-of-control spectators making everyone miserable. (See Chapter 19 for more on dealing with disruptive parents.)

Many leagues have policies in place for the removal of spectators; make sure you're aware of what steps are required for doing so. (See Chapter 2 for more on knowing your league's rules.)

✔ **Discourage parents from yelling at officials, opposing coaches, and opposing players.** Comments from the audience should be positive and encouraging. If a player on the opposing team makes a nice shot or a great pass, everyone should applaud the play to let that child know she did something well. Showing support for all the kids makes for a great day of basketball. Also, make sure parents are aware that they're not allowed to make comments to the opposing coach at any time. Let the parents know that you — and only you — will deal with issues that come up, such as rough play, that involve the opposing coach.

In all levels, from the NBA to youth league games, coaches and refs make mistakes. Beginning-level games typically are officiated by teenagers who, despite their best intentions, may make questionable calls from time to time due to inexperience. Make parents aware of this fact, and let them know that yelling or publicly questioning a call — no matter how bad it may seem — is totally unacceptable.

✔ **Ask parents to refrain from shouting directions.** Hearing multiple sets of instructions confuses the kids. Children are easily distracted and don't perform as well — or have as much fun — when they're being screamed at in all directions. Remind the parents that you're the coach and that all instruction needs to come from you. They should limit their comments to acknowledging good plays and hustle.

Determining playing time and positions

Informing parents during the preseason about how you'll determine positions and playing time will save you many trips to the cabinets for headache medicine. These two topics will grab a parent's attention as much as a bad grade on a report card. The more information you can relay about how these aspects fit into your coaching philosophy, the less you'll have to deal with upset parents in the future. The following sections walk you through these two touchy topics.

Playing time through the ages

Outlining your policy on playing time before the season can help you avoid conflicts with parents during the season. Share with the parents the qualities you'll be keeping a close eye on this season — such as sportsmanship and practice attendance — and how they'll affect playing time, and make sure you stress that equality is paramount in youth leagues (see Chapter 2).

Whether you have seven kids or a dozen, one of your top priorities on game day as a youth league basketball coach is making sure that you divide playing time equally among the kids — especially at the younger age levels (12 and under). As long as your players meet your expectations in terms of practice attendance and sportsmanship, they should receive an equal amount of playing time, regardless of their skills. Explain to the parents that it isn't fair to the kids who show up for every practice to share equal playing time with teammates who show up only on game day.

At the more competitive levels of youth basketball (usually around ages 13 and above), where winning games is more important to the youngsters, parents, and coaches, you should base playing time more on your players' abilities. Parents must clearly understand your policies — regardless of how talented they think their kids are; if your philosophy doesn't meet their needs, they can look for a different program.

Of course, even at the most competitive levels of play, other areas factor in to the amount of playing time a child should receive, including

- ✔ Whether she pays attention and listens to instructions
- ✔ Whether she's a supportive teammate
- ✔ Whether she gives maximum effort during practices and games
- ✔ Whether she abides by the rules of the game and is a good sport

Who plays where and why

Just like with playing time, the age of your kids determines who plays where and why. At the younger age levels, choosing positions for the kids to play is like deciding on an entrée at a really good restaurant: Whatever you choose will probably work out just fine. With the younger kids, your goal is to give your players a taste — excuse the pun — of at least a few different positions.

Use the meeting to share your philosophy for introducing kids to the different positions on the basketball floor. Most parents will appreciate your interest in giving the kids the chance to experience different aspects of the game. In fact, let them know that opening a child's eyes to a new position may spark a more enthusiastic response from the youngster; the new position may end up being what keeps her actively involved in the game for years to come. Parents who feel disappointed that their child won't get to play a specific position as much may be pleasantly surprised to see her excel at an unexpected position — especially if they didn't realize she had the talent to play so well.

Let the parents of your beginning-level players know that you'll also constantly change your lineup so that all the kids get a chance to start some games, come off the bench as subs, and experience different positions on the floor. Even if your team works really well together one week, you won't lock in those starters and use the exact same lineup the rest of the season.

Parents who had designs on their child playing point guard all season long won't be too thrilled upon hearing that you're planning on moving her around. However, telling them up front at least gives them the chance to come to peace with your philosophy or sign up their child elsewhere.

At the more advanced levels of play, figuring out where your kids are best suited to play is more important. The position decisions you make impact how much success your team will enjoy and how much fun your players will have. Let parents know that basketball is a team game and your job is to evaluate the kids' skills and fit them into slots that give the team the best chance to win. (Chapter 5 discusses evaluating your players.) Stress to the parents that the bottom line is the team. You may have four or five kids who desperately want to play shooting guard; your job is to figure out which player(s) has the talent, work ethic, and attitude to handle that position, and which player gives the team the best chance to perform up to its ability. Some kids have to start the game on the bench, but that doesn't mean they're not valued members of the team; they can still make huge contributions when they take the floor.

Putting Together the Paperwork

In most youth basketball leagues, parents are required to sign a series of forms before their children are allowed to participate in games or practices. Parents typically fill out these papers during the registration, but sometimes the responsibility of securing the proper paperwork is dropped in the coach's lap. Although the content and style of these forms varies from league to league, the purpose generally is the same: to inform all parties about necessary info and keep the kids safe. The following sections give you a rundown of the forms you may need to distribute to parents.

Beyond the required league paperwork, you can make your job easier (and keep your sanity in the process) by distributing homemade packets of information to the parents. In these packets, you can include a team roster and contact information, a copy of the practice and game schedule, basic info on basketball for parents who aren't familiar with the sport (see Chapter 3), and a list of the rules that your league has modified.

Doing your duty with league paperwork

Your league will require that your parents receive and fill out a variety of forms before their kids can lace 'em up. If your league doesn't give them the forms or have them fill out the forms during registration, you have to get them the forms and collect them for your league. The end of your preseason meeting is a perfect time for this duty. Take a closer look at these required forms:

✔ **Game and practice schedules:** Leagues typically set the schedules for their seasons well in advance; be sure your parents get copies of the schedule so they can plan ahead accordingly. Also, if your league determines what days and times your team gets to practice, make sure you include that information for parents as well. Provide as much info about what's coming each week as possible. Encourage parents to let you know if they spot any dates that pose scheduling conflicts.

✔ **Consent forms:** A consent form makes clear the risk that a child may get hurt during a basketball practice or game, and it states that in the event of an injury, the league isn't responsible. Most youth leagues carry insurance against possible litigation. Be sure you ask your league director about the league's coverage and your own status under the policy, and relay this information to the parents at your meeting. The National Youth Sports Coaches Association, a program of the National Alliance for Youth Sports, for instance, provides coverage to coaches who complete its training program.

✔ **Medical evaluation forms:** A medical evaluation form, which must be signed by the child's physician, basically states that the youngster is physically healthy enough to participate in the sport. In many cases, the league distributes these forms to the parents during registration. If the child has a condition such as asthma or diabetes that you must be aware of (see the section "Meeting Your Players' Special Needs"), this sheet will list it.

Distributing info with personal packets

Distributing a personal packet not only provides the parents with convenient access to all the important league and team information, but also makes a great impression. Coaches who put in the effort to include parents every step of the way are rewarded with the parents' respect, admiration, and assistance during the season. The following sections present some options for information you can include in the personal packets.

A parent's rules primer

Most of your parents will be fairly familiar with the rules and terms of basketball, but you can't rely on this assumption. Some parents may not have played the game growing up and don't watch it. You simply don't have enough time to go over the entire game in detail during the preseason meeting. What you can do is give the parents a rules primer that covers the basics of the game. Educating your parents will make them more eager to practice with their kids and more excited to watch their games. Encourage them to touch base with you after they've reviewed the rules if they need further clarification on anything.

Don't turn assembling a rules primer into a huge project that keeps you up all night scribbling, cutting, and pasting. Just try to put together a couple pages on some of the basics. You can include a rough sketch of the court and its markings, define some basic terms associated with the game, and list the official's hand signals (you can copy them from Chapter 3).

In the personal packet, include a page that notes any special rules your league has introduced or altered. This page is especially important at the younger age levels, where the rules are very basic (see Chapters 2 and 3). Alerting the parents to any special modifications to the rules during your meeting and in the packet greatly reduces confusion at the games.

A phone list and contact information

A single sheet with all the kids' names and telephone numbers (both home and parent's cell), along with your own, can be a pretty handy piece of paper for parents, coaches, and players. Parents can use the phone list to contact each other, and the players can use the numbers to call new friends. Plus, at some point, parents may need to contact you or another parent to arrange a ride or to discuss an issue.

As a coach, you want to be able to reach your players' parents. Many times, you'll need to talk directly to them, so you can use the phone list. However, you may want to share basic information that isn't urgent, such as plans for a postseason gathering or updates in your league standings. An easy way to communicate this type of information is through e-mail. During the preseason meeting, ask that all parents give an e-mail address.

An emergency treatment authorization form

Including an emergency treatment authorization form in the packets you hand out at the preseason meeting is a good idea. A lot of times, the league will distribute these forms to parents during the registration period, too. A child's parent or guardian fills out the form, which provides the names of three people to contact if the child gets injured and requires emergency medical treatment. The form usually gives you the authority to seek medical treatment for the child if you can't reach any of the people listed on the form.

Assembling Your Assisting Posse

Parents or friends whom you recruit to assist you can be wonderful resources and can help make the season a success, alleviating your workload in the process — *if* you find the right people and the right spots for them to fill. Most parents are more than willing to lend a hand on occasion, but you have to use your discretion to pick the right parents for the right jobs. Of course, you have to speak with them and do some research to know for sure. This section gives you a quick overview on how to get the right people to help.

Recruiting assistant coaches

Even though you'll probably be supervising a small number of youth basketball players, the responsibilities that come with the job are quite big and varied. Recruiting people you're comfortable working with to assist you or appointing parents to assistant coaching positions can help you run your practices more efficiently, which benefits the kids. If you have knowledgeable adults helping out, your drills will be more effective and you'll accomplish more each session, which translates into greater skill development and more fun for the players.

In addition to helping during practices, assistant coaches can be valuable resources on game day. Having additional sets of eyes and ears helps you in many areas, such as the following:

- ✔ **Tracking playing time:** An assistant can monitor your substitution patterns and track each child's playing time to ensure that you're giving everyone an equal amount of time on the court. This info comes in handy if a parent ever questions the amount of playing time his or her child is receiving.

- ✔ **Running pre-game warm-ups:** You have many duties to fulfill on game day before the opening tip — like meeting with the officials and the opposing coach (see Chapter 7) — so being able to rely on an assistant to run your warm-ups and oversee the stretching routine (see Chapter 18) is a huge help.

- ✔ **Policing parents:** During the game, your focus is on the game and the kids, so you may not hear inappropriate comments made by parents. An assistant coach can alert you to transgressions and help ensure that parents exhibit model behavior in the stands at all times.

- ✔ **Scouting the opposition:** At more advanced levels of play (with older kids), you can have your assistants check out the opposition as it warms up. Maybe a coach will notice that the point guard isn't a very good ball handler with his weaker hand or that the center spins only to his right to take shots. These little nuggets of information can help your players during the game.

Chances are, you won't know most (if any) of the parents before the season, so proceed cautiously before you ask who may be interested in filling assistant positions. And definitely hold off on naming your assistants at the preseason meeting. Take a little time to get to know the parents during the first few practices of the season, because you'll only be as good as your worst assistant, and this extra time will give you a chance to get a true indication of the parents' personalities. Observe how they interact with their children and gauge their interest and enthusiasm for the sport. By going this route, you're more likely to select parents who will support your coaching philosophy and emphasize the fun and learning you want to stress. You can even set aside some time after the first few practices to interview any interested parents to make sure their approaches and philosophies match yours.

Some parents who seem like perfect assistant candidates may surprise you the first time they step on the court. They may start acting overzealous and try to take over your practices by imposing their own ideals, techniques, and philosophies. Some seemingly great assistants will require so much mentoring that they'll actually detract from your time with the kids. And, a mistake you want to avoid at all costs is choosing a dad who seems laid-back at your preseason meeting and early practices but turns out to be a yeller as soon as the games begin. If you somehow make a bad judgment call on a parent, you must solve this touchy problem immediately. Meet with the parent in private and thank him for his willingness to help, but let him know that you think it's best if he steps down because your philosophies on working with kids don't quite mesh. Encourage him to continue coming to practices and games and being supportive to his child, as well as the rest of the team.

At the more advanced levels, you want to find out in advance who's interested in assisting and set times to interview them. Question their experience playing and coaching the game, why they want to be involved, and how they think they can be assets to your program. Through interviews, determine who's going to be helpful and who's going to be a hindrance.

Filling supporting roles

You may have parents who don't follow or play the sport of basketball and naturally wouldn't feel comfortable assisting in practices or providing instruction, but that doesn't mean these parents can't help you out in other areas. Most parents want to be involved in their kids' experience; they just want to help where they feel the most comfortable and where they can be the most helpful. The following list presents some of the jobs that your non-assisting parents can help out with during the season:

> ✔ **Telephone list coordinator:** Once in awhile, unforeseen circumstances make it necessary to reschedule a practice or game. It can be time-consuming for a coach to try to get in contact with every parent to inform them of scheduling changes. To wipe out those headaches, you can appoint a phone list coordinator. The coordinator oversees the phone

list to ensure that messages are communicated to every parent as efficiently as possible.

✔ **Team parent:** A great way to wrap up a practice session or game is to gather your troops for a refreshing beverage and tasty snack. You can choose a team parent who can assign parents to certain games or practices for snack duty. This parent also can organize an end-of-season pizza party or make arrangements to take the entire team to watch a high school, college, or professional basketball game.

✔ **Photo coordinator:** Team and action-shot photos are great keepsakes for the children, who years from now will get a real kick out of seeing themselves and their friends all decked out in their uniforms and in action. Besides working with you to select a convenient time for the team photo, a photo coordinator can arrange for a photographer to come out for a game or two to snap some action shots of the kids (if your league doesn't work with a specific photographer).

✔ **Fundraising coordinator:** Many youth basketball teams rely on fundraisers to offset the cost of uniforms or to purchase new basketballs, shoes, or warm-up gear. Fundraisers range from traditional car washes to selling candy and magazine subscriptions. The position of fundraising coordinator entails extensive work and may require a couple parents who are willing to share the duties.

✔ **Trophy coordinator:** If the league you're coaching in doesn't have the resources to provide trophies or participation certificates to the kids, you may want to assign a trophy coordinator who can collect funds and arrange to have small participation trophies or plaques made. You can hold a banquet and present the trophies to each child at the end of the season. Of course, you need to get each parent's approval before setting this in motion, because it involves an additional expense for them.

✔ **Travel coordinator:** This position is appropriate only for older and more experienced teams that compete against teams in other cities. The travel coordinator books the most cost-effective and convenient hotels for the team and arranges a team bus for travel (or coordinates car pools made up of families and friends).

During the preseason meeting, circulate a list of responsibilities that you want to have filled so parents can sign up for duties they're comfortable with. You can deal with any issues after you see the results. For instance, if five parents express interest in being the team parent, have them work together as a committee. If no one signs up to be the fundraising coordinator, mention that you appreciate the parents' willingness to help and ask if anyone would be willing to fill that role rather than their first preferences.

Meeting Your Players' Special Needs

Coaching youth basketball requires that you work with kids who have vastly different personalities, abilities, body types, and needs. You'll coach some kids who are gifted ball handlers, some who are natural-born shooters, and others who are uncoordinated and have difficulty learning basic skills. You may even have a child on your team who has special needs, such as a hearing or vision problem or a learning disability. (Head to Chapter 5 for a look at all the different types of kids you may be coaching this season.) As a coach, you must provide opportunity to all your players and do what you can to make the season fun for *everyone*.

During your preseason meeting, find out whether any of the children on your team have medical conditions that you need to make special accommodations for. You need to be aware of any unique situation, no matter how minor, so you can make the necessary adjustments and preparations.

This venture may be the child's first experience in an organized team setting, and the parents will be in unfamiliar territory on how to handle the situation. Be honest during your meeting, and make it clear that you want to meet the needs of every child, whatever they may be. Explore with the parents any ideas they may have to make the season more rewarding for their child. Parents whose kids have played basketball before often don't want their child treated any differently. Follow their wishes and focus on making the season a fun and rewarding one for every child.

Often, parents don't feel comfortable divulging personal information about their kids in front of the other parents. That's why you should set aside time at the end of the preseason meeting for one-on-one discussions where parents can talk to you in private. You never want to make any parents feel uncomfortable, so just let them know that you'll be available after the meeting if they want to talk. Or, if they would prefer to call you later to discuss anything, let them know that option is available, too.

Concluding the Meeting with Q & A

Near the end of the preseason meeting, you want to give the parents a public forum to ask any questions that they may have. Don't be alarmed if parents start bombarding you with questions during the course of your meeting — that's a good sign! It shows that they're listening to what you're saying and are deeply interested in their kids' well-being. Let them know that no topic is off limits. The Q & A session also allows parents who were hesitant to interrupt during the meeting to pose their questions and get answers.

Also, let parents know that if they'd feel more comfortable speaking with you in private, you'll be happy to hang around to chat one-on-one (see the previous section for more on private meetings). And if you can't answer any questions posed during your meeting, make a note of them and let the parents know that you'll get back with them with answers as soon as possible.

Be sure to remind the parents that if they have any questions or concerns during the season, you'll be eager to speak with them, either one-on-one, over the phone, or through e-mail. Make sure, however, that they're aware of the times that aren't conducive to productive discussions — such as before and after games when your focus is on the kids and your coaching responsibilities, or when you're about to take the floor to conduct practice.

Part II
Building Your Basketball Coaching Skills

The 5th Wave   By Rich Tennant

I'm sure it _does_ help you control the ball, but I'd still like to do some non-peanut butter dribbling exercises.

In this part . . .

A big part of a coach's job is evaluation, both early in the season and at the midpoint. Recognizing the strengths of your individuals allows you to assign positions and select your lineup. Recognizing the strengths and weaknesses of your team allows you to make adjustments and design and run fun-filled practices that your players can't wait to be a part of. This part has you covered on these fronts.

This part also features all sorts of great tips for planning practices that fuel learning and skill development. It even covers game day and everything that accompanies it, from the pre-game to the post-game talks.

Chapter 5

Evaluating Your Team

The best basketball coaches — regardless of the age or experience level of their players — know how to evaluate the individual skills of their players. They also understand the strengths and weaknesses of their teams as a whole and can determine which positions are right for their youngsters. The decisions you make based on your evaluations help define whether your season is marked by fun and development — your youngsters learn and flourish — or struggles and discontent.

How successfully you can put together the pieces comes down, in part, to your ability to relate to your kids — all of 'em. Your youngsters will have remarkably different abilities, characteristics, wants, and needs. These are some pretty big responsibilities being plopped in your lap! But not to worry. This chapter lays out everything you need to know to evaluate skills, assign positions, and assess your team's abilities. We also show you how to work with the many different types of kids you'll have on your team — ranging from the shy and talented to the outgoing and clumsy.

Putting Your Players (And Team) Under Your Microscope

Accurately evaluating the skills of your players pushes them down the path to greater skill development and allows them to have more fun playing the game. How so, you ask? When you understand what areas of the game individual players need extra practice in, you can target those areas to help them develop into more all-around players.

You also want to recognize what areas of the game your team needs to improve in and where you're pretty well set so you can maximize your practice time. Arriving at the court with a purpose — improving your team's and players' weaknesses — enables you to focus your drills on skills that need bolstering, or at least a nudge in the right direction. How can you accurately evaluate your players and team? This section breaks down the skills that you can focus on and shows you where you can turn for help.

Assessing your players' skills

Playing basketball requires a broad range of skills; being able to assess a youngster's strengths and weaknesses is crucial for determining where he best fits in your lineup. At the younger age levels, where you position the kids doesn't really matter because you want to introduce them to all the basics of the game. They'll move from position to position, and they'll get equal playing time. At the more advanced levels, playing a position that suits him allows a youngster to focus his skill development and make bigger improvements, which makes the game more fun for him. The positions you choose also impact the quality of your team's play.

Your early practices should offer a peek at a player's ability in specific areas. Scrimmages or games involving just a handful of players and drills are ideal ways to gain a real sense of a child's strengths and weaknesses in certain basketball skills. For example, to evaluate a player's ball-handling skills, you can watch him in a one-on-one dribbling drill to see how well he dribbles with his right and left hands and how well he moves in different directions. Chapters 11, 14, and 17 offer beginning, intermediate, and advanced drills that allow you to assess your players' abilities.

After you collect all this information on your players, you can take advantage of it by developing practice plans that focus on improving their weaker areas while enhancing their stronger skills. You also can give them valuable feedback so they can spend time improving on their own as well. The following sections cover a few areas to pay particular attention to when evaluating your players, along with the obvious skills: dribbling, passing, shooting, and defending (see Chapters 9 and 10).

Footwork

Good footwork pays off on the dance floor *and* the basketball court. Players who stand or move flat-footed tend to spend more time watching the action, which really affects their productivity (and fun) at both ends of the floor. Players who constantly move their feet create additional scoring opportunities through screens, cuts to the basket, defensive stops, and so on.

During practice (and games), keep an eye on a player's feet, because footwork dictates how well he'll perform. Watch to see if a player stays on the balls of his feet when he's dribbling and if he shuffles his feet while defending. (For more on proper footwork, see Chapters 9 and 10.)

Competitiveness

At the younger levels of play, how competitive a child is shouldn't be a focus. Many younger kids have never played basketball, or any type of sport for that matter. If they stay involved in the game long enough, most kids will gradually become more competitive. In the meantime, stick to helping them have fun, learn the game, and develop skills.

At the more advanced levels of play, you should monitor how your players respond to challenges and difficult situations. For example, does a player become easily frustrated when facing a really good defender, or does he thrive under the pressure? Does a player quickly lose confidence if a couple of his shots are blocked, or does he improvise and find ways to compensate? If certain players are easily rattled, focus on building their confidence and stoking their competitive juices so they'll always put forth their best effort.

To gauge competitiveness during practice, you can challenge the kids. See how many baskets they can make in a row. Or insert yourself into a drill and challenge the players to score on you or box you out for a rebound (see Chapter 10). Kids love going against their coaches, and if they can perform well against you, it can buoy their confidence.

Range of skills

All five positions on a basketball team require a broad range of skills (see Chapter 3 for more). For example, centers who are good at defending players in the post but lack offensive skills don't help the team as much as more well-rounded centers. To evaluate your players' range of skills, run drills during practice that focus on each of the basic skills. You can use a handful of these drills at each session to get an accurate gauge of which skills your players excel in and which areas need some extra attention.

Throughout the season, you should rely on drills that touch on all different aspects of the game so that your players have a chance to become proficient in all areas (see Chapters 11, 14, and 17).

Body language and demeanor

A basketball player's body language during practice and games speaks volumes. If his head droops or his shoulders sag, you can deduce that he probably isn't thrilled with his or the team's performance. Pay particular attention to the following:

✔ Is he too hard on himself when his shots aren't falling?

✔ Does he get frustrated when his teammates make mistakes?

✔ Does he embrace your suggestions, or is he easily offended by feedback?

You can improve a player's mental approach to the game by imploring him to play each possession as though it's the first of the game. Players who have the ability to push aside prior possessions — whether they involved missed shots or turnovers — and focus entirely on the present put themselves in better position to achieve more success. Also, work with the kids on becoming good sports and teammates. You can single out a player after each practice who exhibited good sportsmanship and provided encouragement to others.

Teamwork

Youngsters who fire up and encourage their teammates, during practice and in games, and play an unselfish style of basketball are really valuable. Even when it isn't their turn to be on the floor or participate in a drill, or the scoreboard isn't in your favor, your players can be inspiring by encouraging teammates and applauding their hustle.

On the flip side, kids who sulk or don't pay attention to the action on the court or your instructions during practice can damage team chemistry and kill morale. Have a chat with these kids, emphasizing the positives they bring to the court and how important it is that they remain upbeat for the team (see Chapter 19 for more tips on disciplining kids who don't heed your advice).

IDing the team's strengths and weaknesses

All teams will begin the season stronger in some areas than others. Some teams start off with excellent passing skills; others may shine at shooting. You just never know what you'll get when you take on coaching a youth team. Regardless of how great a coaching job you do, though, the nature of the game dictates that all teams will struggle at different points during and before the season. These problems can range from turning the ball over to losing confidence; they may be a result of some of your team's weaknesses.

To gain a better read on your team's strengths and weaknesses and to assess why your team is practicing or playing the way it is, refer to the following:

✔ **Go to the tape.** Have an assistant coach or parent videotape your practices and games. Watching tape can give you a fresh perspective on your team's play, and you may notice certain tendencies (maybe all your players drive to the basket on the right side, for instance). You can work on anything that stands out during your upcoming practices.

You also can show a player a quick video segment of his play so that he can understand how he's performing a specific skill and what he needs to do to improve or keep up the good work.

Don't adopt a professional coaching mentality and waste valuable time by making your kids watch the tape after every practice. Children should be on the court working on their skills, not in front of a screen watching video! Making them watch tape constantly is a good way to sap the fun out of playing youth basketball.

✔ **Ask for help.** If you know a coach outside your league who has more experience than you do, ask her to watch one of your practices. She may be able to provide some valuable feedback on areas she believes your team needs to spend additional time on. Experienced assistant coaches are a big help in this regard as well (see Chapter 4 for more on finding good assistant coaching help).

Give Me Five: Choosing Your Lineup

Picking your lineup is a big part of your team evaluation, and much of it depends on the age level of your kids. At the younger levels, choosing your positions and lineup is sort of like deciding between Hawaii and Belize for your next vacation: You really can't go wrong. At the 12-and-under age range, rotate your lineup so your kids get equal amounts of playing time.

However, when kids reach their teenage years, your responsibility shifts to basing your lineup on ability. You hand the starting spots to the better players, and you have to devise substitution patterns that meet the needs of your team. The following sections give you advice on assigning positions and making sure the roles you choose will allow all your youngsters to succeed.

Assigning individual positions

At the beginning levels of basketball — where games are played on scaled-down courts with lower baskets (visit Chapter 3 for the scoop on common league changes) — your main goal is to introduce the kids to the game and its most basic components. At this level, it really doesn't matter who plays center or guard, because the kids will just focus on chasing the ball wherever it goes. Therefore, every player should get a chance to play center, guard, and forward. Confining them to one position for the entire season detracts from their experience and doesn't give them a real clear perspective of the game.

As players gain experience and advance to more competitive levels, a coach's ability to fit them into the positions that best suit their abilities and the team's needs takes on greater importance. When positioning your players, keep in mind that most kids can play, enjoy, and excel at any position; however, if you want some general guidelines simply to get started, check out Chapter 3 for a rundown on the attributes of each position.

When assigning positions, remind your players that they're playing the positions because of the special skills they've demonstrated there. As the season progresses, you may recognize that a player would be better off at a different spot. We cover making midseason adjustments in Chapter 8.

Don't rely entirely on a youngster's physical appearance when choosing a position. Just because a player is tall or lanky doesn't mean he will be an effective center. If he's tall and a good ball handler or passer, he could really cause problems for opponents from the point guard slot. You don't want to pigeonhole a youngster and make him feel like he can succeed in only one area of the game. Evaluation is your job, not stereotyping.

Finding roles so all kids can excel

Chances are not all your kids will be thrilled with the positions you give them — especially because the majority of them want to be shooting guards or point guards! Your challenge as coach is finding roles for the kids that allow them to learn and develop skills, have fun, and be contributing members of the team. These goals are more important than fulfilling a kid's vision of where he should play.

Each child adds something to the team's chemistry — even if his contributions don't lead directly to baskets or defensive stops. You need to find roles for your star players and your role players. A player who may not be the best shooter can really work on setting good screens to free his teammates for shots, for example, thus taking on an important role in the team's offense. Of course, he should continue to work on his shooting, and you should make it clear how valuable his screens are to the team's success. Also, you can make sure that a more talented shooter gets in the habit of acknowledging the work his teammates are doing. The shooter should say "good screen" or point at the screener as a thank you after the play.

When assigning the roles you want your players to play, take advantage of the opportunity to stress the essence of teamwork. Clearly explain that in order for the team to work together as a cohesive unit, the players have to make sacrifices. That means not everyone can play center all the time or run the offense every game from the point guard spot. Make sure they realize that every position on the floor is equally important. To help get your point across, be sure to applaud strong rebounds by your guards as enthusiastically as you do putbacks by your forwards. And don't forget to give rave reviews for the little things, like good screens, steals, and passes.

 If you want to show the kids that every position on the floor is vital to the team, you can take a field trip to a professional, college, or even local high school basketball game. This fun team-bonding activity can be an outstanding learning experience for everyone. Have your kids track the players on the floor who play the same positions they do; this observation will give them a good sense of each position's importance. Your kids may even pick up a few pointers on how to improve their own play.

From Shy to Showboat: Understanding and Interacting with All Kinds of Kids

One of the most interesting, challenging, and, at times, headache-inducing aspects of coaching youth basketball is that every child on your team is remarkably unique in so many ways. It doesn't matter if you're coaching a beginning-level team or an advanced squad that knows all about zone defenses; your kids will test your creativity and patience at times and your ability to interact with all types of personalities on a continuing basis.

Your players' athleticism, physical development, and emotional maturity will cover a broad spectrum. Some kids will be as charismatic and outgoing as used car salesmen; others will be as quiet as mimes. Some will be passionate about playing basketball; others will treat practices like they're receiving shots at the doctor's office. Some kids will be talented and athletic; others will be clumsy and uncoordinated. How you handle this mix determines, to a large extent, how much fun your kids will have playing for you this season. This section provides the inside scoop on understanding and dealing with the many types of kids you may coach (hopefully it will help you avoid making that trip to the medicine cabinet for headache pills!).

The shy child

You're very likely to have a shy child on your team. Shyness is a part of growing up for most kids, and dealing with it is a part of coaching basketball. Be aware that shy kids often try to blend into the background and go unnoticed. They want to avoid eye contact with coaches, don't want to ask for help, and quietly move from drill to drill. Luckily for you, all you need is some patience — okay, sometimes a big dose of it — and understanding. Before long, you can lure the youngster out of his protective shell.

To help a player overcome his shyness, keep the following pointers in mind:

✔ **Always proceed slowly.** Pushing the child too hard and too early in the season may cause him to pull back even further and isolate himself more. If you allow him to get comfortable first, later in the season you can include him in front of others (have him lead warm-ups, for instance; see Chapter 18).

✔ **Be content with the little signs of progress, such as eye contact or a smile.** Your patience will be rewarded when you finally coax the child out and he becomes a more vocal and enthusiastic participant.

✔ **Encourage the child.** Give him a pat on the back after he does something well during drills. The youngster may not enjoy verbal acknowledgements from you that draw attention from other team members; however, small acts that go unnoticed can make a big impact on him and slowly draw him out of his shell. He may even start to crave the verbal acknowledgment.

Shyness isn't life-threatening, but it can handcuff a child's interactions in future social settings. As a coach and a mentoring figure who kids look up to, you're in a great position to help children step out of their protective cocoons and discover an inner courage that they never knew existed.

The uncoordinated child

In general, the younger the kids on your team, the less coordination they're likely to have. Regardless of age, though, chances are pretty good that you'll see a discrepancy among the kids' shooting, passing, and dribbling skills. Uncoordinated kids may struggle with the most basic skills of the sport; no matter how much effort they put in, learning the game doesn't come easy.

Failing to shoot the ball or rebound as well as their teammates can really frustrate uncoordinated kids. A lack of coordination can interfere with a child's self-esteem and result in feelings of inadequacy. Therefore, you should do your best to help an uncoordinated child work through his issues.

Keep in mind that as kids grow and develop, they must constantly adjust to their ever-changing bodies, which will throw off their timing and coordination. Helping a child work through coordination difficulties takes plenty of practice and patience. Here are a couple tips that will help:

✔ **Camouflage your frustration.** Uncoordinated kids often don't pick up demonstrated skills as quickly as you hope. Never make your kids think that you're disappointed in their abilities. Choose your words carefully, and never allow a negative tone to creep into your voice or body language.

> ✓ **Heap on plenty of praise.** Just like youngsters who struggle with addition and subtraction don't look forward to math class, kids who wrestle with coordination difficulties may dread practice and game day. They fear their struggles and don't want to disappoint teammates, coaches, and parents. Praising effort every chance you get lets them know that they're capable of picking up skills and contributing.

The reluctant child

Sometimes, a player may not be interested in returning to the game when you call on him. Perhaps he got knocked down while battling for a rebound earlier in the game, or he hasn't caught his breath from his previous playing time. Maybe the opposing team has done a really good job of defending him all game long, and he's totally frustrated by his lack of success.

Whatever the reason for his reluctance, never embarrass the youngster in front of his teammates or force him back out there against his will. If a child isn't comfortable explaining why he's hesitant to return, speak with him privately after the game to find out what happened. Try to see what you can do to ease his fears before the next practice or game.

The child with a short attention span

With kids, short attention spans are as common as runny noses. The younger your players are, the shorter their attention spans are likely to be. Your job is to create practices that keep their attention, which can be very tricky. As we discuss in Chapter 6, short attention spans place a bigger premium on practice structure and drills that keep the kids' interest and excitement levels high.

The quickest route to losing a young child's attention is spending large amounts of time talking rather than keeping him on the move and actively involved in a wide variety of fun-filled drills. You need to make your drills short, action-packed, and fun to win the kids' attention and keep their eyes away from the stands and clock. (For fun drills, head to Chapters 11, 14, and 17.)

Competitive games are great ways to grab the attention of older kids and keep them focused during practice. You can run creative scrimmages with unique twists — such as no dribbling allowed, or everyone must touch the ball on a possession before taking a shot — to keep the kids really into the action.

The athletically gifted child

You may discover that the talent level of one or two of your players exceeds everyone else's by a substantial margin. Some kids are naturally gifted when it comes to music or art; others already have the package of skills needed to excel on the basketball court. The athletically gifted player — whether he likes that label or not — stands out. Everyone knows he's the best player on the team. So, how do you handle coaching this superior talent?

One of the greatest challenges of coaching the athletically gifted youngster is providing drills that are challenging enough to enhance his skills without compromising the rest of the team in the process. You don't want to isolate the player from his teammates, but you also don't want to stifle his development with drills that don't challenge him.

You must use your creativity to concoct ways to help all your players excel at the same time. For example, if you're doing a shooting drill in which coaches guard the players, make the talented player's shots a little more difficult by putting your hand closer to his face. The other players probably won't recognize the difference, but that player will enjoy the extra challenge involved. (For more advanced drills, check out Chapters 14 and 17.)

You can easily fall into the habit of piling the praise on your best shooter or defender, because his stellar play will naturally grab your attention. You need to control your emotions and refrain from going overboard every time his shot swishes through the net or he forces a turnover. Doling out too much praise on one player can lead to the following problems:

- **Feeling too much pressure:** With all the attention, some kids may begin feeling unnecessary pressure, which can inhibit their performance and bury the fun of the game. They may think that they have to shoulder more of the responsibility for helping the team win, and if they fail, they think they've let their coaches and teammates down.

- **Alienating teammates:** Going overboard with the praise can reverberate throughout the roster. You may start to alienate other less-talented members of the team. They may view the talented player as the coach's favorite and start to think that their contributions are less worthy and their roles are less important. If you allow this to happen, your players may begin resenting you and the talented player, which can sabotage the chemistry you're trying to build.

Coaching athletically gifted youngsters is a lot of fun — as long as they maintain good attitudes and are supportive teammates. Just remember that these players are pieces of a much larger puzzle. You must maintain a proper perspective and encourage, support, and guide every player — not just the ones with the best shooting touch.

The uninterested child

No matter how clever your drills are, how riveting your instructions may seem, or how fun games are under your watch, some kids simply won't want to be on your team. Hey, don't take it personally. It happens to the best coaches. Some of the reasons kids are uninterested — most of which are out of your control — include the following:

- ✔ Mom or dad insisted on signing them up, even though they have no interest whatsoever in basketball.

  This issue is common. If explaining to the parents that their child really isn't interested in basketball and may be better off playing another sport doesn't produce the child's desired result, you have to try to make the game fun for him. For instance, if the child is competitive, issue challenges during practice that appeal to his personality. Find whatever positives you can to help ensure that his season isn't miserable.

- ✔ They watched older siblings participate and saw firsthand the pressure applied by overzealous parents or coaches; therefore, they have zero interest in going through that experience themselves.

- ✔ They've been playing for several seasons now and simply need a break from the sport before their interest burns out completely.

- ✔ Something happened last season that affected their interest (such as a painful injury or playing for an unpleasant coach), and they think that they're in for another long season.

- ✔ They gave basketball a shot but don't think it's the right fit. This is perfectly okay. The only way kids can figure out whether they like basketball is by — excuse the pun — giving it a shot.

If you have a child who just doesn't seem interested in basketball, have a private chat to discover his reason(s). By emotionally connecting with the child, you may be able to help him reestablish his enthusiasm for the game.

The disruptive child

Some of your kids will test your authority, challenge your team rules, and tax your patience at times. These kids usually covet attention, and misbehaving is one way of gaining it. Perhaps you've seen the aerial acrobats at the circus balancing on the tightrope; you'll be performing a similar balancing act when dealing with disruptive players. Lucky for you, your safety net is the information in this section. Coaches often wrestle with a couple scenarios:

✔ Being overly concerned about their kids liking them, which leads them to sacrifice discipline and ignore broken team rules.

✔ Being too harsh and too quick to punish in an effort to keep kids in line, which drains the fun out of the season for everyone. These coaches may have 100 rules and minor infractions may never go unpunished.

The trick is finding an appropriate balance between the two. Children can enjoy playing for you — and like you — while respecting your authority and your rules. Tell your players at the first practice of the season (see Chapter 6) what type of behavior you expect and what the penalties are for straying, and always address disruptive situations immediately without causing embarrassment.

If you have a disruptive player, the following cues can help you handle him (Chapter 19 goes into more detail about actually punishing players):

✔ **Grab control of the situation right away before other players get any bright ideas.** The only way you can maintain your team's respect is by punishing the offending player and letting everyone know that disruptive behavior is unacceptable.

Whenever you punish a child, let the rest of the team know the child is being punished for breaking team rules and that their teammate won't be on the court. This reinforces how serious you are about the team rules and reduces the likelihood of others acting out.

✔ **Be consistent in your discipline with all disruptive players.** Having different rules for different players is the wrong approach. Allowing the best player on the team to get away with inappropriate behavior sends a disturbing message that he's more special than everyone else. (See Chapter 2 for more on molding your coaching philosophy.)

The child with special needs

As a youth basketball coach, you have a responsibility to help all the kids on your team — the tall, the short, the great shooters, the poor ball handlers, and the kids with special needs. These needs can include everything from hearing loss and vision impairment to medical conditions such as diabetes or epilepsy. A player may even have a physical condition in which he doesn't have full use of his arms or legs. Every youngster has a right to a fun experience, and it's up to you to make that happen. Sure, you may have some reservations about working with a child with special needs, and you may question your own qualifications, but you have nothing to fear. Just like you can work with the uncoordinated or shy, you can coach and teach a child with special needs.

In Chapter 4, we discuss the importance of finding out before the season whether any players have conditions you need to be aware of. If any of your players do have special needs, make sure you do the following to ensure that the parents and you are in agreement:

- ✔ **Set aside some time before your first practice to talk to the family about their hopes and expectations.** Opening the lines of communication helps you develop teaching tools and solutions that benefit everyone.

- ✔ **Keep in mind that this season may be the parents' first venture into organized sports, and they may be apprehensive about having their child participate.** They may be counting on you for all the answers. Ask other coaches who have had experiences with special-needs children for advice and for frequently asked questions from their parents.

- ✔ **Figure out ways to include this youngster and make him a valued and contributing member of the team.** Explore all the possibilities.

  If you're coaching an older team, ask your players for their thoughts and ideas on how to include the player. They can be great resources for you, and they may surprise you with their creative suggestions. Regardless of the age or skill level of your team, having a child with special needs on the squad can be enormously beneficial for the other players. Youngsters get a first-hand lesson on having compassion and patience for others, and they learn to accept everyone's differences.

In Chapter 7, we discuss the importance of meeting with the opposing coach prior to a game. At this meeting, you should share any important information about your kids who have special needs, and find out whether any of her players have special needs as well.

The bullying child

You have to be aware that there's a chance a bully and his antagonistic behavior may show up on your roster, ready to create all sorts of trouble for everyone around him. The bully thrives on attention and finds great pleasure in upsetting others. When you identify this behavior, you have to act quickly: If a bully's behavior goes unchecked, it can sabotage the experiences of the kids whom he targets.

Kids who get picked on by bullies typically don't complain for fear of making the situation worse. That means you have to keep a close eye on the interactions among all your kids — and not just during practices and games. You have to be vigilant before and after practice, because bullies wreak the most havoc when adults typically aren't around. Don't allow the horseplay that often unfolds at these times, because they're prime times for bullies to strike and cause emotional distress.

If you're having problems with a bully, make sure you do the following (see Chapter 19 for disciplinary measures you can take):

- ✔ **Speak with the child away from the team to let him know that he needs to change his behavior immediately.** Explain that you admire his tenacity on the court, but that he should use his aggression only within the rules of the game *on* the court.

- ✔ **Refocus his energy away from picking on others.** Work with him to be a more positive influence on the team. Reinforce the fact that he's an important member of the team and that he should focus his energy on encouraging and supporting teammates. Let him know that if he does so, they'll do the same for him in return. Make the conversation a productive one by being friendly yet firm. He may even pick up some pointers from you on how to be a better person.

  You can even run some individual drills for your players a few minutes after the conversation so that the bully doesn't have contact with his teammates right away.

- ✔ **Keep the parents in the loop.** His parents may react negatively to you simply because they don't enjoy anything less than positive words being said about Junior. (In your interactions with his parents, you may even get a glimpse into why the child is behaving this way.) Keep a positive tone and share with the parents that although you enjoy coaching their child, his behavior is unacceptable and must change.

The inexperienced child

For all sorts of different reasons, some kids may get involved in basketball at a much older age than their friends. For example, if you're coaching a 12-and-under team, an 11-year-old who has never played organized basketball before, unlike his seasoned friends, may decide to jump on the bandwagon.

With the short amount of time you have with your team, getting an inexperienced child caught up to the skill level of his teammates simply isn't a reasonable goal (unless he's a born basketball player). You can't squeeze a few seasons' worth of practices, drills, and game experience into a month or two, but you can help the youngster develop skills and become a contributing team member by doing the following:

- ✔ **Consider some one-on-one training.** If you sense that one-on-one training won't bother the child, you can use this type of instruction to help fuel his progress (and advise his parents to do the same at home). Working with the player 15 minutes before practice or staying with him for 15 minutes after practice allows him to work on skills without being singled out. And the youngster will feel special because you're willing to spend extra time with him.

Be aware that the youngster is probably already uncomfortable knowing that he's behind, so singling him out for extra work on the sidelines while a drill is going on may make his feelings more prevalent. You have to be sensitive to each player's feelings.

✔ **Remain cognizant of the player's developing skill level.** If the team is doing a drill for a skill that the inexperienced player may not know (such as taking a charge), be sure that the youngster fully understands the proper techniques before including him. Safety trumps a child's wish to be included. A contact drill could pose an injury risk to him or another player. Perhaps an assistant coach could give the player some one-on-one training during the drill until he's up to speed.

The ball hogging child

A *ball hog* — a player who hangs onto the ball for extended periods of time and always looks to shoot rather than pass — creates real problems for the entire team. For instance, a ball hog ignores open teammates who have worked to get into position to score, which undermines team morale and kills your sense of unity.

If you have a ball hog on your team, you may get frustrated and not know what to do. Here are a couple ways a player can earn the unwanted ball-hog label and actions you can take to help him ditch it:

✔ **He's unaware:** Perhaps the youngster isn't aware that he's hanging onto the ball too much. He watches older players who score a lot and wants to emulate them. Maybe he's new to basketball or hasn't been involved in any type of team setting before, and he needs to get accustomed to how sharing the ball makes for a stronger and more effective unit. Go with drills that emphasize passing (see Chapter 14) to help your players break their habit of dribbling and shooting every time down the floor. You can even hold no-dribble scrimmages, where players can only pass and shoot the ball.

✔ **He receives mixed instructions:** Perhaps the child receives conflicting instructions from his dad or mom at home. A parent may be telling the child that he's the team's best shooter and that he needs to take more shots. How can you tell? If the child seems to be doing everything differently than how you're instructing the team, do some investigating. Ask the child why he isn't listening to your instructions. Perhaps he didn't understand what you were saying.

If he confesses that he's receiving conflicting instructions, that plops the youngster in confusing territory and forces you to step in. Talk to the child about his responsibility to be a team player and to listen to your instructions, and reinforce to the player's parents that they need to support what you're trying to teach the kids. (You should convey your team philosophy at the preseason meeting; see Chapter 4.)

If you have a ball hog on your team, take a closer look at your practices, because they may actually be causing some of the problems. During your drills, double check to make sure that you aren't allowing a player to dribble the ball for extended periods of time or to take the majority of the shots. If you notice inequity in your practices, resort to specific types of drills or scrimmages that eliminate opportunities for ball hogs to flourish.

The average child

The majority of the players on your team will be regular kids who enjoy playing with their friends and teammates. They won't attract the attention of college basketball coaches or wind up playing in the NBA someday. They'll simply show up at your practices ready to play for you, learn from you, and grow as players and individuals under you.

Many youth players may be participating because their friends are playing and they want to be involved, too. Some may develop a real love and passion for the game and continue playing it for years to come. Others will be content to try a new sport next season. Either way, you can give all the kids a handle on the basics of the game that they'll keep well into the future.

Chapter 6

Running a Great Practice

*W*hat's the main recipe for ensuring that your season is filled with fun? Sound practice planning that maximizes your time with your players and makes kids look forward to participating in the future. All it takes from you is a dash of creativity, sprinkled in with your passion for helping youngsters excel.

Practices that continually challenge, entertain, and motivate your kids trigger skill development and enhance their overall enjoyment of basketball. This chapter looks at how you can make these great things and more happen. You find out how to start the season with a great first practice, to provide all the necessary equipment, to craft practice sessions that meet the needs of your players, and to choose the right words to send confidence levels soaring. We also present the best approaches for helping struggling youngsters, squeezing the most out of every minute you spend on the court, and ending practices with a bang.

First Practice: Tipping Off the Season

You have a lot at stake when you step on the court for your first practice of the season. This session sets the tone for the season and gives your kids a glimpse of what's to come. Because of its importance, you want to make sure you handle the first practice the right way.

Running a quality first practice may seem pretty daunting — especially when you have a dozen sets of eyes looking up at you. It's important that you come prepared and make a good first impression with everyone in attendance — from coaches to players to parents. You also need to be prepared to focus on the proper skills — appropriate for the first practice with your kids' age group. This section shares ways to run your first practice that make your kids want to come back for more.

Making a good first impression

First impressions are oh-so-important in all areas of life, and your first youth basketball practice is no exception. Your kids will spend those first 30 seconds of contact evaluating you, and they're likely to make quick evaluations. Pulling off a good first impression will make it much easier to start forging special bonds with your players.

Keep the following suggestions in mind to help make sure your first impression is a positive one:

- ✔ **Beat the kids to the court.** You want to be the first person at the court so you can greet the incoming youngsters and their parents. This sends the message that you're committed to coaching this season. Showing up after some players gives the unwanted impression that you're disorganized and uninterested.

- ✔ **Immediately greet players.** Don't allow youngsters and their parents to stand around uncomfortably with no contact or greeting. Instead, as soon as the kids arrive, welcome them with a friendly smile and hello.

- ✔ **Start conversations.** You can greet older players with a friendly handshake and younger players with a high five. While you wait for the entire team to arrive, strike up conversations with the youngsters who are already there. Ask them why they decided to play this season, who their favorite players are, how long they've been involved with basketball, how their teams did last season, what coaches they played for, and so on.

- ✔ **Keep 'em busy.** Some anxious youngsters may arrive at the court early. If the court is open, encourage these kids to shoot around while waiting for the rest of their teammates — after you greet them and strike up a conversation, of course. This helps them get comfortable with their surroundings — especially if they've never played on that particular court. It also gives you a sneak peek at some of their skills.

Only allow the kids to shoot the ball. You don't want youngsters playing one-on-one against each other unsupervised, because injuries can occur if they haven't warmed up properly. Plus, the competition could get out of hand and become too rough.

Introducing the coaches and players

Every child deserves to have a fun and rewarding experience playing basketball, and you may need to clear a few hurdles to ensure that this happens. One of these hurdles is the nervousness and anxiety that kids may bring to the court for the first practice of the season. It's only natural that the youngsters feel uncomfortable in this situation, for all sorts of reasons: There are new coaches to meet, teammates to adjust to, and skills to learn.

You can begin to relieve everyone's anxiety by introducing yourself to your whole team — in the friendliest manner possible — and covering some of the first-practice-of-the-season basics. Paying close attention to the following small details can make a big difference in calming your players and putting them in the right state of mind:

- **Limit the distractions.** Gather the team in an area with the fewest distractions.

- **Speak on the kids' level.** Make sure you relate to the kids on their level, which means speaking to them at eye level. If you gather the players around and have them sit on the court, bend down on one knee to talk to them. Remember, this season is about them and meeting their needs.

- **Give them the scoop on you.** It's only natural for your kids to want some insight on who will be teaching them this season. Toss out a few quick tidbits about yourself. Just give some basics. Kids don't need to hear your life story and don't care if you were a star player on your high school team years ago.

- **Tell them how to address you.** If you don't specify how you want the kids to address you, you leave the door open to a lot of possibilities — some of which may not be appropriate (even if they do make you giggle). Let the kids know if you prefer being called "Coach," "Coach Jeff," or "Coach Smith." If you have a funny nickname that you think will entertain the kids, you can inform them — at your own risk!

- **Introduce your assistants.** If you have your assistants lined up (see Chapter 4), make sure that you introduce them to the players.

- **Keep the intros short.** When you must address the whole team, make the talk short. The less time they spend listening to you, the more time the kids have to play on the court.

- **Introduce players to each other.** You want to introduce the players to each other, without making it too stressful for everyone. Remember, you want everything about your practices to be fun! While the group is sitting down, quickly go around and have each child say his name. To add some fun to the introductions, have each child say who his favorite basketball player or team is. Doing so can help the kids become familiar with one another in a fun setting.

Give each child a name tag to wear during the first practice (and the second and third practices, too, if you struggle to remember names!). Put one on yourself and your other coaches to foster a sense of unity right off the bat.

Covering the appropriate skills during the first practice

The skills you focus on teaching during the first practice of the season depend on the age group of your kids. If you're coaching a beginning-level team, your kids need to start from the ground up. The only experience many of these kids have had playing the game is shooting the ball in the driveway or dribbling around with friends at the neighborhood park. Because basketball can be fairly complex — with the different fundamentals for offensive and defensive skills (see Chapters 9 and 10), the terminology (Chapter 3), and the many fouls and violations — ease youngsters into your first few practices.

With young, inexperienced kids, devote the first couple weeks of the season to some of the most basic skills. You want to give them a good sense of what basketball is really all about. To start, focus on dribbling the ball during the first practice. Kids won't be able to get in position to take shots if they can't handle the ball. After you cover the proper techniques of ball handling, you can proceed to other basic aspects of the game such as passing and shooting.

If you're coaching a team with older kids who have a little more playing experience, you can use the first practice to focus on some offensive fundamentals, like shooting. Because most kids like offense better than defense, you can put a fun stamp on your first practice by focusing on what youngsters like best about the game — putting the ball in the basket!

Keep in mind that you have the entire season to teach your players all the different aspects of the game, so you don't need to barrage them during the first practice of the season. Stick to teaching a couple of basic fundamentals and then build from there in a logical progression.

All the Balls and Whistles: Coming to Practice Prepared

You expect your players to come to practice prepared, so your kids deserve the same from you. Your players should arrive with their water bottles and mouth guards (see Chapter 2), and you need to show up with your practice plan (see the section "Practice Principles to Live By" later in this chapter) and all the necessary equipment to run a productive practice. Coming prepared is the most basic element of a successful practice. The following sections focus on two elements you need to consider: equipment and the first-aid kit.

Bring balls and other necessary tools

Multiple balls are the fuel of a well-run practice. Some leagues issue each team a set number of basketballs for practices; other leagues leave it up to the coaches to round up balls. Having a large supply of balls makes running drills easier and allows for fewer interruptions. Not having enough balls can detract from the quality of your practices. (For more on this topic, head to Chapter 2.)

Even if the league provides some balls for practice, you can encourage players to bring a basketball to practice (if they have one); if they choose to, make sure their names are clearly marked on the balls for identification purposes. If the job falls squarely on your shoulders, check in your area for a used equipment sports store where you can purchase several basketballs at cheap rates.

You should also make sure you have some small plastic cones, pylons, or other type of safe markers to use for various drills. (For a rundown of some drills that require markers, check out Chapter 11.) Just be sure that whatever items you choose don't pose any injury risk to the children.

Pack your first-aid kit

A part of practice preparation that coaches often overlook is having a properly stocked first-aid kit. Even though your league may provide a first-aid kit or even an on-site athletic trainer, you need to bring your own basic kit with you to practices and games. Basketball is a contact sport. With ten bodies moving in different directions on the court, inevitably someone will get nicked up or injured. Make sure you're prepared for any potential injuries with a well-stocked first-aid kit. (Chapter 18 explains how to treat injuries.)

The following essentials should be in every basketball coach's first-aid kit:

- **Antiseptic spray or wipes:** Use these items to clean cuts and abrasions.
- **Assorted bandages:** Use waterproof bandages to cover cuts or other wounds.
- **Athletic tape:** Use the tape to hold ice bags in place so you can reduce swelling on an injured area.

✓ **CPR mouth barrier:** You use this item in the event that a child needs mouth-to-mouth resuscitation.

✓ **Emergency tooth-preserving system:** Break out this kit if a child has a tooth knocked out.

✓ **Freezer-type storage bags:** Plastic storage bags are great for holding ice packs.

✓ **Latex gloves:** You need to wear these gloves when dealing with cuts and scrapes.

✓ **Nail clippers:** Clippers come in handy for repairing torn nails that result from contact with another player.

✓ **Prescriptions:** If a child has asthma, make sure his parents give you a spare bronchodilator to keep in your first-aid kit. You want to have essential medication in case a child forgets his or if his parents can't make it to the practice or game. (In Chapter 4, we explain the importance of asking parents during the preseason meeting about any medical conditions their children may have.)

✓ **Scissors:** You need scissors to cut bandages and athletic tape.

Here are a few other tips to keep in mind concerning your personal first-aid kit:

✓ **Be realistic.** Basketball injuries aren't like lightning: They can strike in the same place twice. Stock a reasonable amount of supplies in order to treat more than one youngster at a practice or game.

✓ **Keep count of used materials.** If you use any supplies during a practice or game to treat a youngster, restock as soon as possible so you aren't caught off-guard the next time a player or coach needs treatment.

✓ **Organize your supplies.** Make sure your supplies are clearly marked and in some sensible order. If you ask an assistant or a parent to retrieve something from your kit while you're dealing with an injury, you want the helper to be able to tell what's what so no time is wasted. Freezer-type plastic storage bags work great for keeping supplies in order.

Practice Principles to Live By

Putting together a really effective practice plan can be challenging. But with a little — sorry, we have to say it — practice, you'll become an old pro in no time, and your players will reap the benefits. A good practice plan involves knowing the skills you want to teach and what drills and approaches you want to use to teach them. (If you don't know, check out Chapters 9 and 10 for the rundown on a smorgasbord of offensive and defensive skills you can teach, and follow up by visiting Chapter 11 for some basic drills that address those areas.) This section details how you can develop a practice plan to help your team have a successful and fun season.

The more organized you are, the more efficiently your practices will run. Utilizing a *practice planner* can make a huge difference in the quality of your sessions. Simply use a three-ring binder, notebook, or even a legal pad to write down — well in advance of the practice — what you'll do that day. Create two columns to keep track of the following info:

- ✔ In the left column, list the individual drills and how much time you want to devote to each drill you have written down for a practice. This keeps you on track so you don't spend too much time in one area while neglecting others.

- ✔ In the right column, include the plan for that day with respect to a goal you want to achieve — such as teaching the kids the baseball pass — or a style of play you want to stress — such as full-court pressure.

At the bottom of the page, you can list backup drills. This list serves as a handy reference; if one of your drills doesn't accomplish what you intended it to, you can stop it and turn to one of your other drills to replace it.

Naturally, you'll want to run as many practices as possible to help prepare the kids for their games. However, most leagues have policies in place regarding practice length, when you can start practicing, and how many practices a week you can hold. Make sure you're clear on these rules before you begin planning and scheduling practices. (Check out Chapters 2 and 3 for more details on information you should know about your league.)

Set the proper tone

When developing your practice plans, remember that your tone at every practice is important. Make a commitment to yourself before the season starts to never allow what's going on off the court to infringe on your practices and how you deal with your players. The tone you set at the first practice of the season — and in practices throughout the season — should feature a steady diet of encouraging words and positive reinforcement.

To get the most out of your practices, you must arrive in a positive mood. Project an upbeat frame of mind even when you've had a disagreement with your spouse. Pile on the praise even though your boss yelled at you earlier in the day. Keep a smile on your face despite the fact that your car died on the way to work. Kids can read body language and voice tones; if you're in a good mood, you'll put them in the right frame of mind. You're the team leader — the person everyone looks up to. Negativity lays the groundwork for an unproductive hour that your players can't wait to escape.

Warm up before you start

Many kids just don't enjoy stretching. After all, youngsters arrive for practices and games eager to dribble the ball and put up shots — not stretch their hamstrings. Yet your practices should always begin with a segment devoted to warming up and stretching.

A proper warm-up enables players to perform at optimal levels throughout the session; skipping this aspect is sort of like never checking the air in your vehicle's tires. You may not have any trouble for awhile, but eventually you'll run into problems that you could've prevented. Warming up is particularly important for older players, whose muscles are more susceptible to injuries. Warm-up exercises develop muscle flexibility and reduce injury risks by preventing muscles from tiring easily.

The two primary types of stretches are

- ✔ **Static:** These are basic stretches where the body is placed in a specific position and held for several seconds.
- ✔ **Ballistic:** These rely on momentum, and the person has far less control over them.

With youngsters new to basketball, start them out with static stretches to get them used to preparing their bodies for activity. As they get older and more experienced, you can incorporate the ballistic approach to prep them for competition.

Keep the stretching exercises consistent. You don't want to waste valuable practice time introducing new stretches each week of the season. Design a basic warm-up and stretching routine that the kids can stick to all season long. For more on stretching and warming up, head to Chapter 18.

In addition to the warm-up, each practice should wind down with a 5-minute period of light exercise. This cool-down helps players' bodies return to their normal resting state. You can have players work on jump shots or lay-ups for a few minutes, or even work on an inbounds play before concluding with a couple minutes of stretching the large muscles. The cool-down doesn't have to be nearly as focused as the warm-up session, because the purpose is to wind down from the activity rather than build up to it.

Keep the practice age appropriate

The secret to running really good practices — the kind that build skills and allow the players to have plenty of fun — is making them appropriate for the age of the players you're coaching. When developing your practice plan, you need to determine the best way to fill the allotted time you have with the team — all depending on the age level of your players:

- ✔ **The beginning levels (kids ages 8 and under):** With the younger kids, you won't have much time to practice and you may get only a handful of practices before your first game and between games. Therefore, keep your practices simple and focus on the most basic components — like dribbling, passing, defending, and shooting (see Chapters 9, 10, and 11) — during early sessions. You don't want to overwhelm young-sters and leave them more confused than when they arrived for practice.

    As the season progresses, you can build on the kids' developing skills (see Chapters 12 and 13). Young players are a work in progress. Don't overwhelm them, but continue giving them just enough feedback and instruction to spur their development and maintain their interest.

- ✔ **The more advanced levels:** Start your season with a refresher on some of the basics of the game. You can follow the early exercises by jumping right into drills that target specific areas of offense and defense (see Chapters 14 and 17). At this level, you'll probably have the chance to hold many practices before your first game, so you'll have ample time to condition your kids and teach them some plays or certain defenses.

Your number one priority is to meet the needs of your kids. When setting practice plans, determine what's best for them — not what you're most inter-ested in. For example, from your experience playing or watching the game, you may be a big fan of full-court-pressure defense. However, if you're coach-ing a team of 6-year-olds who are new to the game, it makes little sense to allocate practice time to your favorite style of defense. You have so many other important fundamentals to teach first. In the eyes of a 6-year-old, just getting a handle on the game probably seems pretty cool.

Determine how long and how often to practice

Most youth basketball programs have specific policies in place stating how often and how long teams can practice. These rules exist to protect the kids from coaches who want to go overboard and cram the week with NBA-style practices. You need to be aware of your league's policies on practice before creating practice plans for your team (see Chapters 2 and 3).

If your league doesn't have any practice policies in place, use your best judg-ment when devising your team's schedule. Chances are you'll want to spend more time practicing than the kids do, so temper your enthusiasm. Keep the following practice-length suggestions in mind for your team:

- ✔ **Kids 10 and under:** We recommend one hour-long practice per week, along with a game.

- ✔ **Kids older than 10:** Only at the older and more-advanced levels should your practices go longer than an hour. We recommend no more than two 1-hour+ practices a week if the team is playing once a week. If you have two or more games a week, scale the practices back to once a week for an hour.

Establish a flexible schedule

The best practices are planned in advance, but that doesn't mean you can't stray from your plans after the session gets underway. Being flexible and adapting to your team, even in the middle of a practice, is necessary to ensure fun and learning for everyone.

Be flexible as you execute your practices. If you find that your players are having trouble executing a particular skill, you may want to spend a few extra minutes on it rather than just jumping to the next drill in your plan for the day. Conversely, if the kids pick up a particular aspect of the game quicker than you anticipated, you may want to cut the drill short and move on to something else you know the team needs work on. Keep in mind that your goal is to help the kids fully grasp a skill, and sometimes you'll have to modify your plans to achieve that.

Maintain some consistency

Parents often give their kids a set routine to follow during the week. They have kids eat at set times, play at set times, and go to bed the same time every night. This provides much-needed structure that shapes their lives; you should approach your practices the same way. If your players know what to expect when they step on the court for practice, they'll be more likely to have the proper frame of mind and be ready to go when they arrive. If you constantly make changes, you'll waste valuable practice time while your players adjust.

Stick with the same stretches and warm-ups prior to each practice to provide the kids with a nice routine before they jump into the meaty stuff. (See Chapter 18 for more info on warming up.) For instance, your warm-ups can begin with your players dribbling the ball while running a couple laps around the court. You may tweak and change your drills from week to week to accommodate the kids' development or target areas for improvement, so maintaining some order serves as the springboard for productive sessions.

Let the kids help select practice drills

One of the best ways to make every player feel like she's part of the team is to give all your players a say in some of the drills that you run during your practices. Plus, allowing your players to make choices gives you insight into the types of drills the kids tend to prefer. After you go through a portion of your season, consider allocating a 10-minute segment of each practice for the players to select their favorite drill. You can create a schedule so that each player gets the chance to choose a drill during a practice.

As the season rolls along, pay close attention to which drills the kids really enjoy and which ones seem to be duds. In a practice planner, make notes next to the drills you want to keep and those that should be discarded or at least tweaked (try to think of ways to make some of your less-popular drills more action-packed and entertaining if you can). Check out Chapters 11, 14, and 17 for a variety of drills you can use.

If you're coaching a more advanced team, you can let your players introduce a drill that they enjoyed from a past coach. And if they're interested in devising their own drills, you can work with them on the creative process.

Include mom and dad in your practices

As you create a practice plan for your team, you may realize that you can't do everything by yourself. Even with one or two helpful assistant coaches, you may need extra help to carry out your plans. Why not occasionally invite mom and dad into your practices? Doing so — especially if you're coaching a team of kids ages 10 and under — is one of the best ways to get extra help and amplify the fun.

You can incorporate as many interested parents as you want. Here are some tips to make it all happen:

- ✔ **Alert the parents.** Let parents know in advance which practices you'd like to include them in. Chances are, mom won't want to step onto the court in her business suit; if she knows ahead of time, she can bring a pair of athletic shoes and appropriate clothes. You can even gauge the parents' interest at your preseason meeting (see Chapter 4.)

- ✔ **Get the kids and parents fired up.** The week before during a post-practice chat, make an announcement to let them know that their parents will take the floor with them at your next practice.

Scrimmaging during practice: Yes or no?

You may want to incorporate an occasional scrimmage into your practice time. An *intrasquad scrimmage* is an informal game between two units on the same team. Scrimmages can be useful tools to give kids some game-like experience. Scrimmages often work well at the end of practices to give kids the chance to work on the skills they practiced during the sessions.

If you want to add a scrimmage to your practice, consider these ideas:

✔ **Run mini scrimmages.** Instead of conducting one full-scale, five-on-five scrimmage, split the court and run two scrimmages at the same time. Even if you only have enough kids to play three-on-three games, you give them more opportunities to rebound, defend, shoot, and pass.

✔ **Mix up the rules.** Use your creativity to bump up the energy and excitement and to target specific skills by changing the rules. For example, if you've noticed a lack of teamwork in previous games, run a scrimmage where no dribbling is allowed. This forces the kids to work together, because they must rely on passing to be successful.

Scrimmages are effective if you use them in moderation. However, don't fall into the trap of using them at every practice. You can't become lazy and rely on scrimmages to fill valuable minutes of practice time because you don't want to plan or run drills. Overusing scrimmages takes away from your individual teaching and instruction. Spend most of your practice time running the kids through drills that zero in on particular areas of the game (see Chapters 11, 14, and 17 for some examples of drills you can use).

✔ **Pit the kids versus the parents.** Scrimmages pitting the kids against the parents are fun for everyone. You can play two games at once, using half the court for each game, to ensure that everyone gets involved. The coaches can ref the games and watch the excitement up close.

✔ **Pair 'em up.** Have a child partner with his parent in a drill. Doing so not only helps the youngster work on a particular area of his game, but also is a great bonding opportunity for the parent and child. For example, at the beginning levels with younger kids, the parent and child can work together on a basic bounce-pass drill together. (For a look at some good drills to use at this level, check out Chapter 11.)

✔ **Use the parents as pylons.** If you're doing a ball-handling drill that calls for the kids to dribble around pylons, have the parents serve as the markers instead. Your players will get a kick out of dribbling around the dads and moms. You can increase the difficulty level of the drill by having the parents try to steal the ball from the youngsters. This forces the players to keep their dribbles low, just like they need to during a game (see Chapter 9).

Maximizing Your Practice Time

You need to make sure all the drills and activities you include in your practices enable the kids to feel like they're parts of the practice. Set up your practices to minimize the standing-around time or, better yet, make it nonexistent. Kids love running up and down the court, dribbling the ball, and taking shots, and those activities don't happen as frequently when they're stuck in long lines waiting to perform a drill. After all, the kids came to *practice,* right?

Constant motion is what you want to strive for so you can keep your practices going at a good pace and increase the learning and skill development that takes place. If you have assistant coaches or parent volunteers, you can run several drills at once all over the floor. (For tips on choosing assistants, check out Chapter 4.) The following sections touch on some more areas you need to be aware of to maximize practice time.

Schedule plenty of water breaks throughout the practice. When a youngster needs water, encourage him to get a drink. You should never withhold water from a child for any reason. For more on hydration, check out Chapter 18.

Building skills

When coaching youth basketball, you have to work your way along a logical progression to build players' skills one at a time. Teaching a youngster how to box out an opponent for a rebound (see Chapter 10) doesn't make sense if you haven't yet taught him how to handle the ball (see Chapter 9). Also, it makes little sense to devote 50 minutes of a practice to shooting the ball and only 10 minutes to playing defense. The best practices are those that allow kids to gain valuable experience performing a wide variety of drills — namely shooting, ball handling, passing, rebounding, and individual and team defense — as long as they follow a logical progression. Focusing on just one or two areas of the game is counterproductive.

Look at each practice session as a building block in your team's development. Every time you practice, you want to reinforce what you've taught so far and then add to what the kids have learned. This takes a concentrated effort on your part; you have to refrain from jumping too far ahead if you want your youngsters to grasp the basics. Evaluating your team and making the proper adjustments to fit your players' needs allows you to teach the fundamentals in the proper order and build on each skill in your practices. (We cover the art of evaluating your team and making midseason adjustments in Chapters 5 and 8.)

Helping players who need it

No matter how well and efficiently you run your practices, chances are some kids still will struggle with certain aspects of the game. When something doesn't go your way, it's easy to get frustrated and lose interest in what you're doing. The same applies to a child who sees teammates excelling at a skill while she's struggling to keep up. Your job is to make sure these kids' efforts are realized and that you assist them when they need some extra help.

Most kids respond better to physical instruction rather than verbal instruction. When a youngster is having problems, show her exactly what needs to be done. For example, if boxing out is giving her some problems, get in the lane with her and box her out. Show her how it's important to push her butt into the opposing player to establish contact and seal off the defender. Show her that after she establishes contact and sets her feet, the chances of the opponent getting her hands on the ball are greatly diminished. Now she can copy your form and execute it herself (for more, see Chapter 10).

If a child is struggling with a specific skill, and you're struggling to figure out a solution, don't tell her to watch how one of her teammates performs the skill. Although this may seem like a helpful approach, it can stick a dagger into the child's confidence because you're sending the message that the other player is better. Also, avoid giving kids so much instruction and information that they become overwhelmed by the thoughts crammed in their heads. When information overload happens, kids can't perform even the most basic skills because they're deep in thought about every move they make. (For more suggestions on what to do with certain players, see Chapter 5 and the following section.)

But, how do you give extra attention and still maximize your practice time? Every practice you conduct must meet the needs of every child. When you break up the kids for different drills at different areas of the court, you can spend extra time with the group of kids that includes the individual or individuals who are having some difficulty. This way you can closely monitor their progress and make some tweaks to your drills to help them.

What to Do if a Kid Just Doesn't Get It

As your season starts to move along, ideally your kids will be having fun, learning skills, improving, and embracing your teachings. However, some youngsters just may not be able to get a handle on some of the basics of the game. Every team you ever coach will have players who struggle to learn specific skills; how you help them overcome their challenges is the true barometer of your passion and coaching ability.

What can you do to solve this dilemma? You'll take on many roles as a basketball coach, with problem solving being just one of them. Just know that figuring out ways to help a youngster who's struggling with certain skills is vital for keeping his interest and morale high. You may need to change the way you're instructing, or you may need to alter how you're interacting with the player. This section gives you the lowdown on what to look for and what to do to help a youngster improve.

Mix up practice routines

If a player is giving maximum effort and still struggling, the problem usually can be traced to the teaching. Really take a close look at your practice approach. Some children get bored with the same routine in practice. If you have a player who's having difficulty with a concept, you may want to change the way you're teaching the skill. For starters, you can try breaking the kids into smaller groups — if you have assistant coaches (see Chapter 4) — so that youngsters who are struggling have more interaction with coaches as they go through various drills.

Keep the following additional ideas in mind for your practices; you can turn to these techniques when a youngster starts to veer off the learning path:

- ✔ **Rev up the reps:** You may be a great speaker, but kids learn quicker and have more fun when getting plenty of repetitions during a particular drill. Increase their repetitions and the skill development likely will follow.

    You can even arrange to have a struggling player spend a few minutes with you before or after practice to work on a particular skill. Spending extra time with the youngster shows him that you're committed to helping him improve, and it may pay big dividends in his development, too.

- ✔ **Simplify your instructions:** Long-winded or complex instructions bring the learning to a standstill. Keep everything you teach as simple as possible to benefit everyone.

- ✔ **Adjust your lineup:** Mix up the positions the kids get to play to keep things fresh. For example, maybe the struggling youngster had his heart set on playing forward like his brother, but you have him at guard for the first few games of the season. Try slipping him into the forward position and seeing if that sparks his enthusiasm and turns his season around. (For tips on evaluating players and choosing positions, see Chapter 5.)

If you can, teach all your kids the different skills associated with the different positions (see Chapter 3). This helps them become well-rounded players who have a deeper appreciation and respect for the game. Who knows, you may discover that a child has a real knack for playing a specific position that you didn't peg him for.

Modify your interactions with the child

When a child on your team simply can't master a skill, you must take a closer look at how you're interacting with him. Perhaps you're spending too much time talking and not giving him enough opportunities to practice the skill. Maybe you're filling his head with too many thoughts about what to do rather than keeping your instructions simple.

To help a struggling child, you may need to make some changes with *you* first, which in the end could help the child improve greatly. Keep the following in mind:

- ✔ **Never embarrass the child.** Making a spectacle out of a child who's struggling is never acceptable. Most children are well aware of how their skills stack up to their teammates', and the last thing they need is for their deficiencies to stand out even more. For instance, avoid singling out the player for extra work on the sidelines during practice while the other kids move on to new drills.

- ✔ **Maintain an even demeanor.** Don't allow frustration or disappointment to creep into your voice or body language. Remain calm, patient, and understanding as you help the youngster work through his difficulties.

- ✔ **Stick by him.** The child needs your support and encouragement now more than ever. Don't neglect him or give up hope because he hasn't contributed as much during games. Continue applauding his effort and encouraging him every step of the way.

- ✔ **Investigate to find out if he really likes the sport.** Some children may not find basketball to their liking, no matter what you or their parents say, and there's nothing wrong with that. You can speak with a child's parents about whether he should continue. You can suggest other activities that could provide opportunities for fun and athletic achievement. (A child's parents can help you with your research. Head to Chapter 8 for the lowdown.)

One of the benefits of holding a preseason meeting (which we cover in Chapter 4) is to discover if any of the children have special needs that you need to make adjustments for. That takes a lot of the investigative work out of your hands and allows you to prepare before the season starts.

Ending Practice on a High Note

How you end your practices is as important as how you start them. How you start a practice sets the tone for the entire session; how you end a practice helps establish your kids' frame of mind the next time you gather for a practice or game. You want to send players home with motivation to get better *and* with smiles on their faces.

Lucky for you, we have some secrets to share for achieving these goals. To finish your practices on a strong note, consider these suggestions:

- ✔ **Save one of your most popular drills or creative scrimmage ideas for the end of practice.** If this method goes over really big, you may have trouble coaxing the kids off the court! That's a really nice problem to have, because it shows how into the game your players are.

- ✔ **Give a post-practice chat — a quick one — to instill some good feelings.** Tell the players that you appreciate the hard work and effort they put in and that you're pleased to see the strides they've made.

Keep your talk general and focused on the entire team. The post-practice chat usually isn't the time to recognize individual efforts because you run the risk of alienating the other kids.

Don't use your post-practice chat to provide constructive criticism or rehash a drill that didn't go well. You never want to send your kids home feeling like they disappointed you. Even after practices where nothing seemed to go right — and you'll have days like that — search for some nugget to highlight so you can focus on the positives. You can pin your praise on all sorts of areas, such as work ethic or the way they encouraged their teammates.

- ✔ **Wrap up the session with a quick review of the upcoming schedule.** This is particularly important if any practice dates or game-day starting times have changed. If the next time you'll see the players is at a game, make sure that everyone can attend so you can plan your lineup (see Chapter 5) and structure your substitution patterns for that day (see Chapter 7).

- ✔ **Thank the team for their hard work and conclude with a team cheer (if you have one).** Now you can call it a day after the excitement dies down!

Put the "I" in positive role model

You have to determine for yourself when individual recognition is appropriate in a practice setting. Say, for example, a player who has struggled all season long with a particular skill finally gets it in a late-season practice, and you want to recognize him. Pointing out what a great job he did while in the midst of praising your entire team may do wonders for his morale. Plus, that serves as a fitting end to a special day in his young basketball career. Use your best discretion when recognizing individuals; as you get to know the kids, you'll develop a pretty good sense of what works best in different situations.

Unfortunately, you may be the only positive role model in some kids' lives. That just makes it all the more important to develop a connection that results in you sending the kids home feeling really good about themselves. Your struggles to instill confidence will be well worth the effort.

Make it a habit to evaluate your practices on the same day you hold them. Keep track of this info in your practice notebook, where you keep your plan for the session. Leave some space in each practice plan to jot down some post-practice thoughts, where you can make notes to yourself on everything from which drills the kids liked and didn't like to what you want to focus on at your next session. (Check out the earlier section "Practice Principles to Live By" for more on how to use a practice notebook.) You want to jot down the basics of the practice while they're still vivid in your mind.

Chapter 7

Game Day

Game day provides youngsters and coaches with all sorts of new and exciting challenges. Your players will be anxious to take the court in their colorful uniforms and use the skills they've learned in practice, and you'll be anxious to watch them flourish and use some in-game strategy. However, as a coach, you also have to handle quite an array of responsibilities before and after the game. Don't worry; your list of responsibilities may be long, but after reading this chapter, you'll see that it's manageable.

This chapter shows you the importance of a variety of pre-game duties, from meeting with the opposing coach to conducting sound warm-ups. You also find plenty of info to use after the game begins; we cover everything from motivating players to orchestrating substitutions. We devote sections to the halftime talk, how to tweak your game-day strategies when necessary, working with the refs, and ending game day with a team gathering. Finally, we explain the importance of good sportsmanship and winning and losing with class. Good luck!

Putting the Press on Your Pre-Game Responsibilities

Before your team can take the court for tip-off, you and your players have to tend to all sorts of pre-game responsibilities. You have to get on the same page with the refs, the opposing coach, and your team. You have to get your players warmed up and fired up. But first you have to actually get to the gym, and get there early. This section gives you the lowdown to guide you through your maze of pre-game duties.

Arriving early

As the head coach, you're responsible for all your players, so you want to arrive on game day before all your players do. That way, when your players pull in, they'll see that you care and that you're ready for the game. Plus, they won't be able to horseplay in your absence and risk injury (for more injury prevention tips, see Chapter 18).

Before your players have a chance to take the court, take a moment to inspect the playing area for any spots that could pose injury risks to the players — such as an area where water may have been spilled. Every step that you can take to help ensure the kids' safety is crucial.

In many youth basketball programs, games are played in rapid succession; however, you can't skirt a pre-game court check because another game just took place there.

Meeting the opposing coaches and officials

Before the game tips off, greeting the opposing coach and the game officials with friendly handshakes is a nice act of sportsmanship you can display. These meetings set a good example for the players on both teams, as well as for the parents and other spectators. And they can be functional, too. During your chat with the opposing coach, find out whether any of her players have special needs that you and your players should be aware of; with this knowledge, you can make any necessary accommodations during the game. And if any of your players have special needs, be sure to relay that information as well (see Chapter 4 for more on finding this out).

Meeting with the game officials also sets the tone for a good game — regardless of whether they're teenagers working an 8-and-under game or licensed officials working an advanced-level game. While speaking with the officials, make sure you share the following info:

> ✔ **Let them know that you want to be informed if any of your players behave in an unsportsmanlike manner.** The same goes for parents making inappropriate comments that you can't hear. (See Chapter 19 for tips on dealing with problematic parents.)

✔ **Let them know if any child on your team has special needs.** Officials can make the proper adjustments when they know this information beforehand. For example, if one of your players has a hearing problem, the officials can use hand signals to alert this child that play has stopped or a foul has been called instead of using their whistles.

You want to work with the officials, not against them. Even though they wear striped shirts and their job is different than yours, you all have the same goals: Ensuring that the kids have a good experience, have fun, and stay safe. (Head to the "Working with the Refs" section later in this chapter for more on how to interact with the officials during and after the game.)

Holding a pre-game team meeting

A pre-game team meeting puts all your players and coaches in the right frame of mind prior to the pre-game warm-ups and the opening tip-off. After your team arrives, you've inspected the court, and you've met with other coaches and officials, gather your players for a quick pre-game team meeting. Keep in mind these general pointers to hold a successful meeting:

✔ **Gather the team in a spot with the fewest distractions.** The younger your players, the shorter their attention spans. Your players won't listen to what you're saying if they can see and interact with their parents or friends who've shown up for the game.

✔ **Keep it short and simple.** Save your long-winded speeches for presentations at work. Keep your pre-game talk under five minutes; otherwise, you risk deflating your kids' energy and enthusiasm.

If you find yourself repeating the same instructions regarding a particular area of the game, you can deduce that your kids need additional work in that area. Make sure you devote time at your next practice to improving it.

✔ **Speak to the team in a calm and relaxed manner.** If you're nervous and uptight, your players will be, too, and those feelings will affect their performance. If you're smiling and laughing, the players can feed off your energy and approach the game in a much more relaxed manner.

✔ **Remember the fun factor.** Whatever you do, leave no doubt in the kids' minds that you want them to have fun — regardless of the score or their performance. When kids genuinely believe that having fun is the most important thing to you, they won't be afraid of making mistakes or losing games. (For more on forming a coaching philosophy, head to Chapter 2.)

✔ **Run down the warm-up.** Discuss your pre-game warm-up to refresh the kids' memories on the order of the drills. (For more on the pre-game warm-up, see the next section. For more on selecting stretches for the warm-up, see Chapter 18.)

✔ **Remind players of the importance of being good sports.** You want your team to be a model of good sportsmanship at all times. Ask your kids to show nothing but respect toward the officials — regardless of what calls are made — and the other players.

Warming up

Just like warming up before every practice, warming up before every game is important and effective. Creating and implementing a sound pre-game warm-up routine that stretches the kids' muscles, loosens their bodies, and gradually elevates their heart rates is necessary for safe competition. The older the players on your team, the more susceptible they are to pulling or straining muscles — injuries that can sideline them for extended periods of time. And time on the bench = no fun.

The goals of your pre-game warm-up are to reduce the chance of injury and prep the kids to play their best. The process is important, but you can keep it light-hearted, upbeat, and positive. Warm-ups conducted in a positive environment will give players confidence and have them looking forward to performing their skills during the game.

The pre-game warm-up should consist of some light activity to get the kids' hearts pumping, some stretching of the primary muscles, and then some drills that target basic skills they'll use during the game. Keep the following in mind when putting together your pre-game warm-up routine:

✔ **Begin with some light exercises.** You can have the players perform some light running in place or some basic jumping jacks, for instance.

✔ **Hit all the muscle groups when stretching.** Your pre-game stretching should cover all the major muscle groups used in basketball, including the hamstrings, calves, arms, and back. Chapter 18 presents some specific stretches you can use.

✔ **Cover all the skills.** Besides getting your team loosened up, you want to get them comfortable performing the skills that will be required of them during the game. Think dribbling, passing, shooting, rebounding, and defending. For example, you don't want to send players into the game without letting them take some shots beforehand.

✔ **Set the kids free at the end.** It's a good idea to end the warm-up by allowing the kids to shoot around on their own. Giving them a bit of freedom allows them to get in their own shooting rhythm. And if they want to work on their free-throw shooting during this time, they can do that as well (see Chapter 9 for more on free-throw shooting).

You can do your part to make the exercises, stretches, and drills as safe, fun, and effective as possible through preparation and motivation. Here are some tips you can use:

- ✔ **Rely on light drills.** If kids go full speed throughout the entire warm-up, they'll be gasping for breath by the time the game arrives. Keep the pre-game drills light.

- ✔ **Bump up the confidence levels during warm-ups.** While your players are stretching and going through drills, work your way around to each player and provide a little extra encouragement. A pat on the back, a wink of the eye, or a quick comment about how a kid played well in practice gives him an extra shot of confidence, which can make a big difference in his play and how much he enjoys the game.

- ✔ **Rehearse the warm-ups.** During the practice sessions leading up to game day, spend a few minutes rehearsing your pre-game warm-up so the kids understand the concepts and the order you want them to follow.

You have to adjust your pre-game warm-ups according to the type of league you're in. Some programs allow for an ample amount of warm-up time — 15 minutes or so — but others may give teams only a couple of minutes to get their kids ready. Make sure you know in advance how much time you'll have to prep your players for games. (Chapters 2 and 3 detail the important information you must discover about your league.)

Don't conduct your pre-game warm-ups right up until the start of the game. Give the kids a moment to drink some water and get themselves focused before the game begins. This brief intermission is a perfect time to give your last-minute talk (see the following section for advice).

Inspiring your team with a pep talk

Inspiring your players to give you their best effort during every game of the season is one of the many challenges you'll face as a basketball coach. The best way to motivate them is to give a pep talk at the end of your pre-game meeting, during which you ask them to give 100-percent effort. Motivational talks are great tools to get players excited about doing their best.

Your motivational talk needs to pull everyone together as a team. If you handle the talk the right way, you'll find your players embracing what you have to say. Accomplish that, and the focus and positive energy will spill over onto the court where it really pays big dividends for your team. Here are some suggestions to help ensure that your final pre-game words motivate and inspire:

✔ **Step into the kids' shoes.** Keep in mind that these are kids, and mold your message to fit their needs. Your best bet is to think about what you'd want to hear from an adult if you were in their position. What would get you excited and pumped up to play your best? For instance, if you coach 7- to 8-year-old kids, you can get them focused on hustling by joking with them that you want to see them running up and down the court like the Road Runner. You'll get laughs *and* a team full of energized kids who will give you their best effort.

✔ **Steer clear of pressure phrases.** You want to motivate your kids, not burden them with pressure-packed goals, before they step on the floor. Avoid saying, for example, "Let's go score 30 points today" or "Let's hold them to fewer than 20 points." No matter how hard the kids try, they can't control performance outcomes. All they can (and should) do is give you their best effort.

✔ **Center the talk on your team.** Focus on your team, your players, and your confidence in them. Positive reinforcement of your players' skills can instill extra confidence.

✔ **Always keep your talk positive.** Focus on areas of the game that the team has excelled in and how you can't wait to see the players put those skills into action. Every word should be positive and upbeat, because you never want any doubt or insecurity to creep into the players' minds before they take the floor.

Tip-Off! Time to Play

When a referee tosses the ball up in the air for the opening tip and the game begins, your job is just beginning, too. While the opposing players are putting your players' skills to the test on the court, your game-management skills are on display for all to see.

As a youth basketball coach, you have many in-game duties to attend to. You have to continue motivating your players, rotate them in and out to juggle playing time, and manage your timeouts. This section helps you handle and master these in-game coaching tasks. (For more on actual game strategy and plays you can use during a game, head to Chapters 12, 13, 15, and 16.)

Motivating your players

Motivating kids is a never-ending job when you're a basketball coach. Even if you deliver the world's best pre-game speech (see the previous section), it will be meaningless if you don't keep motivating the players during the game. During games, kids can get frustrated when skills that they mastered during practice aren't nearly as easy. You have to convince your players that effort and fun are what matters and give them confidence to keep working hard out there.

No matter the circumstances, do your best to convince your players that working hard will eventually turn things in their favor. Granted, this can be a tough pitch to sell, especially when your team is trailing by double digits in the first quarter and the opposing players look like they're all headed to the NBA, but you have to try. Call a timeout and tell the kids to forget about the deficit. Ask them to focus on getting a quality shot on the next possession and then go from there. And all the while, pile on the praise for their effort.

The following list outlines a few more tips to keep in mind when you're motivating players during the game:

- ✔ **Allow players to make mistakes.** Your players *will* make mistakes, because mistakes are just part of playing basketball. Slip-ups are fine as long as your players learn from them. And they can't learn if you're constantly yelling out corrective instructions.

- ✔ **Turn down the volume.** It isn't a good sign if you're grabbing for the throat lozenges after games. Refrain from shouting instructions to your team. Part of being a good coach entails keeping your emotions in check.

  Of course, with older kids at the more advanced levels of play, you may need to get a player's attention by raising your voice. As play gets more competitive, your coaching style must change. Just be sure to convey the instructions in the lowest tone you can.

- ✔ **Limit your sideline pacing.** Use your gym membership to get in your aerobic workout, not the front of your team's bench during a game. Coaches who pace back and forth all game long can be major distractions to players who are doing their best to focus on the game.

  If you want to get up to applaud good plays or spark some passion among your players, occasional trips off the bench are fine. If it isn't overbearing, and you use it at different points during the game, communicating on your feet can fuel a solid performance from your team. At the youngest levels of play, where coaches often are allowed on the court to help the youngsters, you want to provide a steady diet of praise. You also want to include some instruction to help the kids learn the basics of the game.

- ✔ **Be positive with your corrections.** Making corrections to a child's technique is different on game day than in practice because of all the spectators on hand. Try not to single out any youngster who may feel uncomfortable in front of family, strangers, and the opposing team, because it's much different from getting attention during a practice in front of teammates.

✓ **Reward effort.** Be sure to reward the kids' hustle with applause and praise. The team that chases down loose balls and hustles down the court no matter what often finds itself in position to win games. And your least talented players can have the biggest impact on a game by hustling and giving it their all. Let your kids know that it's perfectly okay to make mistakes as long as the mistakes happen while they're playing with 100-percent effort.

After you instill this attitude in your entire team, your players will be more likely to respond with their best effort every time down the floor, and that will be a real feather in your coaching cap.

Substituting players

One of the many cool things about coaching basketball is that you can make unlimited substitutions throughout a game. You should take full advantage of this, too. Moving players in and out of the game helps ensure that younger kids receive an equal amount of playing time and that you don't leave a youngster of any age stranded on the bench for an unfair period of time.

In nearly all leagues, you can make substitutions during the following situations:

✓ During a timeout

✓ Following a made free throw

✓ When play stops because of a ball going out of bounds

✓ When a foul is called

Of course, be sure to check with your league regarding any special substitution policies it has in place. Being familiar with your league's rules, which we discuss in Chapters 2 and 3, is crucial. You need to determine a system for tracking the playing time based on the age and experience level of your players. The following sections break down the differences.

Try to bring kids out of a game after they've done something well rather than after they've made a mistake. If you take a youngster out after he has just committed a turnover, he may look at the miscue as the reason he's headed to the bench, which can take away his confidence. It may also make him less likely to want the ball in his hands the next time he's in the game. Also, when bringing a player to the sideline, give him a pat on the back or a high-five to recognize the effort he put forth. Kids love those kinds of receptions.

For younger, less-experienced kids

With young, inexperienced kids, you need to make sure that everyone —
regardless of how well they play — receives an equal amount of playing time.
If you have an assistant coach or parent who can help out, you can have the
assistant keep a tally sheet of each youngster's playing time so that no child is
denied his fair share of court time. Keeping track of minutes played can be —
we have to say it — time consuming, so it helps to have help! It's also great to
have a written record in the event that a parent questions you on the playing
time his or her child is receiving. (For more details on dealing with parent
issues, check out Chapter 19.)

Your best bet is to run the kids in and out of the game every few minutes.
This keeps the kids actively focused on the game and fresh because they
won't be running up and down the floor for long stretches at a time without a
breather. For example, you can switch out a few players every two minutes of
the game, or you can replace the entire squad to get five new players on the
floor. The bottom line is that you want the minutes equally distributed.

You also can handle the distribution of playing time based on the number of
kids on your roster. For instance, if you have 15 kids on your team, you basically have three mini-teams, and you can send each one out for an equal
amount of playing time. And if your league features four quarters, you can
determine before the game which kids will play specific quarters. One of the
drawbacks of this approach, though, is that it may be difficult to keep the
kids interested and focused on the game for long stretches. You can try split-
ting the quarters in half so that the kids stay actively involved in the game
and don't have to sit for extended periods of time.

At the beginning levels of play, don't send your five best players out on the
floor at one time. Because every player gets an equal amount of playing time,
it doesn't matter to them where their minutes come from. But if your five best
kids play together all the time, your second unit may really struggle and lose
confidence if they can't rely on one or two players to get the ball down the
floor so they have a chance to score, for instance.

For older, more-experienced kids

For older kids, you should have a substitution plan in place before games, but
be prepared to make adjustments according to game situations. Your substitutions should be based on several factors. If you're coaching in a recreational youth league, you'll put your better players in the starting lineup (see
Chapter 5). However, you still have a responsibility to get all the kids on the
floor for some game action. The most talented kids may get the bulk of the
playing time, but you need to track playing time and rotate all the other kids
into the game regardless of how well they shoot, rebound, and defend.

At the most advanced and competitive levels of play — on an all-star or travel team, for instance (see Chapter 20) — the best players should receive the overwhelming majority of the minutes. The lesser-skilled kids will play more supportive roles — giving the starters a rest, coming in when the starters get in foul trouble, coming in to run certain plays, and so on. When your team is winning or losing by large margins, you can take these opportune times to insert all the other kids into the lineup so they get to enjoy some game action.

Using timeouts

Timeouts are stoppages in play called by coaches or players when their teams have possession of the ball. You can call a timeout for a variety of reasons:

- ✔ To give your players a short breather if they've been on the court for a long time
- ✔ To set up a specific play
- ✔ To make adjustments in your strategy
- ✔ To slow down the momentum of an opposing team

The number of timeouts you get depends on your league, but the standard is three full timeouts and two 30-second timeouts per game. Some leagues, in order to keep games moving along, may allow only one timeout per half. No matter the case, you need to exercise great care when choosing when to use your timeouts (see Chapter 2 for more on reviewing league rules).

During a timeout, you can discuss strategy or keep it general and motivational. For instance, you may focus on the following, depending on your team's situation in the game:

- ✔ If your team is tired, use the timeout to let the players catch their breath and get some water.

  If you coach kids at the younger age levels, you'll rarely use timeouts for any purpose other than this (along with piling on the praise). At this level, you don't need to talk much strategy, because the leagues are all about having fun and learning skills.

- ✔ If your team keeps getting beat by the same play, you can use the timeout to change your defense (see Chapters 13 and 16) or how you want to approach stopping that particular play.

✔ If your team's energy seems down or your players are frustrated, you can use the timeout to applaud the kids for their effort, which serves as motivation for them to continue playing hard throughout the rest of the game.

✔ If your team is struggling to score points, set up a play that your team executes well. By using it during a game, you can send confidence levels soaring. (For more on set plays, see Chapters 12 and 15.)

✔ If the opposing team has called a timeout to set up a play in the closing seconds of a tight game, use your timeout to switch up your defense. If you've been playing a certain defense for the majority of the game, the opposing coach is probably setting up a play to go against that type of defense. By switching your defense, you can catch the other coach off-guard and make it more difficult for the opposing team to execute a shot.

Make sure that your kids return to the court pumped up and reenergized rather than put down and feeling like they've disappointed you. Applaud their effort, point out the positives on the court, and encourage them to continue giving their best.

Working with the Refs

On game day, the best youth basketball coaches do more than give goose-bump-filled speeches and draw up strategies that give their teams the best chance to win; they also work with the referees who are officiating the game. Communicating with the refs while showing respect for the important and challenging job they do sets the tone for a fun day of basketball — for the kids, the spectators, and you. If you don't get along with the refs (or don't understand their job), you'll become a distraction. This section gives you pointers on interacting respectfully with the refs.

Communicate with respect

Before, during, and after your game, you want to work with the officials — not against them — which means treating them with respect. Inevitably, you'll disagree with a call or the lack of a call during a game. How you carry yourself in subsequent interactions with the refs can go a long way. There's nothing wrong with asking an official for clarification on a made call — as long as you do it without a negative tone or your hands flailing away at your sides. Speak to the official in a calm manner without taking a confrontational approach with your body language.

When you introduce yourself to the officials before the game (see the first section of this chapter), be sure to get their names. During the game, use them judiciously — not every single time they make a call you disagree with. Doing so sets the tone for positive communication throughout the game.

For example, you should never scream across the court to an official. Instead, if you seek clarification on a call, wait until you can talk calmly with the ref face to face. Perhaps the official had a different angle and saw the play differently. Say something like, "Joe, could you please tell me what my player did to warrant that call?"

Know the rules before you question a call

You lose a lot of respect with an official when you question calls or non-calls without knowing the rules of the game or your league. For example, you can't start yelling for a three-second call — where offensive players can't remain in the lane for more than three seconds — when it isn't a violation in your league. You'll feel pretty embarrassed and look unprepared in this situation. The more knowledgeable you are, the more effective you'll be as a coach and a communicator.

Chapter 3 discusses all the rules of the game that you need to be aware of. You also must be aware of any rule modifications your league has made. For more on the rules of your league, check out Chapter 2.

Remind yourself that refs make mistakes

Referees are human beings who will make some mistakes during the course of a game. Officials are just like you (and the players on your team). Every decision that you make as a coach won't turn out to be right. Maybe you'll discover that a player you tabbed to play at one position actually is better suited to play another (see Chapter 8 for more details on conducting a mid-season review), or that you should switch your defense to better match up against an opponent (see Chapter 13).

Whether the refs are teenagers wearing a striped shirt for the first time or veterans calling a 13- and 14-year-old game in an advanced league, you must learn to accept that referee mistakes are part of the game. For instance, say the official calls a charging foul on your player when, from your vantage point, it looked like the call should've been blocking (see Chapter 3). Remind yourself that the official had a different angle than you did. Referees must make split-second calls constantly throughout the game, and it's completely unfair to expect that every call will be 100-percent accurate.

Halftime: Delivering an Effective Speech and Adjusting Your Strategy

During the first half of a basketball game, you'll see all sorts of things unfold on the court, and you'll have to take those things into account when chatting with your team during the halftime break. Much of what you do during halftime depends on the age and experience level of your kids. In a lower-level youth game, some kids will be making and missing shots, grabbing rebounds, and stealing passes. Other youngsters may be more interested in waving to their parents in the stands. Your job at halftime is to keep the kids focused and motivated to do their best in the second half. Acknowledge all the good plays that took place in order to build their confidence for a strong second-half performance.

If you're coaching at a more advanced level, you should spend the first half monitoring and evaluating your team and your strategies. At halftime, you should give a speech similar to the one given to younger kids (though shorter) in addition to making any necessary adjustments.

As you can see, you have a lot of information to cover and not much time to relay it to your team. At the younger levels, you may get only five minutes at the half; at the older levels of play, you can count on having ten minutes to spend with the kids. This section helps you relay the important info to your team in the time you have and make the necessary adjustments so you're ready for the second half.

Addressing kids of all ages

What are your speech responsibilities during halftime, and how can you make the most out of the little time you have? Foremost, you should adjust your message to fit the needs and mood of your team, based on what you saw during the first half. For example,

✔ **Did your time play lazy defense?** If so, you need to inject your speech with an extra dose of enthusiasm to fire up the kids.

✔ **Did you have trouble scoring points?** Your best route is to take a more supportive approach. Remind the kids how well they shot the ball in practice and that they'll get their shooting touch back if they continue being positive.

> ✔ **Did you simply get outplayed by a good team?** Heap on the praise and stay supportive. They should know that winning takes a backseat to fun and learning. Acknowledge that the opposition played a strong first half, but remind your players that if they stay focused, they can get back in the game.
>
> ✔ **Did you play a perfect half of basketball?** Congratulate the kids on their strong play, but remind them to stay focused and to try to play just as well in the second half.

No matter how the first half went, though, what you say during your halftime chat should be clear, concise, and uplifting. You don't have to verbally replay the entire first half for the team. After all, your players were out on the court, and they're well aware of what happened.

Concentrate on making your chat with your team productive. The following list presents some tips to keep in mind when gathering your team for a talk at halftime:

> ✔ **Get feedback from assistants.** Have a brief chat with your assistants to get their input on the first half. They may have spotted something useful that you didn't catch.
>
> ✔ **Let 'em catch their breath.** Kids will be more receptive to your comments if you give them a moment to drink some fluids, catch their breath, and wipe off with a towel before you dive in.
>
> ✔ **Improvise.** Because every game will be different, you can't rely on the same speech for every halftime. On your way to the locker room or to the far corner of the gym, determine a couple major points that you want to get across based on what you saw in the first half.
>
> ✔ **Don't stray from the key points.** If you limit how much information you discuss, what you say will be more likely to sink in. You don't want to send your team back on the court with too many details to digest, because you'll make it really difficult for them to execute.
>
> ✔ **Hide any disappointment.** If you're frustrated at your team's level of execution, don't let the team know it by the look on your face. Don't let your emotions detract from your ability to coach and interact effectively with your players.
>
> ✔ **Focus on the good stuff.** Piling on the praise for the hard work your players have put forth is a great tool for building passion to continue those efforts in the second half. Regardless of whether your team is ahead or behind, maintain a positive attitude and demeanor at all times. After all, at the younger levels, fun and learning are all that matter.
>
> ✔ **Focus on your team.** Try not to get wrapped up in what the other team is doing and lose focus on what you worked on with your team in practice. Try to play to your team's strengths.

Making adjustments with experienced teams

At the more advanced levels of youth basketball, one of a coach's biggest challenges is making halftime adjustments based on what went right and wrong during the first half. At this level, you should focus on finding solutions and fixing problems rather than making lengthy halftime speeches. Recognizing the adjustments that will help your team and being able to share them with your players during your brief halftime period is one of the cornerstones of good coaching.

Here are some samples of what you can discuss with your assistants and players at halftime; this list certainly isn't exhaustive, but it should give you a good idea of what goes on during halftime:

- ✔ Decide if your current defense is able to get the job done or if you should switch to a different defense (see Chapter 13).

- ✔ Alert your players about kids on the opposing team who may be suspect defenders and focus your attack on them (see Chapters 12 and 15).

- ✔ Remind your players about their foul situations.

- ✔ Decide what players you should rotate in to rest your starters for the second half.

Sometimes, you'll have the chance to coach in games in which the kids execute everything that you worked on in practice perfectly. In this case, you want to recognize their outstanding play and challenge them to match that level again when they return to the floor.

Winning and Losing Gracefully

There will be a winner and a loser every time two basketball teams take the court — unless, of course, you coach in a beginning-level program that doesn't keep score (in which case this section doesn't really apply to you!). As a youth league basketball coach, teaching your team how to win and lose with class and dignity transcends your duty to teach players the basics of offense and defense.

Discussing sportsmanship lays the foundation for behavior that will make you proud. You need to spend time talking to your team about playing fairly, abiding by the rules, and behaving with class in both victory and defeat. Review the right ways to congratulate a winning team, and cover how to behave when celebrating a victory. This section shows you the way.

How to win with grace

As a youth basketball coach, you have plenty of challenges you must face during the season. One of the most overlooked challenges is teaching children the art of winning with class. Even though grandstanding routinely occurs at the professional, collegiate, and high school ranks, there's no room in youth basketball for excessive celebrating, taunting, trash talking, or belittling.

The "winning with class" requirement also applies to you. In most youth basketball programs, you'll see a pretty big discrepancy in the skills of the players. If you find your team dominating an opponent that simply doesn't have the talent to compete, do everything you can not to pile on the points and embarrass the other players. Running up the score reflects terribly on you and your team and serves no purpose in the development of your players. You wouldn't want your kids to feel demoralized against a superior opponent, either.

If your team is on the winning side of a lopsided game, consider implementing some of the following approaches to keep your team's interest level high, to work on a broad range of skills, and to avoid humiliating the opponent:

- **Shift players around.** Give your players the chance to play different positions. For example, moving your center to point guard gives him the chance to use different skills and see the game from a new perspective. (For tips on assigning positions, see Chapter 5.)

- **Put in the backups.** If you're coaching in a league where playing time is dictated by playing ability, you can put your nonstarters into the game when the score gets out of hand.

After you remove your starters from the game, never put them back in just because you want to win by a specific margin. That's a terrible display of sportsmanship. Only reinsert your starters if you're in danger of losing the game with your backups.

- **Call off your offensive and defensive pressure.** If your team has played suffocating defense that resulted in many turnovers and easy baskets, ease up when you have the game in hand. Likewise, if you have a big cushion, don't allow your players on offense to launch three-point shots to pile on more points.

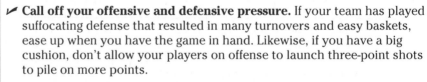

Use the noncompetitive time to work on a different aspect of offense or defense that doesn't exploit the other team's weaknesses. For example, you could work on a zone defense and making sure your players are in the proper positions for this type of defense. (For the scoop on different types of zone defenses, check out Chapters 13 and 16.)

The habits your players pick up from you are the ones they'll carry with them during their future years in the game. Knowing that you instilled positive traits in them will make you feel great — and deservedly so.

How to lose with grace

You'd love to win every game your team takes the floor to play, but that simply won't happen. The best coaches and the best teams at all levels suffer losses. There's nothing wrong with losing a game, but there's plenty wrong with you, your players, and their parents behaving like a loss is the worst thing that could happen. Your players need to learn to hold their heads up high in defeat when they know in their hearts that they gave their best effort, and the same goes for their parents (see Chapter 4 for more on conveying this in the preseason meeting). And teaching your team to show respect for opponents and the officials is important for their overall development as young basketball players and as people.

Regardless of what happens on the court, your players should always line up after the game to shake hands with the opposing team, its coaches, and the referees. You and your assistants also should be in the line to shake the kids' and the coaches' hands. Encourage your players to acknowledge a well-played game from the opposition by saying "good game" or "good luck."

Showing respect can be especially difficult if the other team shows no class. No matter how cocky the opposing players may be, or how much inappropriate celebrating they do, your team should rise above that type of behavior. As difficult as this is — and that goes for you, too — you should always offer a congratulatory handshake or high-five. Being sincere in the face of adversity is a great attribute.

Wrapping Up with a Post-Game Talk

What you say to your team — and how you say it — following a game is the message that resonates in their young heads until the next time they take the court. Regardless of the outcome, one of your most important tasks is sending the kids home feeling good about themselves and the effort they gave. Pats on the back, encouraging words, and genuine smiles are what you should be giving players in any post-game chat.

When giving your post-game talk, use the following pointers to send your team away feeling appreciated and satisfied. When kids feel appreciated, they'll continue to give you their best effort, which is all you can ask for. (Chapter 2 provides some info that can help you develop your coaching philosophy and interact with your players.)

✔ **Focus on the fun you had.** When it comes to fun, always take the time to solicit feedback, gauge feelings, and probe for answers. One of the most obvious and effective ways to gauge the level of fun during the game is asking the kids directly whether they had a good time. If some kids don't answer as enthusiastically as you'd hoped, try to find out why. Sometimes, part of being a good basketball coach is being a detective. Do whatever you can to make sure that their experiences continue to be fun — or return to being fun prior to your next game.

✔ **Accentuate the positive.** Whether your team played its best game of the season or got beat by double digits, point out some of the good things that happened and use subsequent practices to build on them. Wins and losses shouldn't define your team's effort or what areas of the game you're making improvements in.

✔ **Recognize good sportsmanship.** How your team behaves on the court is a direct reflection of you as a coach, so be sure to touch on sportsmanship in your post-game chat. Point out displays of good sportsmanship and show your appreciation for them to reinforce their importance. Be sure to make mental notes of these instances when they occur during the course of play.

Chapter 8

Refining Your Coaching Strategies

. . . .

In This Chapter

▶ Adjusting to your changing team

▶ Holding a midseason review to judge your goals

▶ Working with the parents to keep the kids happy

. . . .

*E*ven if you begin the season on a great note and your kids are having fun and showing improvement, you can't assume that the remainder of the season will naturally take care of itself. You expect your kids to put forth a strong effort in the second halves of games and practices; you should expect the same from yourself during the second half of the season. Just like you want the kids to improve in all areas of the game, you should want to improve your practice planning, on-court decisions, and handling of players. You must make the necessary adjustments to account for the ever-changing dynamics of your team.

This chapter looks at how your coaching responsibilities change when the season hits the halfway mark. Here you find all sorts of useful info on revising your game-day strategies to match your players' development, reviewing your players' progress, using goal setting as motivation, adjusting practice plans, and fine-tuning drills to meet your team's changing needs. Use the information in this chapter to fill the remainder of your season with plenty of fun and learning. (If problems arise in the first half and you must deal with behavioral issues, head to Chapter 19 for advice.)

Dealing with Shifting Team Dynamics

During the first several practices and the first few games of the season, you'll see players excel in different areas of the game, and you'll be able to identify areas that need improvement. Some players will show pretty good range from the perimeter; some will be tenacious defenders; and still others will emerge as reliable rebounders who work hard on both ends.

Perhaps you had a player penciled in at one position, but he's shown that he has the skills to handle a different position where he can help the team more. For example, say a youngster whom you started at power forward has shown a real knack for handling the ball and finding open teammates; he seems to be the perfect candidate to run your offense from the point guard position (see Chapter 5). Of course, chances are pretty good that some youngsters will have difficulty picking up some or all the skills you teach. In some cases, they'll be a lot further behind their teammates (see Chapter 6 for some advice).

As you begin to identify the kids' true skills and abilities, and as these skills change, you need to evaluate the makeup of your team — especially at the older age levels. You need make revisions to your lineup, shuffle kids into different positions, adjust practice drills, and tweak your offensive and defensive approaches to match your team's evolving strengths. This section helps you identify these potential changes and what you may need to do to adjust to them. It also addresses the importance of recognizing improvement in your players.

Recognizing team/player improvements

Recognizing and acknowledging player improvement, no matter how big or small, is essential for building your kids' skills and confidence all season long. Developments that may seem minor to you may be life-changing in a child's eyes. Make a big deal out of the smallest gains, particularly at the youngest age levels; be there to deliver a high-five and enthusiastic praise, from the least talented player to the most talented kid. The alternative — disappointing a child by overlooking his efforts — can cause a player to wonder, "What's the point?"

The achievement may be something subtle — how a player gets into good position to box out on a rebound (see Chapter 10) — or something more obvious — such as a youngster's ability to make free throws (see Chapter 9). As a youth basketball coach, few things are more thrilling than seeing your players learning, developing, and even excelling in the different areas of the game. A player who struggled when handling the ball at the start of the season may start to zip around the court, dribbling and weaving; this will bring a huge smile to your face.

The scoreboard is a terrible gauge for analyzing whether your players are making strides in certain areas of the game. Also, you should pay no attention to your team's win-loss record when measuring development. Ignore your record and the final score and take a closer look at what unfolded during a game. Your observations may reveal an outstanding effort by your players, even in a loss; be sure to praise your players for it.

For example, you can look past a loss and recognize that your players may have turned in their best defensive outing of the season. The reason for your opponent's scoring outburst could be that the players' shots were falling from everywhere on the floor. Some days, even great defense isn't enough to offset a hot shooting hand. Or perhaps you spent time in practice working on getting through screens, and your players did a good job of that during the game; heap on the praise!

Revising your early plans

As your season progresses, you need to observe how your team is performing in practices and during games. Some kids may be picking up skills faster than others, and some kids may start to develop new skills. As a result, you need to revise your practice drills and game-day strategy to account for your players' improvement in different areas of the game.

When you're ready to revise your practice and game-day plans, keep the following points in mind to help your team continue to improve and have fun:

- ✔ **Switching positions:** You have to be a constant evaluator of talent, and you have to be willing to make changes to your lineup if you think you can strengthen your team's performance — but only if you're coaching at an advanced level of play. At the beginning levels, you want to rotate the kids around to all the different positions.

  During practices and games, pay close attention to the smallest details. You may discover that a child who's playing in the backcourt has emerged as the team's best rebounder, for example. If he's a strong rebounder from a guard position, you may start to wonder how much more effective he (and your team) could be if he played closer to the basket as a forward. Who knows, you may also recognize that one of your forwards handles the ball really well against pressure, which means he may be better suited for a guard position. (For more on assigning positions, see Chapter 5.)

- ✔ **Changing your strategies:** As you change positions and team dynamics, you need to adjust your coaching strategies accordingly. For example, if your offensive approach has centered predominantly on bringing the ball up the court methodically and running screens to get a shot (see Chapters 12 and 15), but you've observed that you have some really good ball handlers who can move down the court quickly, you may want to change to a fast-paced attack to take advantage of these skills. And if you plan on changing to a faster offense, you need to incorporate more practice drills that emphasize moving the ball at higher speeds. (If you're in need of these types of drills and more, check out Chapters 14 and 17.)

✔ **Protecting your players' feelings:** Discovering that a youngster is better suited for a different position brings good news and bad news. The good news is that the player will be an asset to the team at his new position; the bad news (at the older age levels) is that you have to move around other players who may not want to move, too (at the younger levels, kids should play everywhere equally).

You can help make the transition smoother for the player being displaced by explaining to him that the ability to play more than one position is a great asset to the team. If you're lucky, the child will look forward to trying out a new position. Quite often, though, the youngster's feelings will be hurt and his self-esteem will sag. And you may have the unpleasant task of bumping a youngster to backup status and taking away some of his playing time.

If you coach older kids, explain to the youngster in private after practice that the move is for the benefit of the team and you want him to accept this new role. Talk about the skills he's shown that impress you the most and how he can be a strong factor in his new position. Don't make it a conversation about how another player is better; concentrate on how you think he's suited to handle the challenges of playing elsewhere.

✔ **Informing the parents about changes:** When you make changes on your team, save yourself a headache by letting the parents know about your plans. You want to keep those vital communication lines open so you don't catch the parents by surprise on game day. (For more info on working with parents, check out Chapter 4.) Use the same tactics when discussing the changes that you use when informing the kids. (You can also refer to the section on meeting with parents later in this chapter.)

Tweaking your practices as the season progresses doesn't have to be a time-consuming burden. You can take some of the kids' favorite drills and make some simple modifications to increase the difficulty level and refresh your practices. (Jump to Chapters 11, 14, and 17 for some drills you can use.) For example, when having your players dribble the length of the court against a defender, you can add another defender to the mix so the dribbler gets practice dealing with double teams. Or, you can position the extra defender in front of the basket so the dribbler must try to score against him. All it takes is a little creativity to spice up your drills.

Conducting a Midseason Review

By midseason, the basketball team that you welcomed to your first practice will seem like a distant memory. The team you have at the midpoint will be dramatically different. Your players will evolve right before your eyes, and your team (hopefully) will emerge as a cohesive unit. Reviewing your team's progress at the midpoint of the season helps keep a successful season on track and throws a life preserver to a season that's drifting off course. Look at the process of the midseason review like you're examining a road map to avoid making any aggravating wrong turns.

Pointing out progress and areas for improvement

Schedule meetings with the kids and their parents — private one-on-one sessions — either before or after a mid-season practice to discuss their progress. Even just a brief chat, in which you run down their progress and the areas you feel they should focus on in the coming weeks to help them in their development, is a great way to keep the parents informed and the season headed in the right direction. Failing to acknowledge progress and make suggestions sends the message that setting goals, working hard, and improving really isn't that important to you. Also, you should welcome any questions from the parents or players.

What you say to kids, and how you say it, goes a long way toward impacting their experiences with you. Whenever you're discussing a child's abilities and setting goals, tread carefully. You want to build the kids up and encourage them so that you don't drain their enthusiasm for participating the remainder of the season. When sharing with players their possible areas of improvement, make sure you sprinkle the conversation with bits on how proud you are of them and that you know that through their hard work and dedication to the game they'll improve.

Redefining your team goals

Midway through your team's season, you need to take a step back and look at your progress. During this time, you should re-evaluate your team's goals. Depending on how well you've met expectations, you may need to tweak some of your goals.

Your team's playing level affects how you should redefine your team's goals:

  ✔ **Beginning-level team:** You can set some basic goals for the entire team that shift the focus away from winning and losing. Your primary goals are having fun and teaching basic skills, and your goal changes should reflect this. They should be simple, attainable goals. For example, you can ask players to get five quality shots a half or hustle to get back on defense to prevent easy baskets. These are team-oriented goals that foster the importance of working together as a unit. Another goal is forcing the opposition into more turnovers than your team commits.

You may find that your expectations turn out to be too high for the kids, many of which probably haven't dribbled a basketball in an organized setting before. If that's the case, you can tweak the goals to getting two quality shots in a half instead, for instance. This way the kids can reach the goal and be congratulated for it.

✔ **More advanced team:** When the goals you set for older, more advanced players are realistic, your share of wins will come and — more importantly — your players will reap the rewards of playing together. Samples of goals you can use include shooting 75 percent as a team from the free-throw line or limiting the opposition to a set number of offensive rebounds per game.

Keeping team statistics can be useful for pointing out to players that they really are improving, even if they aren't collecting many wins. They can be shooting a higher percentage than they were earlier in the season, for example. Keep both offensive and defensive statistics so you can detail improvements in all different areas.

If your team is unable to reach its goals, you can restructure them. Drop the free-throw percentage down to 60 percent, for example. This way, if the players reach it, you can applaud their effort and they'll pick up some confidence in this area of the game. Then, you can gradually increase the level you want them to strive for as the season nears its end.

With older and more advanced players, you can monitor progress with team goal boards. *Goal boards* simply list several different goals that you've outlined for the team to focus on. Goal boards help steer some of the attention away from winning the game to giving their best effort. With goal boards, coaches can pinpoint certain areas of the game that they really want the teams to focus on improving; on the board, you can redefine and alter the goals from game to game.

Setting team goals that revolve around winning (capturing the league title or finishing above 0.500, for example) may seem like a good idea, but these goals can lead to all sorts of problems. For instance, losing may make some of your goals suddenly unreachable. What if your team plays two of its best games at the end of the season, yet your players are disappointed because the goal of winning the league is out of reach? Instead, focus on weekly improvement and playing hard on both offense and defense. Aim for team-performance goals, such as cutting down on turnovers or taking the best shot possible each time down the floor. Positive team goals really make a difference in raising the level of the kids' games.

Adjusting your players' individual goals

In addition to tweaking your team's goals (see the previous section), you want to take a close look at each individual player's goals at the midpoint of your season. When you do it correctly, setting goals is one of the most effective ways to motivate and get the most out of your players. Setting the right goals keeps their attention during a long season, gives them something to strive for, and presents a chance for them to feel satisfaction when they achieve a goal.

At the midseason mark, take advantage of the knowledge you've gained about your players — their skills, interests, and personalities — and set specific goals and revise others as needed for the remainder of the season. To make your goal setting successful, keep the following tips in mind:

- ✔ **Set attainable goals.** Establish goals that fit within the framework of your team's goals. Setting a goal of scoring ten points a game is unrealistic for many reasons — one being that the child has little control over how to achieve it. And even if you advise your team to pass the ball around on offense, this player may begin taking bad shots simply because he's focused on reaching the scoring level.

  Instead, give the player the goal of notching two assists a game. This way, the youngster is looking to make good passes that lead to scoring opportunities for his teammates. That's the essence of teamwork that benefits everyone involved. If the player has become a proficient passer, revise the goal by increasing the assist total per game from two to four. Again, the more good passes he makes, the more it benefits his teammates on the floor.

- ✔ **Focus on short-term goals.** The younger the child, the shorter his attention span, so you're better off setting a series of short-term goals so he (and you) can see a lot of progress right away. For instance, you can set a goal for a youngster in a beginning-level program of dribbling the ball up the floor during a game without losing control or having it stolen.

- ✔ **Institute several different goals.** If a player doesn't reach his most desired goal but still makes strides, he can gain a sense of accomplishment. Having just one goal to shoot for turns the process into an all-or-nothing proposition.

- ✔ **Find a proper balance.** Choose goals that aren't too easy or too difficult so that you keep the child's interest while minimizing frustration. For instance, for an advanced-level player handling the point guard position, set a goal of him having more assists than turnovers during the game.

✔ **Get player feedback.** You can make goal setting more effective and enjoyable if you have a short discussion with a player on the areas in which he wants to improve. Maybe one of your guards wants to improve his defense; if you ask for his feedback and tell him to focus on his defense, his effort may be quite enthusiastic.

✔ **Factor in injuries.** If a youngster has been injured early in the season and misses some playing time, take that injury into account when setting midseason goals. Give the youngster time to get back up to his desired level and adjust the goals accordingly. When you sense that he's back to normal, you can revisit the goals and adjust them to coincide with his improved health.

Encourage all players to practice skills with their parents or friends at home in order to work toward the goals you set. Just a few minutes of practice in the driveway a couple times a week can pay big dividends. Never force it, though — you don't want it to feel like homework. Just give gentle reminders about spending time on certain skills at home to nudge kids in the right direction. If you have a player on your team who has improved his play by practicing at home, point him out to the team to demonstrate that they can improve through hard work, too.

You can involve the parents in this goal setting. For instance, you can include them in your chats with the kids so they're kept in the loop on what you want to achieve. Encourage them to be creative in working with their youngsters. Goal setting should be a fun activity that allows parents and kids to bond. The parents and children can even make colorful charts to hang on their refrigerators that monitor the players' progress toward the set goals you come up with.

Holding Parent-Coach Conferences

Maintaining close contact with the parents of your players is especially important when you evaluate the kids' progress during the midseason review. You'll be making adjustments to help the kids for the rest of the way, and the parents deserve to know about these changes. In Chapter 4, we discuss opening the lines of communication with a preseason meeting; you don't want the foundation you've built to crumble after the first few practices and games.

As your season approaches the halfway point, let the parents know that you want to set aside a few moments to speak to them about their children and their thoughts on the season so far. A good time to make this announcement is following a game, when most parents are likely to be on hand. Schedule a good time to call during the week or, if it's convenient, schedule a time before or after practice to chat in person.

During this conversation, you can gain some valuable insight into what their child thinks about playing for you so far. You also can use this time to update the parents on their child's progress and identify areas of the game you'll be focusing on with him for the remainder of the season.

Determining if Junior is having fun

You should solicit feedback from parents to find out whether their child is excited for games and is wearing his uniform around the house two hours early or needs to be coaxed to get ready for practices and games.

No matter how great of a teacher and person you are, there may come a time when a player doesn't have fun on your team. It may sting your ego a bit, but that's okay. You want an honest and open conversation with the parents. What's not okay is failing to address the situation. If something isn't working and the youngster is rapidly losing interest in playing for you (or, worse, the game in general), you owe it to the child to explore the reasons and find ways to reignite his interest and restore the fun.

The following list presents a couple fairly common situations that arise to drain the fun from the game:

- ✔ **He isn't close to any of his teammates.** If you notice kids who haven't been able to forge friendships on the team, try to incorporate more partner activities into your practices to help your players get to know one another better (see Chapter 11 for some basic drills you can use). Developing closer bonds with teammates leads to improved teamwork.

- ✔ **He feels like he does too much running.** Basketball requires plenty of running, which is a turnoff for some kids. If this is the reason for the child's lack of interest, your best option is to work with the child to help him get in better shape so that he doesn't feel as miserable when exerting energy. If that doesn't appeal to him, consider suggesting to his parents some other sports that may better suit his personality (if you feel comfortable making those types of recommendations).

It's never too late to turn a child's season around. After speaking with the parents and uncovering a concern, don't allow it to linger. Act quickly to determine the best course of action to address the issue. The child's parents may be able to suggest a solution for you, or you can meet with the child to determine what to do.

Finding a different position for Junior

One of the most common issues for youngsters is not getting the chance to play coveted positions. Kids watch their favorite stars in action all the time, and they want to emulate them by playing the same positions. Also, parents sometimes have expectations of where they want their child to play, and many will share them with you.

Often, the solution is as easy as giving the child a shot at a different position (something you should be doing at the younger levels of play anyway). You can give her a taste of the new position during practice. You may discover that she has the skills to play that new position and will benefit the team by moving. Or perhaps the child will discover that the position isn't what she envisioned after all, and she'll be more than anxious to return to her regular spot. Another option is to give kids experience playing different positions in the fourth quarter of games that aren't close. At the advanced levels of play when the game is out of reach, that's a valuable time to give the kids a shot at a new position.

Helping Junior conquer his fears

Sometimes what happens on the court puts a stranglehold on the kids' enjoyment of the game. Perhaps a youngster misses a couple free throws in the final minute of a close game or gets flattened by a defender when driving to the basket. Kids can hold themselves responsible for losses or feel embarrassed by blocked shots (just like adults).

After discussing the issue with the child and his parents, the ball is in your court, so to speak, when it comes to addressing his fear. Sometimes, your best bet is to use your discretion when addressing an embarrassing incident. Perhaps the less attention you give the situation, the less likely it is that the child will worry about it. If you do feel the need to soothe a child's bruised feelings, try sharing a similar incident that happened to you. Explain to the player that basketball is a team game and that his shots won't always fall. Every athlete experiences failure and disappointment; it's how an athlete bounces back that really defines him. The unexpected twists and turns are part of what makes playing basketball so much fun. Work with the child to push the past out of his mind and help him focus on the present.

Part III

Working with Beginning and Intermediate Players

"Excellent job defending the ball, Adam, but you can stop now. Practice is over. These balls are coming home with me."

In this part . . .

A basketball coach who doesn't understand the fundamentals of the game and how to teach them will be about as successful as a medical student who cringes at the sight of blood. In this part, we provide you with chapters that help you teach the offensive and defensive fundamentals of the game. And if you have a team full of intermediate players, not to worry; we bump up the coverage to Offense and Defense 101 to account for your little scholars.

We also arm you with an assortment of basic drills that you can use to teach your players the fundamental elements of offensive and defensive play. We follow that up with some more challenging drills to help your intermediate players compete.

Chapter 9

Teaching the Offensive Fundamentals

*W*hen children first learn how to write, parents and teachers don't expect them to suddenly start scribbling legible, complete sentences right away. Instead, teachers show them how to write the letter "a" and go from there, allowing them to make mistakes and build on their knowledge. The same approach works for coaching the fundamental offensive skills of basketball. In order for a child to enjoy success, have fun, and develop a love for the sport, you have to start with the basics and build a strong foundation.

In most cases, youth coaches can be with their teams for only one to three hours each week, so you have to have realistic expectations of what you can accomplish. If you can provide the young kids with a good understanding of the most basic offensive skills, you're well on your way to accomplishing the goals of youth basketball: fun and skill development. You'll also be a quality coach who kids really enjoy playing for. This chapter examines the basics of executing at the offensive end of the court, including dribbling, making (and catching) basic passes, shooting, and rebounding.

Working and Protecting the Ball

Teaching your players how to execute on offense is one of the most enjoyable and, at times, most challenging aspects of coaching basketball. Before (and while) you start helping your youngsters get a handle on the offensive fundamentals, you should sit them down and explain to them how all the different skills are woven into a team concept. Let them know that if they all work together, play unselfishly, and give it their all, they'll produce quality shots and hopefully score some points.

Share the following pointers with your players to help enhance your team's offensive productivity:

- ✔ **Keep moving.** Stationary players are easy for opponents to guard, while players who are constantly on the move are difficult to keep up with. During your initial practices, in which you'll teach the fundamentals, remind your players not to get caught flat-footed. You can explain it in a fun way — letting the kids know that you don't want to catch them looking like statues, for instance. (For more tips on running effective practices, check out Chapter 6.)

- ✔ **Always look for open teammates.** Although all kids love scoring, your offense will be much more effective and *all* your kids will have more fun if you teach your players to work as a team. Teach them to derive as much satisfaction from seeing a teammate score as they do from dropping shots through the net themselves.

- ✔ **Stick to the safe passes.** Making risky passes — like trying to feed the ball to a player who's double teamed (guarded by two players) — usually isn't as productive as making safer passes to open teammates.

- ✔ **Limit your turnovers.** Turnovers take away scoring chances from your team while giving your opponent additional opportunities to score — an exchange that definitely doesn't work out in your favor.

As you can tell, basketball has a unique language all its own, peppered with all sorts of colorful terms and phrases. You'll see many of these terms throughout this chapter, such as *turnover,* the *hole,* and the *boards.* Check out Chapter 3 for a complete rundown of the common terms and phrases. Relying on these while coaching can be counterproductive if your players don't know their meaning. Stick to terms that you know all the kids fully understand.

Build on the Basics: Dribbling Skills

Dribbling skills are extremely important to a basketball player. Kids who can maneuver around the court gain a lot more enjoyment from the sport and can progress more quickly with other skills.

As you're running through dribbling instruction and drills during your time as a coach, keep a couple things in mind — things dribbling-related that all coaches should be aware of. Although you may not focus on these things while you teach the bare-bones basics, you can progress to them during your teachings as your players pick up the fundamentals:

✔ The best ball handlers can dribble the ball with either hand without actually looking at the ball. When a player looks down to dribble, he's at a big disadvantage because he can't spot open teammates or react quickly if defenders swipe at the ball.

✔ Players shouldn't pick up their dribbles unless they have a specific plan — such as passing to a teammate or shooting. When players pick up their dribbles without action, they put themselves at greater risk of being trapped by defenders, with nowhere to go with the ball.

The rest of this section covers the basic dribbling skills that all players, regardless of their position (see Chapter 5), need to be able to call upon.

The controlled dribble

Understanding the basic dribbling stance, and being able to execute out of it, is imperative for dribbling without losing control of the ball or having it stolen by the opposition. The following list outlines the proper dribbling stance you can teach to your players:

1. **The player moves her knees slightly beyond shoulder-width apart and flexes them so that she maintains a semi-crouched position (see Figure 9-1).**

    The player's off foot should be a little forward. How much the player crouches depends on the type of dribble she's using. This is called the *basketball position* — the basic position a player should assume when dribbling, passing, cutting, screening, defending, and preparing to shoot.

Figure 9-1: The player maintains a semi-crouched position while dribbling.

2. **She looks straight ahead so she can scan the floor and watch the defenders and her teammates.**

   Looking up allows for vision of the offensive end of the court.

3. **The player controls the ball with the tips of her fingers and thumb.**

   Her knees are flexed and her body is a bit hunched over.

4. **She bounces the ball slightly forward.**

   She keeps contact with the top of the ball, toward the back half, while dribbling. She holds her non-dribbling hand at waist level, with her palm facing down. She can easily shift to dribble with her other hand from this position.

5. **She controls the direction and velocity of the dribble by flexing her wrist and fingers.**

   Her arm, from her elbow to her fingertips, moves up and down to bounce the ball.

6. **She should dribble the ball back up about knee high.**

   The lower the dribble, the more difficult it is for the defender to make a steal or deflection.

7. **When a defender approaches, the player turns her body so that the arm that isn't dribbling is nearest the defender.**

   The free arm, held up and used like a bar, provides an extra layer of protection to better maintain possession of the ball.

The speed dribble

A player uses the *speed dribble* to push the ball down the court quickly — on a fast break, for instance (see Chapter 15) — or to drive through the defense to the basket (called *taking it to the hole*), among other reasons. Check out the following steps to see how to execute it:

1. **From the standard dribbling stance, the player leans his body forward (see Figure 9-2a).**

2. **After taking off on a run, the player dribbles the ball out in front of his body when a defender isn't nearby.**

   When a defender is nearby, the player should dribble the ball a little off to the side to protect it from steals (see Figure 9-2b).

3. **He bounces the ball between waist- and chest-level at this speed.**

   As he moves, he keeps his head up and shoulders square to where he's heading.

Figure 9-2:
The proper stance when executing the speed dribble.

a

b

Are your players having trouble controlling the speed dribble? This is simply an issue of timing, because they haven't adjusted the dribble to how fast they're moving up the court. Work with a player to push the ball farther out in front of him so that each time he dribbles, he doesn't have to slow down, break his stride, or reach back for the ball.

Addressing Passing and Catching Skills

Players have many options for moving the ball around to teammates to attack opposing defenses. Chest, bounce, and overhead passes are the most effective and fundamental ways to distribute the ball all over the court. Don't pass up this section, which provides instruction for making and catching these passes.

Delivering a chest pass

A *chest pass* is — you guessed it — when a player passes the ball from chest-level to a teammate's chest. Here are the steps for executing this pass:

1. **The player faces the teammate she wants to pass to.**

   Her head is up, her shoulders are square, her feet are a little more than shoulder-width apart, her knees are bent, her weight is on the balls of her feet, and her eyes are focused on the intended recipient.

2. **She holds the ball at chest-level with both hands.**

3. **The player grips the ball with the tips of her fingers and thumbs, slightly behind the center of the ball.**

   Her elbows are bent in this position (see Figure 9-3a).

a   b

4. **The player steps toward her target and releases the ball forcefully, rotating her wrists inward.**

   Her arms should extend straight out toward her teammate's chest. The thumbs should face down upon release (see Figure 9-3b).

Are your players' chest passes missing their targets? If so, check the followthrough with their arms and hands. You want them extending out toward the recipient's chest.

Executing a bounce pass

Sometimes, the best (or only) way to get the ball to a teammate is by using a *bounce pass* — when the pass bounces once on the court before reaching the intended recipient. The type of defense an opponent plays often dictates when your players should use bounce passes.

Here are the basics for executing a bounce pass:

1. **The player faces the target and holds the ball similar to the way he holds the chest pass — at chest-level with the tips of his fingers and thumbs.**

   His body position also should be similar.

2. **The player steps toward the target and pushes the ball downward, extending his hands toward the floor (see Figure 9-4).**

The ball should bounce about two-thirds of the way between the passer and his teammate and reach the teammate at waist-level. Your players must consider this when aiming the pass.

Figure 9-4: The bounce pass is an effective tool for getting the ball inside to a teammate.

Are your players' bounce passes missing the mark? The solution may be as simple as having the recipient help out the passer. Make sure the recipient holds his hands up and gives the passer a good target around waist-level.

Making an overhead pass

An *overhead pass* comes in handy when a player needs to get the ball over a defender's head or get it down the court quickly over a longer distance. The following list runs down how you deliver the overhead pass:

1. **The player holds the ball above her head with both hands (see Figure 9-5a).**

She shouldn't bring the ball any farther back than the top of her head. If she holds the ball around her neck, she can't protect it as well from pesky defenders.

She grips the ball with the tips of her fingers and thumbs. Her thumbs should be behind the ball.

Figure 9-5:
Overhead
passes
allow
players to
get the ball
down the
court
quickly.

a

b

2. **The player takes one step toward her target and aims to deliver the ball at her teammate's chest or toward the target the receiver gives her.**

   The inside of her elbows should be facing toward the target as an aiming device.

3. **She extends her elbows and uncocks his wrists to release the ball.**

   Her thumbs should wind up pointing down at the court (see Figure 9-5b). This helps ensure that the player follows through.

If a player's overhead passes are coming up short, have her aim for her teammate's head. Because overhead passes often fall short, having your kids adjust their targets usually is enough to offset the problem. The strength of the player's wrist snap also can be a factor.

Catching a chest pass

An accurate chest pass goes to waste if the intended target can't handle it. Spend time working on the following techniques so your players will develop the skills to corral chest passes:

1. **The player holds his hands open at chest-level to provide a good target for his teammate.**

2. **When the pass is delivered, the recipient takes a step or two toward the ball.**

   This step shortens the distance the ball has to travel and minimizes the chances of it being stolen.

3. **The player extends his arms out and watches the ball into his hands (see Figure 9-6), allowing for a little give in his hands and arms so the ball doesn't bounce off.**

   He should catch the ball with two hands whenever possible.

Figure 9-6: A player extends his hands toward the ball to receive a chest pass.

4. **After catching the ball, he should come to a stop with his feet shoulder-width apart.**

   From this position, he can pivot (see Chapter 3) to face the basket so he has the option to drive to the basket, pass to a teammate, or take a shot. People in the know often call this the *triple-threat* offensive position.

Kids often try to look at what they want to do next too quickly, especially if they're anxious to attack the basket or put up a shot. Remind your players to watch the ball into their hands before they make their next moves.

Handling a bounce pass

Players use bounce passes in many different situations — such as when teammates cut to the basket or when making an entry pass into the post — but you can only take advantage of these opportunities if your players can catch these passes. The following list looks at how to handle bounce passes:

1. **The intended recipient holds his hands open at waist-level to give the passer a target.**

2. **When the pass is delivered, the recipient takes a step toward the ball.**

   This helps prevent the defender from stepping in and swiping the pass before it reaches the intended recipient.

If the bounce pass is an entry pass into the post, you want the target reaching out to receive the pass before the defender can reach around and knock the ball away. You don't want him taking a big step toward the passer, or he may relinquish the post position he has established.

3. **The player extends his arms to greet the ball, with his fingers spread comfortably.**

   He keeps his eyes on the ball and watches it into his hands.

4. **After the ball contacts his fingers, the player bends his elbows and brings the ball up toward his chest.**

5. **With the ball in his possession, he pivots to face the basket to put himself in position to dribble, pass, or shoot.**

   A player in the lane may not have an opportunity to turn and face the basket, what with so many defenders swarming around him. For a peek at some more advanced moves for post players, see Chapter 12.

Look to Score: Shooting Skills

Youngsters can score baskets in several different ways, using basic fundamental shots. Each shot requires different techniques, and teaching those techniques to your players is an important job. The good news is that this job is one of the most fun parts of practice, because the kids' attention and excitement levels will perk up when you transition to shooting drills.

Your beginning-level players have four basic types of shots they can take during a live ball. Those shots include

- ✔ **Lay-up:** The most basic shot in basketball.

- ✔ **Set shot:** A shot where the player's feet don't leave the floor. One version of the set shot is the free throw.

- ✔ **Jump shot:** The most popular type of shot, especially at the older and more advanced levels of play. It's taken from mid- to long-range. The player jumps into the air and releases the ball at the highest point of his jump.

- ✔ **Hook shot:** This shot is more advanced, and we cover it in Chapter 12.

This section gives you all the shooting basics. We explain how to show your players the standard shooting position, and you find out how to teach your players the most fundamental shots.

During your shooting instructions, be sure to point out that when your kids don't have an opening to shoot, they should look to pass to teammates who may be in better positions to score.

Demonstrating the basic shooting position

Before your players can learn specialized types of shots *and* expect to see their shots consistently fall, they need to develop a good understanding of the proper shooting position. To show your players the correct shooting position, keep these key points in mind:

- ✔ **Feet:** Good shooting begins from the floor up. The kids' shoes should not only be tied (a very important consideration at the youngest levels!), but also positioned shoulder-width apart. The heel of the foot of the player's shooting-side hand should be even with her off-side toes, and her weight should be equally distributed on the balls of her feet.

- ✔ **Knees:** Slightly bent. The strength for the shot comes from the legs, not the upper body.

- ✔ **Hands:** Shooters hold the ball with two hands but actually shoot it with just one. Prior to release, the shooting hand is underneath the ball with the fingers spread and the thumb pointed toward the player's non-dominant hand. The non-shooting hand cups the ball on the side (see Figure 9-7).

Figure 9-7: The proper hand positioning for shooting the ball.

- ✔ **Elbows:** The shooter's elbow on her dominant arm should be bent at almost 90 degrees and held close to the body, though not perfectly under the ball. Her opposite elbow points down to the side at an angle toward the floor.

- ✔ **Shoulders:** Square and facing the basket.

✔ **Eyes:** Focused on the target — either just over the front of the rim or at the back of the rim. The eyes should stay zeroed in on a spot without straying to the ball, its flight path, or to Grandma taking pictures!

When going over proper shooting technique with your players, always start them close to the basket. Allow them to feel the success of seeing the ball drop through the net so they can gain confidence. Have them focus on holding the ball properly, because if kids stray from this basic fundamental, they're bound to miss more often than they make. Why? The ball will never be in the proper scoring position upon release.

Converting a lay-up

The *lay-up,* one of the most basic shots in basketball, is a shot taken right next to the basket. Players use lay-ups throughout the game, such as when driving to the basket or finishing a fast break.

Here's the scoop on teaching your players how to convert lay-ups (for beginners, start on the side of the basket that mirrors their shooting hands):

1. **The player plants the foot opposite his shooting hand a few feet in front of the basket and to the side of the rim.**

   A right-hander plants his left foot, and lefty plants his right.

2. **He jumps into the air off his plant foot toward the basket, much like when a child jumps over a puddle.**

3. **He raises up his dominant knee, hand, and arm at the same time as he jumps, as if they're all connected with the same string.**

   He uses his non-dominant hand to protect and control the ball while bringing it up into position to shoot.

4. **At the highest point of the jump, the player releases the ball against the square on the backboard.**

   The index finger of his shooting hand should be pointed directly at the basket or the square on the backboard — whichever is his target as he releases.

After your players become comfortable making lay-ups in the basic fashion, you can work with them on shooting left-handed when they're on the left side of the basket and right-handed when they're on the right side. A righty simply switches the moves to the opposite limbs, and vice versa. The reason for the switch is to protect the ball with your body so the shot is less likely to get blocked by a defender.

Taking a set shot

For youngsters who are new to the game, as well as for any player at the beginning levels of youth basketball, you want to lay a shooting foundation on which to build. Teaching players the *set shot* is the best, most fundamental route for helping them get the ball through the basket. The basics of the set shot are as follows:

1. **The player positions his feet shoulder-width apart and moves up slightly forward on the balls of his feet.**

   His weight should be distributed evenly. He should have his head up and his eyes focused on the front of the rim.

2. **If the youngster is right-handed, he places his right foot slightly ahead of his left foot — with the heel of his shooting-side foot even with the toes of his opposite foot.**

   For a left-handed shooter, his left foot should be ahead of his right foot.

3. **He bends his knees and sticks out his butt slightly (see Figure 9-8a) while bringing the ball up into shooting position (see the section "Demonstrating the basic shooting position").**

Figure 9-8: The body positions for executing a set shot.

a

b

The space between his forefinger and middle finger on his shooting hand should line up with the middle of his face. His fingers should be spread comfortably.

4. **He cocks back his shooting wrist and locks it.**

5. **He transfers his weight onto the toes of his front foot while straightening his body, extending his arms, and snapping his shooting wrist to release the ball (see Figure 9-8b).**

   The ball should roll off his index and middle fingers last, creating backspin so the ball arcs toward the basket.

6. **He follows through with his fingers pointing at the basket and his palm facing down.**

   He should pretend that he's reaching into the center of the basket.

Firing a jump shot

After your players gain some experience with the set shot, and if their bodies are strong enough, you can introduce them to the jump shot. A *jump shot* allows them to shoot over the top of defenders by jumping into the air before releasing the ball. It also allows a player to get the ball to the basket from mid- to long-range distances. This is the most popular type of shot for players in intermediate and advanced leagues. Here's a look at the techniques for executing the jump shot:

1. **The shooter faces the basket with his shoulders, hips, and feet square to the rim.**

   The middle of the rim should be the player's target on most jump shots. His feet are in a position similar to the set-shot position (see the previous section).

2. **He grips the ball with the fingers of each hand (see Figure 9-9a). His shooting hand is slightly underneath the ball, and his non-shooting hand helps balance the ball from the side.**

   The fingers of the non-shooting hand are spread and pointed straight up. The thumbs of each hand should come close to forming the letter "T."

3. **The player moves the elbow on his shooting hand directly under the ball.**

   His forearm and upper arm should form a 90-degree angle. His wrist is cocked, holding the ball in the shooting position slightly above his forehead.

4. **He bends his knees to generate the force needed to jump into the air.**

   If a player wants to increase his shooting range, he must increase his knee bend to generate more power and lift. *Note:* The jump should be comfortable, not one that makes him strain to get in the air.

5. **He jumps straight up, keeping his body facing the basket (see Figure 9-9b). As he jumps, he straightens his legs, and before reaching the top of the jump, he extends his arms and brings his wrists forward to release the ball.**

Figure 9-9:
The ball rests on the fingers and pads of the player's hands, and he follows through with his fingers pointing toward the basket.

a   b   c

6. **He moves the fingers of his shooting hand up and through the ball and snaps his wrist.**

   The ball should come off the index and middle fingers last. This motion gives the ball a slight backspin.

   His non-shooting arm and hand should maintain their supportive positions on the side of the ball until after release.

7. **The player finishes the release by following through with his hand and wrist, pretending that he's reaching into the basket.**

   The fingers of his shooting hand should wind up pointing at the basket (see Figure 9-9c); his elbow should be above his eyebrows.

8. **He lands on both feet, still facing the basket.**

Because there are so many steps involved in making jump shots, problems are likely to pop up. Here are some of the struggles that often come up, along with tips on how you can get your kids back on track:

✔ **Shots don't have much arc:** Shots without arc have little chance of dropping through the basket. As a general rule, the ball should be on its upward flight until it reaches about two-thirds the distance to the basket. To correct a problem with arc, check the position of the ball in the player's hands before release. Often, kids will rest the ball in their palms rather than on their fingertips, which takes away a lot of their control and reduces the loft of the ball in the air.

✔ **Shots aren't reaching the rim:** The likely cause is the player shooting the ball on the way down from his jump rather than on the way up. When a youngster shoots the ball on the descent, he can't generate as much strength or be as accurate. A shooter's legs are what give him power on longer shots.

✔ **Players aren't getting very high off the floor:** To help get a little more air under the player's feet, make a slight adjustment to his standing position. Slide up the foot on his shooting side about 6 inches in front of the other foot. This gives him a more comfortable base to take off from.

✔ **Shots aren't accurate:** When shots are drifting off target, you can trace the problem to the position of the player's shooting arm before release. If his elbow is pointing inward or outward — rather than positioned directly below the ball — he'll likely force shots to the left or right.

Sinking free throws

When the referee awards your team with free throws (see Chapter 3), you want to capitalize on the scoring opportunity because no defenders are harassing the shots or obstructing the view of the basket. Youngsters who step up to the free-throw line should stick with the same basic shooting fundamentals we cover in the section "Taking a set shot" — with just a couple slight variations. Here you find a few more tips to help your kids increase their free-throw proficiency:

✔ **Align the feet.** The player's foot on the side of his shooting hand should be aligned with the middle of the rim. His other foot should be a couple inches behind (the standard heel/toe set up) the dominant foot, and he should leave about 12 inches between his feet (see Figure 9-10).

Figure 9-10:
Having the proper foot position is key for sinking free throws.

✔ **Stay on the floor.** Although the shooter rolls his weight up onto his toes while shooting the free throw, his feet should never totally leave the floor. After he releases the ball and follows through, he returns to the exact position he started from.

✔ **Focus.** Teach your players to concentrate on the front of the rim and dropping the ball over it.

✔ **Develop a routine and stick with it.** Establishing a pre-shot routine and sticking to it is important to free-throw success. A routine helps players get into a comfortable rhythm and establish a consistent shot. For instance, they could dribble the ball three times before shooting or take a deep breath and picture the ball going through the net. Whatever routine they come up with, make sure they use it during practice and not just on game day.

When a player misses a free throw, have him step away from the free-throw line for a moment to take a breath and reset his position. He then goes through his routine all over again.

Take It to the Hole: Driving to the Basket

The closer your ball handlers can get to the basket on offense, the easier the scoring opportunities tend to be. Having the skills to drive to the basket can help a player generate a lot of coveted shots from close range and make him extra difficult for defenders to guard. *Drive* refers to a player quickly dribbling the ball toward the basket (or the *hole*) — down the lane or from the baseline — against the player who's guarding him. (For more details on the terms of the game, check out Chapter 3.) This section includes a few basics you can teach your kids about attacking the basket.

Driving (to the hole) with confidence

During games, it isn't uncommon for teams to sputter on offense. They have trouble generating good scoring chances. This is when having the ability to drive to the basket comes in handy, because your players can generate shots from close range or force opposing players to leave their men to provide defensive support, which creates openings for passes to teammates. Players who can take the ball to the basket with confidence can attack from anywhere on the floor and give your whole offense confidence. Good results often follow in the form of made shots or free-throw attempts.

A shot fake is a great way to get defenders off-balance, which can lead to open lanes to drive to the basket. See Chapter 15 for more on executing shot fakes.

It requires a lot of timing, coordination, and — of course — practice for a player to become comfortable driving to the basket. You can help your players solve the following problems that can drain their confidence when they first learn this skill:

- ✔ **They commit charging fouls:** This often happens when the defender doesn't go for a shot fake. When the offensive player doesn't have or hasn't created an advantage to dribble past the defender (with his quickness, for instance) and he goes to drive the basket, he'll dribble right into the defender and get called for charging (see Chapter 3). Also, players on good defensive teams will slide over into the lane to help their teammates by attempting to draw charges.

  Work with your players on their shot fakes to make them more realistic so defensive players will give openings to attack. Sometimes, a youngster may have to use several shot fakes against a good defender in order to create a shot opportunity.

- ✔ **They travel on the way to the hoop:** In a player's anxiousness to get past the defender, he may drag his pivot foot, or pick it up, before beginning his dribble (see Chapter 3 for more on the rules of the game). Work with your players during practice to get them in the habit of dribbling the ball before lifting the pivot foot. Through plenty of repetitions, you can reduce the amount of traveling calls whistled on your team.

Using the crossover drive

Players who can use a *crossover* drive to get to the basket can cause big problems for a defense. The technique puts the defender guarding the ball handler off-balance so he can't get a read on which direction the player is headed. The other defenders are then forced to help, caving in the entire defense's walls. Here are the techniques for helping your kids add the crossover drive to their offensive arsenal:

1. **When the ball handler has established her left foot as her pivot foot, she fakes the defender by lunging to her left while dribbling with her left hand, as if she'll dribble that way. (A lefty begins by lunging and dribbling to her right.)**

   She should be in good basketball position — her feet shoulder-width apart, knees bent, body balanced, and head up.

2. **She then pulls the ball across her body in the direction she intends to go — in this case, to the right of the defender.**

3. **She takes a long, low, and strong step with her right foot and explodes past the defender to drive at a sharp angle to the basket.**

   She should dribble the ball to her right hand before picking up her pivot foot (the left) so she doesn't get called for traveling.

4. **She continues past the defender and toward the basket, looking to take a close-range shot or deliver a pass to an open teammate.**

Hitting the Boards: Offensive Rebounding Skills

How important is rebounding in basketball? Consider this: Even if your team is pretty skilled on offense and defense, you probably won't fare that well on game day if you get only one shot every time down the court. More offensive rebounds equals more scoring opportunities.

Being a good offensive rebounder requires determination, hustle, and anticipation. These traits may be innate in some players and absent in others, but you can do your part to put your players in the right position to box out and grab rebounds. From there, the hustle and anticipation they show will lead to rebounding success. This section reviews the basics of offensive rebounding.

Getting in position

The real key to pulling down offensive rebounds is getting in the proper position to be able to grab them — not being tall or a great jumper (although these traits certainly are assets). Two basic moves are the *step over* and the *spin*. The step over is effective against defenders who haven't established good box-out positioning (see Chapter 10); the spin, on the other hand, is effective against opponents who are in good rebounding position. The following lists present the techniques for teaching these moves to your players:

1. **To execute the step over, the offensive player lifts up his arm nearest the defender after coming in from behind him.**

   He moves it over the defender's arm (see Figure 9-11a). This move is called a *swimmer's move,* because it simulates a swimming stroke.

Figure 9-11:
The step over works against opponents who have poor rebounding position.

a   b

2. **He moves his inside foot in front of the opponent (see Figure 9-11b).**

3. **Keeping his arms up in the air, he bends his knees and pushes his butt into the opponent's waist to establish inside position.**

   From here, he can keep himself between the defender and the basket (see Figure 9-11b).

When the opponent shuts down the step over move (see Figure 9-12a), your offensive player can switch to the spin move:

a   b

Figure 9-12:
The spin move works when the defender seals off the step over attempt.

c

1. **As soon as the defensive player seals off the step over by sliding in front of the offensive player, your player can counter by spinning back in the opposite direction (see Figure 9-12b).**

   For a split second, he faces away from the basket and is back-to-back with the defender.

2. **He then executes the step over with the opposite arm (see Figure 9-12c) and swings his other leg around in front of the opponent, using his butt to establish position.**

Grabbing offensive rebounds is one of the most difficult parts of the game for kids to learn, because success requires using the right techniques, anticipating where the ball will come off the rim, and hustling to battle the opponent for the ball. Keep an eye out for the following problems:

✓ **The defender continually seals off your player's step over move:** Often, the offensive player isn't executing the move quickly enough. As soon as he begins lifting his arm over the opponent's, he should move his inside leg into position to overtake the defender. If he waits too long to move his feet, the opponent can simply slide a half-step in front of your player to seal him off.

✓ **Poor footwork on the spin move:** The spin move is a challenging technique to master because it involves a lot of footwork and coordination. Plus, it isn't natural for young kids to turn their backs on the basket. Kids tend to shuffle their feet when their backs are touching the opponents', which slows them down and allows the defenders to keep them out of position. The trick is to get your players to understand that you want their backs touching the opponents' for the shortest amount of time possible.

Boxing out

After your offensive players work and struggle to get in position (see the previous section), they certainly don't want to give it up. They need to work to keep themselves positioned between the opponent and the basket. This position is called the *box-out position*. Here are the techniques for teaching your kids how to box out at the offensive end of the floor:

1. **As soon as the player gains position between the basket and the opponent, he pushes his butt into the player's thighs.**

2. **He moves his feet shoulder-width apart so that the opponent can't push him too far underneath the basket.**

For information on boxing out players at the defensive end of the floor, check out Chapter 10.

3. **He raises his hands up to head level.**

Keeping his hands up allows him to react to the ball when it ricochets off the rim. His palms should be facing the basket, and his elbows should be extended out. His head is tilted back slightly to follow the flight of the ball.

Chapter 10

Teaching the Defensive Fundamentals

....

In This Chapter

▶ Hammering home the importance of defense

▶ Coaching the basic defensive techniques

▶ Crashing the boards for rebounds

▶ Showing your players the art of stealing

....

*W*hen you send your players out on the floor, you want them to play good offense *and* defense; you don't want them to be a team of one-dimensional players. Your job is to help your kids understand and become proficient in all areas of the game — and one major area is playing good team defense. This chapter dives into teaching the defensive fundamentals your players need. We begin with the most basic defensive element of the game — guarding a player who's dribbling the ball — and then zero in on other important aspects, such as defending drives to the basket, making shots more difficult, taking charges, and going for steals. We also introduce the basics of rebounding, from boxing out on normal shots to grabbing the ball after missed free throws.

Emphasizing the Importance of Defense

In basketball, like in many walks of life (war, relationships, and so on), playing defense is necessary for success. Because your players will spend roughly half of each game trying to prevent opponents from putting points on the scoreboard — or, in the case of younger players, trying to get the ball back so they can play offense — the more they understand the necessary defensive techniques, the more success they'll have. Playing good team defense also paves the way for your players to enjoy playing the game more.

Playing defense is isn't very appealing to many youngsters (and even older players). However, teaching defense doesn't have to be an unpleasant experience for all parties — as long as you handle it the right way. The following list presents a few tactics you can use to emphasize the importance of playing defense; if you teach with enthusiasm and heap on the praise, your kids will embrace learning the fundamentals of good defense:

- ✔ **Constantly remind that good defense leads to more time on offense.** Think about it. Every time your team grabs a rebound or makes a steal, your opponent has one less possession that you have to defend. That translates into valuable (and fun) scoring opportunities that your kids can capitalize on.

- ✔ **Make playing defense fun.** The enthusiasm in your voice, the praise you hand out, and the energy you bring to teaching defensive skills must match how you act when teaching offensive skills. If you applaud a pass deflection as passionately as you do a nice pass, your kids will embrace playing defense.

- ✔ **Use appropriate defensive drills.** Pack your practices with fun defensive drills that give your kids the best chance to learn a wide variety of skills. Check out Chapters 11, 14, and 17, which present some great drills that you can incorporate into your practices. *Note:* When coaching older kids, using competitive drills helps create added interest and enthusiasm among them.

Many youngsters new to the sport probably don't realize the important role defense plays in the game. You can signal its importance by making sure your team practices defense every time you get together. You can even start off your practices with a defensive drill to make its importance clear.

Break Down! Teaching the Basic Stances

Playing good defense requires your players to use a variety of skills and defensive stances when contending with opponents. For instance, your players need to employ different tactics when an opponent is dribbling along the perimeter, driving to the basket, delivering a pass to a teammate, and so on.

Of course, the younger your players are, and the less experience they have, the less technical your teachings must be. The older and more experienced your players are, the more exact you can get when working with them on these fundamentals. In this section, we dig into the basic techniques your players need to master so that they're always operating from a solid defensive foundation. Teaching these techniques helps turn your team into one that drives opponents crazy on game day.

Battling with a ball handler

Players guarding *ball handlers* — offensive players either dribbling or holding the ball — are at a disadvantage: They don't know where the ball handler will go when dribbling or what his plans are for shooting or passing. The way to minimize this disadvantage and prevent scores is to stick to sound defensive fundamentals when guarding ball handlers. Specifically, maintaining proper body position and reacting to whatever the opponent does is key.

The following list outlines the techniques you can teach your players who must defend ball handlers:

1. **The defender places his feet shoulder-width apart.**

   He flexes his knees and stays on the balls of his feet with his heels lightly brushing the floor. His weight is equally distributed (see Figure 10-1a for an example).

2. **The defender keeps his foot opposite the ball handler's dominant hand about six inches in front of his other foot.**

   For example, if the ball handler is right-handed, the defender's left foot should be extended out.

3. **He positions his body just beyond an arm's reach away from the ball handler, in between the offensive player and the basket.**

   He should be able to reach out and touch the player he's guarding.

4. **He raises his arm that's ball-side, with the palm facing the ball handler.**

   His opposite hand is extended out to cut down on the passing lanes and to distract the player and hinder his court vision.

Figure 10-1:
The proper stance for guarding a ball handler.

a

b

5. **He keeps his head up and his eyes focused straight ahead at the player he's guarding.**

6. **If the ball handler dribbles to his right, the defender pushes off his right foot and moves his left foot out to the side (see Figure 10-1b).**

    When the ball handler moves to his left, the defender pushes off his left foot and moves his right foot out.

    His right foot then slides toward his left in a shuffling motion.

7. **As he moves laterally, the defender keeps his left hand to the side with his right hand forward at waist-level.**

    If the player picks up his dribble, the defender can close in on him because the ball handler can't dribble past him to create an opening.

8. **If the ball handler gains an advantage and gets by your player, your defender must turn and run as fast as possible to recover and reestablish position between the player and the basket (see the following section for more).**

    No matter how good a defensive player is, opponents will get by him sometimes. It's just part of the game.

Advise your defenders to always try to force the dribblers away from their intended destinations and make it as difficult as possible for them to find openings, take shots, or deliver passes. You also want your players to force the offense to take wide angles away from the basket. If your defender is in the middle of the court, for instance, you want him moving toward the sidelines to put the offense in a weaker attacking position farther away from the basket. Also, if your defenders can force ball handlers to use their weaker hands, that increases your defense's chances of getting a stop or creating a turnover.

Guarding ball handlers, especially quick ones, presents many problems for youngsters. Here are some of the common issues kids encounter with this aspect of playing defense:

- ✔ **Players dribble right by them:** If this happens often, have your defender slide a half step to the dribbler's dominant side. Doing so forces the ball handler to dribble with his less-dominant hand, meaning he won't be quite as efficient. This technique is known as *overplaying* a ball handler.

- ✔ **Players aren't getting any steals:** If a defender can't apply much pressure, make sure he has his foot that's opposite the ball handler's dominant hand several inches in front of his other foot. Proper foot position allows players to flick at the ball and create turnovers. Also, take a look at the position of his hands to make sure they're palms up.

Defending a drive toward the basket

Defending opponents who are driving toward the basket is all about anticipation and reaction. If defenders can't stop a player from driving to the basket, or at least make his route a lot more difficult, they can be in for a pretty rough day. Teach the following steps to your players so they can stop the drivers and slashers:

1. **The defensive player stays in his basic defensive stance (see the previous section).**

2. **The defender pivots in the direction the ball handler moves by dropping the proper foot back (called the *drop step*) in the same direction (see Figure 10-2).**

   For example, if the opponent is driving to the hoop on the left side of the defender's body, the defender's first step should be with his left foot in that direction.

Figure 10-2:
Players must react quickly when defending drives to the basket.

3. **He slides at an angle with his next step and begins to shuffle to stay between the player and the basket.**

   His feet shouldn't contact each other or cross. Shuffling with many small steps ensures that both his feet are never off the ground at the same time, allowing him to change direction quickly and efficiently.

4. **He keeps his eyes focused on, and his upper body facing, the offensive player's chest, with his hands out and his palms up.**

   When a defender keeps his eyes on the ball handler's chest, he's less likely to go for any head or shoulder fakes (see Chapter 15).

Guarding drivers is a difficult assignment for any defender. When a player is on the move, he's more difficult to guard than a player who's standing still or moving laterally. Plus, if the ball handler is quick, tall, or athletic, it increases the difficulty of sticking with him. Here's a look at the most common problems kids have with this skill:

- ✔ **Player drives by the defender with ease:** The main culprit for this is taking long strides when reacting to moves made by the ball handler. Remind your defenders to use short, choppy steps, which enable them to make quicker lateral movements. If a defender gets beat, teach him to sprint back into position and get in front of the ball handler again in his defensive crouch.

- ✔ **The defender gets called for reach-in fouls:** Defenders often get whistled for reaching in (see Chapter 3) because they're out of position and try to compensate by reaching their arms out to contact the ball handlers. When working with your defenders, stress the importance of keeping their bodies facing the ball handlers. If they turn sideways, they create larger openings for the ball handlers to drive past them.

Making a shot more difficult

When an offensive player is taking a shot, you want your defender to apply as much pressure as possible to increase the difficulty — without fouling. The following list explains how your defenders can make shooting the ball more challenging for the opposition:

1. **When the offensive player leaves his feet to attempt a shot, the defender should extend the arm that's closest to the player into the air.**

   His other arm is at waist level and can swipe at the ball if the player is executing a fake (see Figure 10-3a).

2. **As he raises his arm, the defender moves at a slight angle toward the shooter.**

   If he isn't in position to block the shot, he can put his hand in the defender's face to obstruct his vision.

3. **He reaches his arm to try to shadow the ball as it leaves the shooter's hand.**

   He must maintain good body position so that he doesn't allow his momentum to carry him into the shooter, which is a foul.

Kids can derive a lot of satisfaction in rejecting another player's shot. However, it's an advanced skill that requires a lot of timing, coordination, and patience. Still, it's a good skill to be able to rely on in certain situations when players can avoid fouling. Advise your defenders to try to keep the ball on the court when they block shots. If a shot blocker keeps the ball on the court, he gives his team a chance to grab possession and perhaps create a fast break.

Figure 10-3:
Contesting
shots makes
scoring
more
difficult.

a   b

When an offensive player picks up his dribble and is close enough to the basket to put up a shot, the defender should extend one arm in front of the player's face and keep the other stretched at waist level to cut down on the opponent's available passing lanes (see Figure 10-3b). If the player leaves his feet to take a shot, the defender leaps with him to attempt to block the shot, or at least to impair his vision and make the shot more difficult.

Defending a shooter is pretty challenging, and players can get themselves into trouble. Here are some areas of concern when it comes to shot blocking:

✔ **The player fouls the shooter:** The defender may be jumping directly at the shooter, which often causes him to make contact with the arm. If you teach him to take more of an angle (see Step 2), he'll be less likely to contact any part of the shooter's body.

✔ **The player goes for a shooter's pump fakes:** Youngsters, in their enthusiasm for defending shots, often have a tough time keeping their feet on the floor, which makes them vulnerable to fakes. The pump fake (see Chapter 15) is one of the best weapons offensive players have for creating advantages. A defender shouldn't leave his feet until he sees the offensive player commit to going in the air.

The best way to solve the problem is to shift the focus away from blocking shots and put it on being in good defensive position at all times.

Obstructing passes

For kids — especially the younger ones — guarding players who don't have the ball isn't very exciting. Your job is to encourage the practice and make it exciting, because the better your youngsters are at denying passes, the fewer quality shots they'll allow opponents to take. The key to denying passes is having the four defenders off the ball handler maintain their positions between the ball handler and the players they're guarding.

The following list tells a player what to do when defending passes:

1. **The defensive player keeps his eyes on the ball handler *and* the player he's guarding.**

   He should be in the basic defensive stance, with his feet spread comfortably apart, his knees flexed, and his hands up. If a youngster turns his back to the ball handler, the player he's guarding has an advantage. And even if the youngster maintains sight of the ball handler at all times, he still has to be quick on his feet to react to his player's moves and cuts.

2. **The defender keeps himself between the player he's guarding and the basket.**

   The farther away the ball is from the defender, the farther away the defender can take his stance from the player he's guarding. Likewise, the farther away the offensive player is from the basket, the farther away the defender can play from him.

3. **When the opposing player makes a cut, the defender, keeping his arms active and between the passer and the player, tries to prevent (by shuffling) or deflect any passes.**

   Even if he can't get a steal himself, by simply deflecting the ball he can create opportunities for his teammates to scoop up loose balls.

Guarding players who don't have possession of the ball can be challenging to teach, mainly because kids' eyes naturally follow the ball handler. The following list helps you address some common problems youngsters have when trying to defend passes:

- **Defender loses track of the player he's guarding:** This isn't unusual at any level of play. Defenders can get lost in the maze of players running, cutting, and setting screens. Most likely, your defender is too focused on watching the ball handler, which gives the player he's guarding a little extra room to maneuver. Redirect your defender's primary focus to shadowing the player he's guarding and then gradually work with him on keeping an eye on the ball handler, too.

- **Defender gets beat on back-door plays:** The *back-door play,* in which an offensive player cuts to the basket behind a defender and receives a pass to convert a lay-up (see Chapter 12), often is the result of the defensive player being a little too aggressive. If your defender is always looking to make a steal, he may find himself out of position and be susceptible to this type of play.

Guarding post players

When defending players in the *post* (the area on the court comprised of the lane), your players have a couple different options. (For more information on the markings on the court, refer to Chapter 3.) Specifically, defenders have the option of playing behind the offensive players, in front of them, or even beside them.

In the middle or high post

When guarding players in the *mid-* and *high-post areas* — the areas in the lane farthest away from the basket — defenders usually should stick to playing behind the opponents (between them and the basket). When an offensive player has the ball in this area, he isn't in great scoring position because of his distance from the basket — especially if he has his back to the basket, which often is the case.

After the opponent receives the ball in the mid- to high-post area, the defender should use the following techniques:

1. **The defender maintains about an arm's length distance from the offensive player.**

   If the player with the ball is a good shooter from this range, the defender should play him a little closer; if the opponent doesn't pose much of a scoring threat, the defender can back off even farther if he chooses. As the game unfolds, you and your players will begin recognizing which kids are good shooters and which aren't.

2. **He extends his arm on the ball side at a 45-degree angle toward the shooter's face (see Figure 10-4) while maintaining his defensive positioning.**

Figure 10-4:
Post defenders must be active with their hands to stop the opponent.

Doing so provides a distraction if the player attempts a shot.

3. **He extends his other arm out at waist level.**

    This makes it more difficult for the opponent to pass or dribble the ball effectively.

4. **He keeps his feet shoulder-width apart as he shuffles to maintain position with the opponent if he moves.**

    He can overplay the opponent by sliding a half-step in the direction of the player's shooting hand to make it more difficult for the offensive player to rely on this hand for dribbling and driving to the basket.

In the low post

When defending players in the *low post* — the area in the lane near the basket — your players can guard the opponents from behind, from in front, or even on the side (though not often). The choice depends on the offensive player's skills to a large degree. If your defender is quite a bit shorter, he should probably play in front to deny the pass; otherwise, if he's behind him and the player receives the ball, the opponent can simply turn and shoot over the defender. If the offensive player doesn't have a lot of moves and tends to dribble a lot, your defender is better off playing behind him.

When defending from the front in the post, your players should follow these instructions:

1. **The defender positions his body in front of the opponent — between the player and the ball handler — with his legs about shoulder-width apart.**

2. **He should press his butt against the player's midsection.**

   Maintaining this contact allows him to follow the player as he moves around.

3. **He extends his arms straight up in the air to cut down on the available passing lanes and to make an entry pass into the post more difficult to execute.**

   When a player is guarding this way, he also has to be concerned with bounce passes and keeping his hands low, as well as passes delivered through the air where he needs to have his hands higher.

   Because he's playing in front of the opponent, the defender's top priority is preventing him from receiving the ball, which his outstretched hands can do. If the opponent does get his hands on a pass, he'll likely have a path to a great scoring opportunity — unless you have teammates there to help (see Chapter 16). If the player puts up a shot, the defender tries to box out the shooter to grab the rebound.

If the defender plays behind the opponent in the low post, he must maintain tight position (also known as *bodying up*) because of his proximity to the basket. This is how he should handle the position:

1. **He keeps his feet shoulder-width apart and his knees flexed.**

   This position allows him to shift quickly to his left or right if the offensive player attempts to spin and drive to the basket or move to another passing lane. Establishing a strong base also helps prevent the defender from being backed down underneath the basket by the offensive player.

2. **He keeps his hands straight up in the air.**

   This makes the defender taller, which makes it more difficult for the opponent to take a shot and draw a foul on the defender.

3. **He keeps his midsection in contact with the opponent's backside — called *bellying up*.**

   This allows him to react more quickly to sudden moves and puts him in good position to box out if an opponent chooses to take a shot. (Check out the section "Boxing out opposing players" for more hands-on info about teaching this technique.)

Defending in the post is difficult, particularly if an opponent has a height or quickness advantage. Kids often have trouble adapting in the following areas:

✔ **Gets beat on spin moves in the low post:** This often happens when the defender leaves a gap between him and the opponent; in this position, the opponent has a better chance of attacking and creating a good scoring opportunity with a spin move. Remind your defender to belly up and maintain contact as the opponent moves.

✔ **Gets beat off the dribble in the high post:** Offensive players who catch the ball in the high post don't have to be defended as tightly as players in the low post, unless they're really accurate shooters from that range. If your defender plays close, the opponent may be able to dribble right by him if he's a little quicker. Instruct your player to maintain good defensive positioning, with his knees flexed and his hand up (refer to the section "Defending a drive toward the basket").

All wood, no plastic: Taking the charge

Players who are willing to take a *charge* — which means establishing legal defending position and allowing offensive players to displace or run into them, usually knocking them to the floor — are real assets to a defense. (For more info on the terms of the game, check out Chapter 3.)

Here's how to teach your players the art of taking the charge:

1. **When the ball handler is on the move — driving toward the basket, perhaps — the defensive player should slide in front of her and attempt to beat her to a spot between her and the basket.**

2. **She should move her feet shoulder-width apart and plant them when she gets to the spot.**

   Players can draw charging fouls without having their feet planted if they slide with the offensive players and maintain legal guarding position.

3. **She keeps her arms at her side or crossed at waist level (see Figure 10-5).**

   If she's more comfortable having her arms extended straight up in the air, she can do that, too.

When the offensive player makes contact, the defensive player will probably get knocked backward. Encourage your players to maintain control of their bodies as they fall on their butts and put out their hands as a cushion, making sure not to lock their elbows so they don't risk injury.

One of the drawbacks of trying to draw a charge is not getting the call from the referee. When this happens, play may continue (if the defender isn't called for a blocking foul), putting your defense at a big disadvantage because you have to defend five offensive players with only four defenders. You can't control the refs, though, so just take the good and the bad and have your players use this technique whenever the situation is right.

Figure 10-5:
Taking a charge requires beating the offensive player to a spot — and staying sturdy.

Young kids often encounter the following problems when learning to take charges:

- ✔ **Afraid of getting hurt:** Who can blame children for being a little reluctant to initiate physical contact? Taking a charge usually won't feel that great. To help your kids get over this mental hurdle, make sure you teach them how to fall. Use a mat or several fluffy pillows when introducing kids to the hardwood. Have them get used to falling backward on a soft surface before you incorporate an offensive player into the mix.

- ✔ **Flops before the contact:** Sometimes kids (and pros) *flop,* meaning they fall backward in an exaggerated motion right before any contact occurs. Remind the youngsters to allow the offensive players to initiate contact before going down.

- ✔ **Gets called for blocking fouls:** Kids have a tendency to stick out limbs in order to brace for contact or initiate it, which usually results in the ref calling a foul. Remind your players of the importance of not leaning into the offensive players or sticking out their elbows or legs.

Rebounding the Ball after a Missed Shot

Rebounding the ball on defense is as important as making shots on offense. Teams that rebound well pose plenty of problems for opponents, and at the advanced levels of play, these teams usually are pretty successful when it comes to wins and losses. Your team can play great defense on the floor and force opponents to take bad shots, but if your players don't snare the rebounds, their effort goes to waste. Even worse, your opponents will get offensive rebounds and more opportunities to score points.

The following sections show you the way. But first, here are some tips to share with your players; these tips will explain how they can get their hands on more rebounds:

- ✔ **Consider the distance of the shot.** Usually, the farther away from the basket a shooter is, the longer the rebound will bounce on a missed shot.

- ✔ **React to the arc of shot.** Shots with a high arc tend to bounce high off the rim and stay in the vicinity of the lane. Shots with a line-drive arc tend to bounce low off the rim and deflect farther away from the basket.

- ✔ **Play the angles.** The angles at which players take shots can help your defenders predict the likely landings spots of rebounds:

   - • Shots taken from the wings often end up bouncing to the opposite side of the basket.

   - • Shots taken along the baseline often carom to the opposite side of the basket.

   - • Shots taken from the top of the lane and perimeter are much more difficult to predict because they can hit short or long or deflect to the left or right. Players should pay attention to the other factors in this list for these shots.

- ✔ **Sense the short shots.** Noticing that a shot will come up short is helpful, because these shots will either glance off the rim and drop straight down or bounce directly back to the areas they were taken from.

   Instruct your defenders who sense a short shot to yell out "short." This alerts teammates that the shot could be an air ball or a short rebound. Yelling "short" is especially important if a defender deflects the shot, which may cause the ball to come up way short.

- ✔ **Keep your hands ready.** When a shot goes up, your defenders' hands should go up with their elbows out. This position ensures that they're ready for any rebound — especially tricky ones that hit off the front of the rim and drop straight down.

✔ **Box out the shooter.** The shooter is always a threat to snare an offensive rebound because he has a pretty good idea of where the ball is going (see the following section for more).

✔ **Focus during the final seconds.** During the final seconds of close games, young kids tend to stand around when shots go up, anxiously waiting to see if the balls drop through the net. If they get lackadaisical in their rebounding responsibilities, your kids could allow an opposing player to rebound a missed shot and make the winning basket.

✔ **Assume that shooters will miss every shot.** Instill the mindset that your players constantly need to be in good rebounding position.

✔ **Rebound with your heart.** Good rebounders come in all shapes and sizes. Short players with big hearts who really covet the ball, hustle, and are tenacious will get their fair share of rebounds.

Boxing out opposing players

The most basic and important defensive fundamental for securing rebounds is *boxing out* (also called *blocking out* or *checking out*). This term refers to a defender keeping himself between the basket and an opposing player when a shot goes up. Quite simply, a defender tries to block the opposing player's path to the basket so that he can get his hands on the ball and prevent the other team from getting another shot attempt.

The following list explains how to teach your players the art of boxing out:

1. **As soon as the ball leaves the shooter's hands, the defender should locate the player he's assigned to guard.**

   In a man-to-man defense (see Chapter 13), this player is the one the defender is responsible for guarding, so he shouldn't have to look too far! If he's playing in a zone defense, he turns and boxes out the player nearest to him.

2. **When he nears his opponent, he extends the hand that's farthest away from the basket across his opponent's shoulders (see Figure 10-6a).**

3. **He takes a step backward into the opponent, spreads his feet shoulder-width apart, and pushes his back and butt into the player's abdomen and thighs (see Figure 10-6b).**

   He keeps his hands up and his elbows out. This position helps ensure that the opponent will have difficulty getting to the rebound and helps prevent the rebounder from getting whistled for a holding foul.

Because the defender is pressed against his opponent's legs, he limits the player's ability to jump for the ball and to push the rebounder toward the basket. He also can slide in any direction the opponent attempts to move in.

If the opposing player doesn't fight for position to go for the rebound, the defender can simply stay in position and use an arm bar (see Figure 10-6c). The arm bar blocks the player's path so that he can't make a play if the missed shot results in a loose ball.

Figure 10-6: The defender sets his position by extending his arm across the opponent's shoulders.

4. **He raises his hands up to head level, with his palms facing the basket, as the shot caroms off the rim.**

   He should extend his elbows out and tilt his head back slightly to track the ball. He should grab the ball at its highest point (or the player's highest jumping point!) with both hands (see Figure 10-6d).

Are your players having a difficult time boxing out? The following areas often give kids trouble; read on to find out what you can do to help:

✔ **Offensive players can get around his box out:** Make sure your player's butt is in contact with the opposing player and his hands are up with his elbows out so he can move left or right to seal off his opponent. You want your players to *feel* where the opponents are rather than see them, because if they keep their eyes on the opposition, they won't be able to react to the ball.

✔ **Taller kids are reaching over him to grab rebounds:** The taller a player is, the farther you want to keep him from the basket. If your players can box out farther from the basket, they'll neutralize height advantages and make it difficult for opponents to get their hands on rebounds.

Boxing out on free throws

There are many unique aspects to boxing out on free-throw attempts, because different players have different responsibilities. For example, the two players nearest the basket must box out the opponents standing next to them, while the player nearest the shooter — usually one of your guards — must step into the lane to prevent the shooter from getting his hands on any missed shot.

The following list presents the techniques for boxing out on free-throw attempts for the defenders nearest the basket:

1. **The defender on the free-throw shooter's right positions his left foot as near as possible to the opposing player; the defender on the left moves his right foot.**

   A defender's feet must remain between the tabs (see Chapter 3 for a look at the markings on the court).

2. **Before the shot is released, each player stands with his feet shoulder-width apart and his elbows out.**

   His body should be leaning slightly forward. Offensive players have trouble getting around players whose arms are out.

3. **When the free-throw shooter releases the ball, each defender slides the foot that's nearest to his opponent into the lane at a slight angle toward the basket.**

   Some leagues don't allow any movement into the lane until the ball hits the rim, so be sure to check so you can teach your players the proper techniques (see Chapters 2 and 3).

4. **Each player lowers the arm nearest the opposing player and extends it across the player's chest.**

5. **Each player moves his feet back to shoulder-width position to maintain a strong base so the opposing player can't take him out of position.**

The defenders in the top two lane positions (nearest the shooter) have different responsibilities. One player must box out the shooter. As soon as the player lofts the shot, the defender steps in front of him, extends his arm across the shooter's mid-section (see the previous section), and positions himself as close as possible to the player.

The following are the problems youngsters often face when learning how to box out on free throws:

✔ **Unable to establish good position:** When your defensive players step into the lane, make sure they do so at a slight angle while making contact with the opponents.

✔ **Getting pushed under the basket:** Your defenders nearest the basket may get pushed underneath it, where they can't get their hands on the ball, if they don't establish a strong foundation with their legs. Make sure they keep their feet shoulder-width apart so they can maintain their spots in the lane, along with having their hands up and elbows out.

Protecting the ball after a rebound

After one of your players has effectively boxed out her opponent and grabbed a rebound, you don't want all her hard work to go to waste. You must teach your players to prevent opposing players from stealing the ball back. Teach the following protection techniques to your players so that they don't surrender their well-earned rebounds:

1. **When the player grabs a rebound (see the previous section), she should bring it down below her chin and hold it against her chest (called *chinning the ball;* see Figure 10-7).**

   She should hold the ball with the pads of her fingers and not her palms.

Figure 10-7:
Players hold
rebounds
close to
their chests
to provide
maximum
protection.

2. She extends her elbows out to her sides.

Doing so provides extra protection against opposing players who may try to reach in to swipe the ball.

3. She bends her knees and pushes her butt out while keeping her head up and her eyes looking down the court for open teammates.

The bended-knee position allows her to dribble, pivot, or pass the ball. After the player secures the rebound, she can look to make an *outlet pass* (when a player who has just gained possession of the ball passes to a teammate moving down the court) to one of her teammates to help get the ball down the floor.

The following list presents some problems kids typically deal with when learning how to protect rebounds:

- ✔ **Called for flagrant fouls:** You want a player's elbows pointed away from her body to keep defenders from getting too close, but you don't want the youngster swinging her elbows wildly and putting opponents at risk of injury.

- ✔ **Ball gets knocked away:** This happens when a player holds the ball away from her body after she pulls down the rebound. Instruct your players to hold the ball against their chests, which takes away the room opponents have to grab at it.

Teaching On-Court Thievery: Steals

Stealing is bad when it involves taking another child's toys or lunch money, but on the basketball court, stealing is applauded. Good defensive teams and players can create more turnovers than the local bakery. The most obvious benefit is that it denies the opposition a shot attempt and a chance to score points. An added bonus is that a steal — especially one that occurs along the perimeter — can lead to a fast-break opportunity (see Chapter 15).

The following list explains how to teach your players the art of the steal:

1. **The defender maintains good position in front of the ball handler and keeps his eyes on him as he dribbles.**

   When you tell your players that successful steals begin with their feet, you may get a few weird looks — and understandably so! After all, this is basketball, not soccer. However, they must understand that the better their footwork, the better position they'll be in to harass ball handlers and make steals (refer to the section "Battling with a ball handler").

2. **When the ball handler brings the ball in front of him, it presents an opportunity for the defender to attempt a steal.**

   If the ball is well-protected, the defender should simply maintain good position and not reach for the ball, because that usually results in a foul.

3. **The defender reaches for the ball in a side-to-side motion to knock it away.**

   If he uses an up-and-down motion, he risks slapping the ball handler's hands and being called for a foul.

4. **After he knocks away the ball, the defender must quickly make a grab for it before his opponent can recover.**

Early in games, encourage your players to fake reaching in for the ball as they guard ball handlers. This action gives them a sense of how the opposing players will react to steal attempts. If a defender can gain some insight on potential reactions — such as which hand the opponent relies on when pressured or how he twists his body to protect the ball — he can increase his chances of making steals.

Becoming a good ball thief takes a lot of practice. A player often must clear the following hurdles along the way:

✔ **Denying himself opportunities to steal the ball:** Inspect his footwork to ensure that he's using short, choppy steps to move from side to side. He shouldn't be crossing his feet because it slows him down and puts him out of position. Secondly, zero in on his hands. Many kids want to play defense with their hands at their sides because it's easier to move around that way. However, to create steals, kids have to keep their hands up and in position to strike.

✔ **Getting whistled for fouls while attempting steals:** Make sure your defender isn't slapping at the ball with an up-and-down motion, which leaves little room for making contact with the ball. Instruct your players to use a side-to-side swatting motion.

Chapter 11

Fundamental Drills for Beginners

● ●

In This Chapter

▶ Educating and entertaining with offensive drills

▶ Utilizing fun-filled defensive drills

▶ Teaching your players to go for rebounds

▶ Determining cool ways to open and close practices

● ●

*O*ne of the secrets of becoming a beloved youth basketball coach that beginning-level players enjoy learning from is running practices that come close to matching the excitement and fun of game day. Sure, coming up with drills that are interesting, challenging, and fun to perform all season long may seem pretty daunting, but not to worry. We have you covered!

This chapter presents a smorgasbord of drills — both offensive and defensive — to give your young, beginning players a wonderful start in mastering the basic elements of the game. We cover everything from dribbling, passing, and shooting drills to work on rebounding and guarding ball handlers, among other topics.

You can modify the drills we present in this chapter to fit the needs of your team and to keep pace with the kids' ever-changing development. Chapter 8 gives a full tutorial on evaluating your team during the season and making adjustments. If you have a group of players who've been playing for several years and have a pretty good understanding of the fundamentals, you may want to jump to Chapters 14 and 17, where we provide a series of intermediate and advanced drills you can use during practice.

Incorporating Offensive Drills to Bolster Scoring Chances

Becoming an efficient offensive team requires that your players have a solid understanding of the basics of dribbling, passing, and shooting. These are the offensive skills you should focus on during practice with young, inexperienced players. If you don't practice the skills often, your players won't develop the ability to execute them while being pressured by opponents. And developing all-around skills on offense — accompanied by the confidence to perform them on game day with spectators in the stands — will lead to more enjoyment of basketball.

Learning and executing all the basic techniques can be overwhelming for beginning players. As you introduce different drills, keep this in mind: the simpler, the better. Don't let your urge to be creative with your practices cause you to lose sight of the fact that you want your players to develop solid offensive fundamentals (which we tackle teaching in Chapter 9). Quality learning will take place only if you provide the players with quality instruction. This section highlights some basic offensive drills you can add to your practices with your inexperienced players.

You can tweak your drills to fit the needs of a player who's struggling with a certain aspect of his game. For example, if one of your players is really struggling with his shot — perhaps he's had several shots blocked and his confidence is sagging — you must build him back up. Don't stick him back in drills where his shot may get blocked. Rather, put him in a drill that doesn't include defenders to help him regain his shooting touch and some confidence. Then, when he seems ready, you can add defenders to the mix so he can work on shooting with a hand in his face.

Of course, you don't want to overlook the needs of the entire team for one player during practice. So, you can split the team in half, with some kids shooting without defenders on one side and some competing in a more intense drill at the opposite end (as long as you have an assistant to cover one end of the floor; see Chapter 4).

Becoming dribbling demons

The ability to dribble and handle the ball in a variety of situations is an important skill for young players to develop. In fact, dribbling is the first skill that players should work to develop. It's even more important than shooting, because if kids can't move the ball down the floor, they'll never get those coveted opportunities to put up shots. This section presents some dribbling drills that you can use to help your players build their skills.

Obstacle course

The *obstacle course* drill teaches kids how to dribble around the court using both hands (not at the same time, of course). The good thing is, as the kids get older and more advanced, you can easily tweak this drill to challenge them and help them further develop their skills.

What you need: A bunch of pylons. Four basketballs.

How it works: Set up four columns of five pylons going across the width of the court. Leave roughly 10 feet between each pylon.

These numbers are simply guidelines. This drill, as well as the others we introduce in this chapter, is just as effective with fewer pylons and with other types of objects at your disposal. If you don't have access to pylons, you can use old t-shirts, towels, and even parents!

Break up your team into four equal groups and position one group at each row of pylons. Give the player at the front of the line in each group a basketball. On your whistle, the first player in each row begins dribbling, weaving back and forth slalom-style between each pylon while switching the ball between his right and left hands. You want the players dribbling with their left hands when they're cutting to their left and with their right hands when they circle around the pylons to their right. When the player returns to where he started, he hands the ball to the next player in his line.

Coaching pointers: Remind the players to keep their heads up to watch where they're going rather than the balls. The young players may need to take it slow to accomplish this, but that's okay. In time, keeping their eyes up will enable them to negotiate the course quicker — and will make them more effective during games.

Relay race

The *relay race* drill helps youngsters practice keeping control of the ball while moving down the court quickly. This sets the foundation for fast-break drills and for late-game situations when teams need to advance the ball quickly (see Chapter 15).

What you need: One basketball for each two-person team

How it works: Break up the team into pairs. Position one half of each team at one end of the floor and give each of these players a basketball. Their partners should line up opposite them at the other end of the floor.

1. **On your whistle, the players with the balls begin dribbling down the court as fast as they can (see Chapter 9 for tips on speed dribbling).**

2. **When they reach their partners, they hand off the balls, and the new ball handlers dribble back down the court.**

   The first player to reach the line where the drill began wins!

Coaching pointers: Make sure the kids are trying to control the balls and not just pushing them far out in front of their bodies. Balls in that position can be stolen by defenders in a game situation. You also can incorporate passing and shooting aspects into this drill. For example, when the first player dribbles down the floor, you can have him stop when he gets within 15 feet of his partner to deliver a chest pass. When the second player heads down the court, you can have him convert a lay-up or stop and take a medium-range shot. (See Chapter 9 for info on performing these techniques.)

Practicing proficient passing

When young kids watch basketball, they love to focus on the scoring, the slam dunks, and the blocked shots. Passing often seems boring and lost in the shuffle. You must impress upon your young team the importance of passing. The following drills help improve your team's passing skills.

Target chest passes

The *target chest passes* drill focuses on enhancing kids' accuracy with their chest passes, which is important because the chest pass is the most common type of pass basketball players use (see Chapter 9).

What you need: One basketball for each two-person team

How it works: Divide the team into two-person groups and have each two-some stand about 15 feet apart. You can adjust the length based on your players' needs. A player in each pair begins with a ball.

1. **The partner with the ball delivers a chest pass to her partner.**

2. **After several repetitions, evaluate whether the players are making accurate passes; if they are, have them take a step backward to increase the difficulty.**

   Another fun option is to turn the drill into a competitive game. After the first round of passes, you can eliminate a pair if they made any off-target passes. Continue moving the kids farther away until only one pair is left.

Coaching pointers: Stress the importance of stepping toward the target when executing the chest pass, as well as following through toward the recipient's chest with the hands. Have the receiver show her hands to give a target where she would like to receive the ball.

Partner bounce

The *partner bounce* drill allows kids to practice delivering accurate bounce passes. A bounce pass can be more advantageous to use during certain game situations, such as when executing fast breaks or passing inside to a post player. (For the basics of teaching the bounce pass, head to Chapter 9.)

What you need: One basketball for each two-person team

How it works: Break up the team into pairs and scatter the pairs around the court. Have each pair begin with 10 feet between the partners and one ball.

1. **On your whistle, the player with the ball steps forward and delivers a bounce pass to his partner.**

2. **Gradually, as the kids become comfortable delivering bounce passes from a short distance, move them back a couple steps.**

   As with the previous chest passes drill, you can turn this into a challenging game by seeing which pair can move back the farthest while maintaining accuracy with their passes.

Coaching pointers: Make sure the bounce passes arrive at a good height (waist-level) for the young players to handle. Have the partners give the passers a target by showing their hands. If the passes come in too high or too low, you need to adjust the spot the youngsters are aiming at on the bounce.

Soft hands

When young players first start at the beginning levels of basketball, many don't have much accuracy with their shots or their passes. A player will be an asset to your team if she can make accurate passes *and* catch off-target passes. Kids get valuable practice corralling passes from all different angles with this *soft hands* drill.

What you need: One player. One coach. One ball.

How it works: The player lines up about 15 feet away from you or an assistant coach/parent helper (see Chapter 4).

1. **The coach begins the drill by delivering a bounce pass a little off-target to the player's left or right.**

   The youngster should react and try to catch the ball; if she does, she sends a bounce pass back to the coach.

2. **The coach follows up with an off-target chest pass to force the child to move her feet.**

   After the player gains possession of the ball, she delivers a chest pass back to the coach.

   You can turn this drill into a challenging game by giving each player ten off-target passes to see who can catch the most without bobbling or dropping them. You also can award points for how many accurate passes players get back to you.

Coaching pointers: Make sure the youngster stays on the balls of her feet with her hands up, ready to react to the errant passes. This position increases the chances of her receiving the balls cleanly. Players waste valuable time moving their hands into proper position while the ball is on the way.

Putting the ball in the basket

For basketball players, nothing matches the thrill of seeing shots drop through the net for baskets — especially for young kids. The following drills zero in on basic shooting skills so that your youngsters develop a shooting touch from different areas on the floor.

Lay-up mania

Lay-ups — whether converted on a drive to the basket, when finishing off a fast break, or when putting up a short shot off a rebound — play a crucial role in a team's effectiveness on offense. The *lay-up mania* drill helps young-sters become more proficient in this area of the game. (For a review of proper lay-up and passing techniques, check out Chapter 9. Chapter 15 covers fast breaks.)

What you need: Your entire team. Two balls.

How it works: Split the team in half; each half heads to one end of the floor. You can supervise by spending time at each end of the floor, or you can have an assistant handle one group while you oversee the other. The more baskets and supervision you have access to, the better, because running the drill on both ends eliminates a lot of standing-around time. Within each group, set up one row of players to the right of the free-throw line, facing the basket, and another row of players to the left.

1. **The player at the head of the right line starts with the ball, and he begins dribbling toward the basket; the first player in the opposite line also jogs toward the basket.**

2. **The player with the ball shoots a lay-up; the other player grabs the rebound or the made shot and delivers a bounce pass to the next player in the right-hand line.**

   The player who took the shot and the rebounder go to the ends of the opposite lines.

Coaching pointers: Run this drill at top speed to make the lay-ups game-like in nature. Make sure the kids use the foot opposite their shooting hands to push themselves into the air.

Spot shots

The more comfortable your players feel when taking shots from all over the court, the more problems they'll pose for defenders. If you help develop this comfort at an early age, you'll set up the kids for great fun and skill develop-ment down the road. The *spot shots* drill is a fun way to develop young kids' shooting touch.

What you need: One player. One ball. Some pylons (or other markers). A stopwatch.

How it works: Set up the pylons at various distances around the basket.

1. **On your whistle, the youngster takes a shot from a spot next to one of the pylons.**

2. **After lofting the shot, he rebounds the ball, dribbles to a different pylon, and takes another shot.**

   See how many shots the player can make in a one-minute span. You can make the drill a fun team contest by awarding different points based on distance from the basket. See which player can accumulate the most points during the time span.

Coaching pointers: Because this drill has a time factor, the kids will tend to sacrifice technique in order to rush shots. Let a player know right away if he isn't using proper form. You want to ensure that the child sticks to the shooting fundamentals (see Chapter 9). You can even ditch the stopwatch and keep the focus on shooting from different spots on the floor.

Free-throw frenzy

Being effective at the free-throw line (or the *charity stripe*) is all about establishing a comfortable routine and having the confidence to convert under any circumstance. (Oh, and practice. Plenty of practice, starting from an early age.) The *free-throw frenzy* drill helps players gain comfort and confidence. (For more on free-throw technique, head to Chapter 9.)

What you need: Your entire team. Four basketballs.

How it works: Divide the team into four groups, and have each group gather near a basket (if possible). Using multiple baskets prevents boredom by eliminating a lot of standing-around time.

1. **Have the first player in each group attempt a free throw.**

2. **After taking the shot, the player retrieves the ball and passes to the next player in his group for another free-throw attempt.**

   Give each group 20 or so shots to see which makes the most free throws.

Coaching pointers: Players should use proper form and stick to the same pre-shot routine before every free throw. You can tweak the drill and have each player take two shots, because during games players often have two free-throw opportunities at a time. Or, if a player makes the first shot, you can award him another. You also can line the rest of the kids in the shooter's group around the lane to help your players get accustomed to the positions they'll assume on game day (see Chapter 3).

Becoming Shut-Down Defenders with Defensive Drills

Playing defense requires skills that are much different from those needed on offense, simply because the emphasis is on reacting to the opposition. Stopping players from penetrating into the lane, disrupting passing lanes, boxing out to grab rebounds, and making shots more difficult are just some of the fundamental skills players need to play defense. (Chapter 10 covers the basics of playing defense; Chapter 3 covers the layout of the court.) Use the drills in this section to help your beginning-level players enhance their defensive skills and create more scoring chances for themselves on offense.

Defending dribblers

A good ball handler can cause many problems for your defense, from penetrating into the lane and going for easy buckets to breaking double teams and passing to open teammates. Disrupting an opposing ball handler's movements requires a broad range of skills. The drills in this section help your players improve those all-important techniques for defending opposing dribblers.

Lateral slides

Good defensive play requires the ability to move in all different directions — quickly — while maintaining proper position. The *lateral slides* drill works to enhance your kids' footwork.

What you need: Your entire team. One coach. One ball.

How it works: Position the team in front of you in rows of four players, with about 10 feet between each player. The players should assume the proper defensive stance. (See Chapter 10 for the scoop on teaching the proper stance.)

You begin the drill by holding the ball out in front of you for everyone to see. When you shift the ball, your kids move based on your movement:

- ✔ When you move the ball to your left, the kids shuffle in that direction (to their right) until you move the ball in another direction, and vice versa for going to the right.
- ✔ When you raise the ball over your head, the kids move forward.
- ✔ When you hold it out in front of you, the kids backpedal.

Coaching pointers: Make sure the kids' eyes remain focused on the ball while they move and that they aren't crossing their feet while shuffling. Straying eyes and crossed feet slow players down and make it tougher to stick with offensive players.

Deny the dribbler

The ability to stop players from driving to the hoop is one of the marks of sound defensive play. The *deny the dribbler* drill helps your kids become stronger in this area of defense.

What you need: One ball for each twosome

How it works: Break the team into pairs and give one player in each twosome a ball. The players with the balls line up along a baseline, leaving approximately 15 to 20 feet between each player. The other players face their partners, standing close enough that if they reach out, they can touch the ball handlers.

1. **On your whistle, the players with the balls begin dribbling upcourt, trying to work their way to the other baseline while their partners try to make their progress as difficult as possible.**

2. **When they reach the other end, the defenders take over on offense, and the ball handlers become the defenders.**

Coaching pointers: The key to defending well in this drill is maintaining good position by shuffling the feet. If the defender gets beat, he needs to sprint at an angle to the dribbler and turn him back and get into good defensive stance again; he can't shuffle and catch up to the offensive player. If an offensive player is getting down the court too easily, advise his defender to move over just a half-step in the direction of the ball handler's stronger hand. This forces the ball handler to dribble more with his less-dominant hand, which takes away a little of his quickness. (Chapter 10 has more tips.)

Guarding passers

Successfully defending all types of passes — whether along the perimeter or in the post area — requires good footwork, proper technique, and quick hands, along with a healthy dose of instinct and anticipation. The drills in this section help your youngsters get comfortable at both denying and deflecting passes. (Chapter 9 gives you a rundown of the different types of passes players can make.)

Denying the dish

Preventing passes into the post area can limit the number of quality scoring chances the opposition can create. The *denying the dish* drill helps kids practice defending passes from behind and from the front of the opponent. An added bonus is that players get practice making passes, too.

What you need: Groups of three kids. One ball per group.

How it works: Break up the team into groups of three — two offensive players and one defender. If possible, each group should perform this drill in front of its own basket, under the supervision of you or an assistant coach. Within each group, position one player with the ball at the top of the key. Her offensive partner positions herself in the middle of the lane, and the defensive player stands between the two offensive players.

1. **The player with the ball attempts to pass it to her partner in the post, while the defender tries to steal or deflect the pass.**

   Don't allow the player with the ball to dribble and change position.

2. **After the ball handler makes the pass, repeat the drill with the defender beginning behind the post player.**

Coaching pointers: Make sure the defender keeps her arms up when she's in front of the offensive player to cut down on the available passing lanes. She needs to keep in contact, with her butt on the post player's thigh, so she knows where she is at all times; this way, she can stay in front of her without having to turn around.

When she's behind the post player, watch to make sure that the defender maintains good position — and doesn't foul by reaching around — so that even if the post player does catch the ball, your defender is ready to contest a shot. And she should try to force the post player as far away from the basket as possible without fouling. If she lets the player catch the ball a few feet from the basket, she'll probably get scored on or commit a foul. (Chapter 10 covers the techniques in more detail.)

Challenging the inbounds pass

Inbounds plays happen many times throughout the course of a game. Making it difficult for the opposition to inbound the ball can lead to turnovers and good scoring chances for your team. The *challenging the inbounds pass* drill makes your players tough from the very first inbound.

What you need: Four players. One ball.

How it works: Choose two players to get the ball inbounds and two to defend. Position the player with the ball along the baseline, with his partner in play ready to receive a pass. One defender guards the inbounder, and the other covers the player who will be receiving the pass.

1. **On your whistle, the inbounder has five seconds to get the ball to his offensive partner.**

2. **The defenders try to deny the inbounds pass; if the pass is made, they attempt to steal or deflect it.**

Coaching pointers: Watch the player guarding the inbounder to ensure that he doesn't step over the baseline and that he keeps his arms up to disrupt the passer's vision and passing lanes. Also, make sure the other defender isn't grabbing at the offensive player; he should be relying on his feet to maintain good defensive position (see Chapter 10).

Suffocating shooters

The foundation of good defensive play is being able to deny offensive players good scoring opportunities. The drills in this section focus on the fundamentals of defending shots: footwork and maintaining good body position.

Slide and stop

The ability to stick close to good shooters is a great skill for youngsters to have in their defensive arsenal. The *slide and stop* drill forces your players to rely on good footwork and balance to defend shooters.

What you need: Four players. One ball.

How it works: Position two offensive players on each side of the lane above the key, facing the basket. The other offensive player starts with the ball and stands a few feet in front of the basket, facing his offensive partners (see Figure 11-1). The defensive player moves to a position just below the free-throw line, with his back to the player with the ball.

1. **On your whistle, the player with the ball passes to one of the two offensive players on the perimeter.**

2. **As soon as the defender sees which direction the ball is going, he moves quickly toward that player to prevent him from getting an open shot.**

   He must determine whether to attempt to block a shot, if he thinks the player will attempt one, or maintain good defensive position so the player can't dribble by him and toward the basket.

3. **The ball handler attempts a shot.**

Coaching pointers: Remind your defender that if he goes to block a shot, he should aim for where the shooter is releasing the ball, and not for the shooter himself. You never want your defenders to allow their momentum to carry them into shooters (see Chapter 13 for the blocking mechanics). Also, you can make modifications to this drill to best suit your team's needs. For example, after the initial pass is made, you can give the offensive player the option of shooting the ball, passing it over to his partner for an open shot (if the defender is closely guarding him), or driving to the basket (to shoot or pass to his partner for an open shot). This further challenges the defensive player.

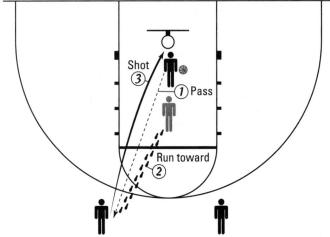

Figure 11-1:
Challenging
perimeter
shots is a
key
component
of playing
good
defense.

Monitoring the motion

The best way to prevent a player from scoring is to keep him from getting his hands on the ball. Of course, that's much more difficult than it sounds! You can use the *monitoring the motion* drill to help your players practice guarding closely and forcing opponents to work extra hard to receive the ball.

What you need: Three players. One ball.

How it works: Position one offensive player with the ball at the top of the key. The other offensive player and one defender begin inside the baseline and underneath the basket. The offensive player stands in front of the defensive player, and both are facing the passer.

1. **On your whistle, the offensive player without the ball begins moving around the court, trying to get free of the defender to receive a pass.**

2. **The player with the ball can't dribble; he must wait for an opening to deliver the pass.**

Coaching pointers: Good defensive play originates with good footwork. Make sure the defender keeps his feet shuffling and his hands up so he's always in position to create chaos — by making a steal, cutting down on the passing angles, or deflecting an attempt. Also, keep a close eye on his hands so that he doesn't use them to grab at the player who's making cuts.

You can play a series of five possessions and then rotate the kids so that each player gets to be a shooter, passer, and defender. You also can turn the drill into a game by awarding the defender two points if he steals the ball and one point if he prevents a basket; you can give one point to both the passer and shooter if they score a basket.

Introducing Effective Rebounding Drills

Proper footwork and body positioning, coupled with good hand-eye coordination and quick reflexes, are valuable skills to have to be able to win the battle for coveted rebounds. The two former, you can develop through practice; the latter two are more innate. The following drills help your youngsters become skilled rebounders. (For the basics on offensive rebounding, head to Chapter 9. For the defensive side of rebounding, head to Chapter 10.)

Rebounding drills can become pretty competitive as kids vie for loose balls, so make sure you keep an eye out for play that's too rough. If players commit fouls in their eagerness to grab rebounds, be sure to stop play, point out the fouls, and make corrections in their technique. Otherwise, the kids will carry bad habits over to game day. (Chapter 3 covers the various fouls in play.)

Free-throw positioning

When an opponent misses a free throw, you don't want to surrender another scoring opportunity by giving up an offensive rebound. The *free-throw positioning* drill allows your players to practice boxing out on free throws.

What you need: Five players. One coach. One basketball.

How it works:

1. **Choose three players to be on Team A and two to be on Team B. You (or an assistant) will assume the role of a player for Team B.**

2. **Take a position at the free-throw line; you're the designated free-throw shooter.**

   You take this role so you can control where the ball goes.

3. **Have your players take their positions in the lane; the players for Team A should be in the slots closest to the basket — the defensive positions.**

   For a look at how the lane is set up, check out Chapter 3.

4. **You loft free throws — intentionally missing them — while the players vie to grab the rebounds.**

Coaching pointers: Make sure the players aren't stepping into the lane too early — before you release the shot. Also, make sure the two players nearest the basket maintain good body position so they aren't susceptible to opponents getting around them. Try to put up a variety of shots that bounce off the rim at all different angles and heights to give the kids plenty of practice going after misses.

Throw a couple line-drive shots off the front of the rim that you can go after. Doing so keeps the Team A player nearest to you alert about his responsibilities for blocking you out.

Box and grab

Whenever an opponent puts up a shot, each defensive player is responsible for boxing out an opposing player. The *box and grab* drill helps your players practice getting in the proper box-out position (see Chapter 10).

What you need: Four players. One ball.

How it works: Designate three players for offense and one player for defense. Position one offensive player behind the baseline to inbound the ball, and have another offensive player set up around the three-point line to be the designated shooter. (For younger kids, you can move them in closer so they can get the ball to the basket.) Put the other offensive player just inside the free-throw line in the lane; the defensive player should set up about five feet away from him (see Figure 11-2).

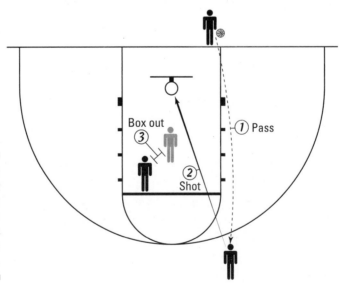

Figure 11-2:
Boxing out players is how you grab rebounds in traffic.

Box out ③

①Pass

②Shot

1. **The inbounder throws the ball to the perimeter shooter.**

2. **He catches the ball and puts up a shot.**

3. **As soon as the shooter releases the ball, the defensive player locates the offensive player in the lane and blocks him out to try to grab the rebound.**

Coaching pointers: The key to boxing out is locating where the opponent is and making contact with his body. Your defender should push his butt into his opponent's midsection so that he's sealed off from making a play on the ball.

To add a little variety to the drill, you can have the shooter move around to different positions on the floor. Also, you can have the inbounder deliver both chest and bounce passes to the shooter so that your players can work on all sorts of skills at once (Chapter 9 covers the basics of these passes).

One-on-one box out

Kids who are relatively new to the sport often require some time and plenty of practice to adjust to the aggressive nature of rebounding. The *one-on-one box out* drill helps speed along their learning process by giving them experience battling for rebounds with just one other player.

What you need: Two players. One coach. One basketball.

How it works: Position two players in the lane near the basket. Have one player face the basket as the defender, and have the other player assume the offensive-rebounding position behind the defender (see Chapter 9). You have the basketball and stand around the three-point line. You loft a shot, and the two players battle for box-out position to see who can come up with the rebound. The players can switch positions after each shot or after a set number of shots. You can even turn this drill into a game by seeing which player can secure five rebounds first.

Coaching pointers: Keep a close eye on how the kids are getting into rebounding position. If they commit fouls in the box-out process, be sure to whistle them and make the necessary corrections with their technique. (Chapter 3 goes through the infractions the kids may make.) Take your shots from a variety of angles, and mix in some different types of shots.

Three-on-three box out

Grabbing rebounds while sandwiched among teammates and defenders is pretty challenging for young players. The *three-on-three box out* drill helps your kids become more comfortable going for rebounds in traffic.

What you need: Seven players. One ball.

How it works: Choose four players to play offense and three to play defense. Position two offensive players to the left and right of the basket, roughly five feet from the lane (see Figure 11-3). Another offensive player begins in the lane a few feet in front of the basket. The final offensive player begins at the top of the key with the ball. The defenders take their places guarding the three offensive players nearest the basket; you leave the ball handler free to shoot.

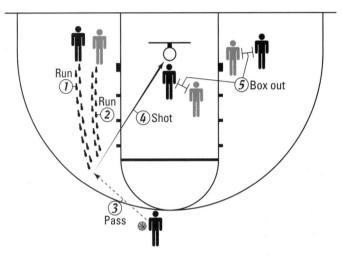

Figure 11-3:
Good defensive play requires boxing out on every shot attempt.

1. **Begin the drill by calling out the name of one of the players standing outside the lane; that player circles around the perimeter.**

2. **The defender guarding that player follows him out and keeps his arms up in the air to distract him.**

3. **The ball handler passes to the player called.**

4. **After receiving the pass, the cutting player takes a shot.**

5. **The other players near the basket battle for position to grab the rebound.**

   Be sure to rotate the players around so that they get a chance to play different positions.

Coaching pointers: As soon as the shot goes up, pay close attention to how the players nearest the basket seal off the opposing players. If they aren't making contact with the players by using their backsides — allowing them to know where the opposition is at all times — they'll have problems keeping the opponents from swiping the majority of the rebounds (see Chapters 9 and 10).

Rebound and outlet pass

Players who can grab rebounds and pass up the court quickly can create good scoring opportunities for their teams (for more on fast breaks, see Chapter 15). The *rebound and outlet pass* drill focuses on making good outlet passes after grabbing rebounds.

What you need: Four players. One ball.

How it works: Choose three players to play on Team A and one player to play on Team B. Position two players from Team A on opposite sides of the lane near the free-throw line, facing the nearest basket. Position the other Team A player in the lane near the basket with the ball, facing her teammates. The Team B player begins several feet in front of that player in the lane, facing the basket (see Figure 11-4).

Figure 11-4: Good outlet passes trigger fast-break opportunities.

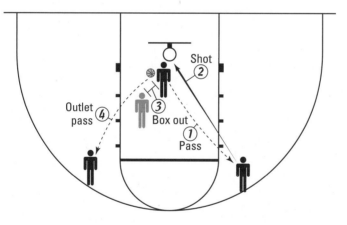

1. **The ball handler delivers a pass to one of her partners outside of the lane.**

2. **That player catches the ball and puts up a shot.**

3. **The offensive player in the lane then boxes out the defensive player and grabs the rebound.**

4. **The rebounder now looks to deliver an outlet pass to one of her two teammates who are running down the court.**

   The Team B player should assume a defensive stance after the other player grabs the rebound. For tips on making long passes, see Chapter 12.

Coaching pointers: For younger, beginning players, you may want to begin the drill by having the outlet passer find teammates who are standing still. You can work up to delivering passes to players on the move. Be patient with the kids, because it may take many repetitions for them to get their timing down in order to connect with players running. Also, make sure the rebounder uses proper form to protect the ball so that her hard work doesn't go to waste by committing a turnover (see Chapter 10).

Making practice fun and building your team's skills

Although game day is what kids look forward to most, your practices are what determine how much learning and skill development will take place this season. If you make your sessions fun-filled and entertaining, your players will be enthusiastic participants who likely will develop more skills that they can transfer to the court on game day. Conversely, if your practices are boring and unimaginative, the kids won't be fired up to attend and learning will be sporadic.

The following is a sample one-hour practice that you can use or model to keep your sessions as fun as game day, and even more productive:

- ✔ **5 minutes:** *Warm-up.* To get the kids' hearts pumping, have them jog around the outside of the court while dribbling. To mix things up, yell out "reverse" when you want them to switch hands or "pivot" when you want them to change direction. (For more on the warm-up process, head to Chapter 18.)

- ✔ **10 minutes:** *Obstacle course.* You can modify the drill you put here to fit your team's needs. Running a popular drill that's a surefire smile-starter is a great way to kick off your practices.

- ✔ **10 minutes:** *Lay-up mania.* Converting lay-ups is a must if you want to become an efficient offensive team. This drill helps kids master the proper techniques for making lay-ups while building their shooting confidence.

- ✔ **15 minutes:** *One-on-one box out.* If you have assistant coaches/helpers, that opens the way for you to run a couple drills at opposite ends of the floor. You can run this rebounding drill at one basket with half the kids while working on inbounding at the other end. After 7 or 8 minutes, rotate the kids so they get a chance to participate in both drills.

- ✔ **5 minutes:** *Lateral slides.* Sometimes, it's a good idea to simply set aside the balls around the midpoint of practice and focus on good footwork, which is the basis for playing sound defense.

- ✔ **10 minutes:** *Deny the dribbler.* This is a great follow-up drill to the lateral slides drill because it allows kids to use a skill they just worked on in a one-on-one setting.

- ✔ **5 minutes:** *Partner bounce.* This drill serves dual purposes: It hones the kids' passing effectiveness while allowing their bodies to cool down.

Chapter 12

Coaching Offense 101

In This Chapter

▶ Kicking your team's offensive skills up a notch

▶ Drawing up plays for the kids to work together

*I*f your youngsters have a pretty good handle on the offensive basics of the game (see Chapters 5 and 8 for tips on evaluating your team and setting goals), you can begin to introduce them to more advanced techniques that will enhance their performance. You can teach different ways of handling the ball, practice a variety of passes to beat different defenses, and demonstrate an array of shots the kids can call upon in various situations.

If you've come to this chapter looking for ways to rev up your offense and give your kids a new challenge, you've hit the jackpot. Here we explain how to help your players upgrade all sorts of offensive skills. Plus, we open up our playbook and share valuable information on running offensive team plays, ranging from setting screens to executing the pick and roll. As your kids latch onto these new and valuable skills, your offense will become more efficient, your opponents will have more difficulty guarding you, and your players' love for the game will flourish.

Upgrading Your Players' Offensive Skills

Players who have mastered the basics of offensive play (covered in Chapter 9) will crave the chance to climb to the next level, and it's up to you to help them get there when they're ready. When players learn new skills — especially ones that make them more effective against defenders — they brim with confidence and enthusiasm.

When players improve their skills and gain confidence, they also gain enormous satisfaction from playing for you, leading to more inspired and effective play. This section shows you how to help your players improve by introducing new offensive skills that build on the basics they've already mastered. If your players continue to advance and want even more offensive challenges, Chapter 15 provides more opportunities.

Deadly dribbling techniques

Dribbling the ball is one of the most basic elements of the game, and the teams that do it best are the toughest to defend. Although dribbling is basic, you can teach different types of dribbles that will make your players more efficient with the ball.

An obvious benefit of being efficient with the ball is that opponents can't force as many turnovers, which translates into more scoring opportunities for your team. Two of the more advanced types of dribbles, the crossover and the reverse pivot dribble, are techniques that can bolster your players' ball-handling skills. (Chapter 9 covers the basic dribbling fundamentals.)

Crossover

The *crossover* dribbling technique allows players to change direction quickly side-to-side in order to maneuver past defenders and create open passing or shooting lanes. This list shows how it's done:

1. **The player dribbles the ball with his dominant hand (in this case, the right) while facing the defender.**

2. **He takes a jab step with his right foot about 12 inches forward while lowering his body closer to the court.**

   A *jab* step is a short, quick step, like what a child does to squish a bug with his shoe. (A left-handed dribbler takes a jab step with his left foot.)

3. **The player shifts his weight to the inside of his right foot.**

   He keeps dribbling the ball ahead of his right leg and to the right of his right foot.

4. **He leans slightly to his right to get the defender's body going in that direction.**

5. **He pushes off his right leg, switches the ball to his left hand by bouncing it low, and dribbles past the defender with his left hand and leg.**

   He must do this quickly because he's exposing the ball to the defender.

Reverse pivot

Many times during the course of the action — especially when a defender is guarding a player closely or the defense is springing a trap (see Chapter 16) — the reverse pivot can be a perfect mode of escape, catching opposing players by surprise. The *reverse-pivot* dribble allows the ball handler to spin away from a defender to generate a scoring (or at least a better passing) opportunity. The following looks at how a player performs the dribble (players should be proficient with both hands):

1. **To start the execution of a reverse pivot, the player dribbles the ball with her right hand (if she's right-handed) while facing the defender.**

   Left-handed players begin the pivot while dribbling with their left hands. The righty's left leg should be about six inches in front of her right leg.

2. **She pivots clockwise on her left foot while swinging her right leg and torso in the clockwise direction.**

   She should keep her body low to the court and stop the spin as her back faces the defender.

3. **The ball handler pulls the ball toward her (see Figure 12-1a) while keeping her body between the defender and the ball.**

   Make sure she keeps her hand off the bottom of the ball to avoid palming (a violation; see Chapter 3).

4. **She switches the ball to her left hand while completing the spin move (see Figure 12-1b).**

   She's now ready to pivot on her right foot to dribble past the defender.

Figure 12-1:
Youngsters can turn to the reverse-pivot dribble to create scoring chances.

a   b

Potent passing outlets

When your team has possession of the ball, you want your players constantly moving and delivering accurate passes to their teammates. The more motion and ball movement your offense features, the more potent your offensive attack will be. The passes covered in this section are more advanced techniques for attacking defenses that your players can turn to during specific situations in the game.

Baseball pass

Players can use the *baseball pass* when they need to deliver the ball over long distances. Usually, you see a baseball pass after a player has broken free down the court and is wide open or when a team must take a chance with a long pass to generate a last-second shot.

Here's how the baseball pass works:

1. **The player takes the ball back over his throwing shoulder and behind his ear.**

   The ball should be resting in the palm of this throwing hand.

   If you coach younger kids, encourage them to use their opposite hands to balance the ball (see Figure 12-2a).

2. **The player takes a step forward with his left foot (if he's right-handed) while transferring his weight from his back to his front foot.**

3. **He releases the ball by extending his throwing arm and snapping his wrist so that the ball darts off his fingertips (see Figure 12-2b).**

   The player's hand should follow through toward his intended target.

Figure 12-2:
The baseball pass pitches the ball to players down the court.

a   b

One-handed flip pass

The *one-handed flip pass* is effective when being closely guarded by an opponent. The pass allows the player to sidestep the defender and deliver the ball past him very quickly. Follow these steps to teach it to your players:

1. **The player picks up his dribble and holds the ball with both hands.**

2. **He steps to the side of the defender where he wants to deliver the pass, keeping his opposite foot planted (see Figure 12-3).**

Figure 12-3:
The one-handed flip pass works well when players have little room to breathe.

3. **If stepping to his right, he rotates his right wrist over the top of the ball and delivers a bounce pass to a teammate by flipping his right hand.**

If stepping to his left, he uses his left wrist and hand in the same manner.

Reach-around pass

The *reach-around pass* is similar to the one-handed flip pass and is just as effective in the right situation. In this case, though, the offensive player's body position allows her to protect the ball a bit more effectively. This is how you teach the pass:

1. **The player picks up her dribble and holds the ball with both hands.**

2. **She turns her body to the side in the direction of the intended pass by using a crossover step (see Figure 12-4).**

She should keep both hands on the ball in this position.

3. **She extends her arm farthest from the defender to the side or around the defender and delivers a bounce pass.**

Figure 12-4:
Players can
deliver safe
and
accurate
passes with
the reach-
around
technique.

Sharp shooting options

The more types of shots your players are comfortable lofting, the more scoring opportunities they'll have. If you teach your young players the shots in this section in addition to the basic shooting fundamentals (see Chapter 9), they'll gain confidence and have tons of fun scoring baskets. If you're in charge of an older, more advanced squad, you want to give them new options to help them score against more complex and tenacious defenders. The techniques in this section should do the trick.

Turnaround jump shot

In order to be a consistent scoring threat close to the basket (in the post; see Chapter 3), a youngster should be able to execute turnaround jump shots. After he receives a pass near the basket with his back facing the defender, he can pose many problems for the defender if he can spin around and get off a quick jump shot. The turnaround gives him this option.

Here are the steps to make it happen:

1. **The player begins with his back to the basket and the defender.**

   He can move to this position while dribbling or catch a pass and start dribbling in this position.

2. **He keeps his knees flexed and parallel and evenly distributes his weight on the balls of his feet.**

   In this position, he can turn in either direction.

3. **If he wants to go to his right (as a right-hander), he picks up his drib-ble as he pivots on his right foot, all while bringing his left foot around clockwise so that it becomes parallel to his pivot foot (see Figure 12-5).**

   He'll wind up holding the ball at chest-level. For a left-handed player who intends to move to his left, he pivots on his left foot while bringing his right foot around.

Figure 12-5:
The turnaround jump shot requires a strong pivot move and a quick shot.

4. **In the same motion, he brings the ball up into shooting position and then jumps into the air to release the shot over the defender.**

Hook shot

Youngsters who play offense close to the basket (particularly centers; see Chapter 5) often encounter problems getting off normal shots against taller or more agile defenders. The *hook shot* helps solve this problem by creating space between the players and giving the shot a higher arc. Here's a look at the proper technique for taking and making hook shots:

1. **The player begins with his back facing the defender and the basket.**

2. **A right-handed shooter takes a lateral step to the left with his left foot and brings the ball up around chest-level (see Figure 12-6a).**

   As he moves to the left, he opens his body counterclockwise and sets his sights on the basket. A left-handed player begins with a lateral step to the right with his right foot.

3. **He brings his right leg up while pushing off his left foot into the air.**

4. **In the same motion, he extends his right arm above his head and releases the ball (see Figure 12-6b).**

Have your shooter flick his wrist and slide the ball off his finger tips. The ball should come off his index and middle finger last, and he should follow through toward the basket.

Figure 12-6:
Hook shots
are difficult
for post
opponents
to defend —
and they're
old school! a

b

Inside power shot

The ability to score baskets in the lane is part of being an effective offense. If you're one-dimensional and stay on the perimeter, you make it too easy for the defenders. The *inside power shot* allows your players to score close to the basket, even when they're being guarded tightly by defenders. The following is what it takes to be successful with the inside power shot:

1. **The player takes a lead step with her foot nearest the basket and grabs the ball with both hands (see Figure 12-7a).**

2. **She then plants her feet close together, shoulder-width apart, and bends her knees so that her body is lower to the court (see Figure 12-7b).**

The shot works best if her body is parallel to the backboard. The defensive player should be behind her, which makes it difficult to defend the shot without fouling.

3. She uses both feet to jump off the floor straight into the air, extending both arms above her head in the process.

4. She uses her nondominant arm to shield the defender while releasing the ball with her shooting hand (see Figure 12-7c).

a

b

c

A player has more control over lay-ups and other inside shots if she banks them off the backboard.

Forming a Cohesive Unit with Basic Offensive Team Plays

As your players develop offensively, you can capitalize on their progress by incorporating offensive plays that you can run during practices and games (see Chapter 8 for more on evaluating your team at midseason). *Offensive plays* are specially designed methods for getting the defense off-balance and generating scoring opportunities. This section runs through some specialized offensive techniques, like moving without the ball and setting screens, that increase the fun and your team's chances of achieving offensive success.

Moving without the ball

One of the keys to running effective practices (see Chapter 6) is keeping the kids involved and limiting the standing-around time. That same principle applies to running your offense. Because only one player can handle the ball at a time, the other four players should be in motion most of the time. The more the kids move — especially when they don't have the ball — the more problems they'll present to opposing defenses. Just ask a hunter what's more difficult: Shooting moving or stationary prey? When players aren't moving, they make the defenders' jobs easy.

One of the best and quickest ways to get open is by *cutting* — making a sharp turn or suddenly changing directions to get away from a defender. You can teach your players several different types of cuts, including the following:

- ✔ **Front cut:** When the defender positions himself between the offensive player and the basket, the offensive player runs past him toward the basket.

- ✔ **Back cut:** The offensive player makes a fake cut toward the player with the ball to get the defender moving in that direction. He then quickly changes direction and steps behind the defender and toward the basket (see Figure 12-8).

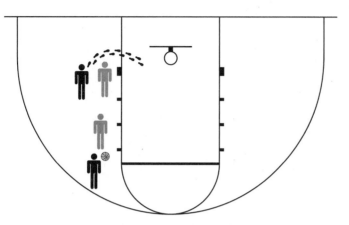

✔ **Curl cut:** The offensive player circles around a teammate (see Figure 12-9) to try to create traffic and get open. This is most effective when the teammate is setting a screen (see the next section) or when the defender is closely tracking the player everywhere he goes on the court.

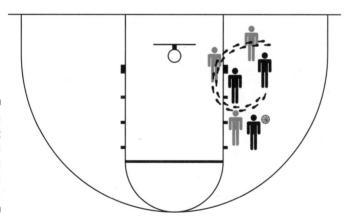

Figure 12-9:
The curl cut
utilizes
teammates
to screen
defenders.

✔ **Flashing cut:** Most often made by a player in the low-post area, the flashing cut calls for a player to quickly step out into the vicinity of the free-throw line with his hands up ready to receive a pass (see Figure 12-10).

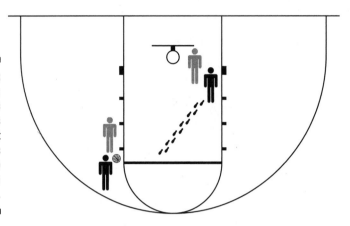

Figure 12-10:
A flashing cut lets teammates know that the player is available to receive a pass.

During your practices (especially during drills), continually stress to your kids that keeping their feet moving is the secret to making it tough for opposing players to guard them. Using the preceding cuts with purpose is important, though. Players shouldn't waste energy just running around the court.

Setting screens

Setting a screen can be an effective way to help a teammate break away from his defender. A *screen* (also called a *pick*) is when an offensive player stands in a set position to block a defender as he's guarding a teammate. The defender literally runs into your player's screen door, freeing the teammate to drive, pass, or shoot.

Whenever teaching kids how to set screens, exercise great caution, because the risk of injury is present whenever kids are running into each other. Never run a drill that includes screens unless every youngster clearly understands how to execute them.

Follow these steps to show your players how to execute screens:

1. **The player setting the screen plants his feet a little wider than shoulder-width apart.**

   His feet will remain stationary through contact.

2. **He crosses his arms across his waist (see Figure 12-11) to protect himself from and brace for the contact.**

   You can teach boys to cross their hands in front of their groin area and females to cross their arms at chest-level for protection.

Figure 12-11:
Setting
screens
helps
players get
free from
defenders.

3. **The offensive player receiving the screen cuts as hard and as close to his teammate as possible.**

   Doing so makes it difficult for the defender to fight through the screen.

4. **The screener leans slightly forward to make contact with the defender he's attempting to block, without fouling by pushing or holding.**

   If the screener doesn't establish body contact, the defender may simply sidestep the screen.

5. **The screener maintains his position until his teammate is clearly past and creating scoring opportunities.**

   If he gives up his position too early, he may allow the defender to get back into the play, which costs your offense its advantage.

Picking and rolling

The *pick and roll* is a play run by two offensive players to disrupt the defense and create an advantage to score a basket. The best time to attempt the pick and roll is when the ball handler and his teammate are on one side of the lane and the other teammates are on the opposite side. Here's how your players execute the pick and roll:

1. **The ball handler dribbles toward a teammate.**

2. **The teammate sets his feet to establish a screen.**

   The ball handler should dribble as close to his teammate as possible (rub shoulder to shoulder) so the player guarding him will run into the screen.

3. **As the ball handler moves past the screener and both defenders scramble to cover ground, the screener pivots on his foot nearest the basket, brings his outside arm around, and extends it toward the basket (like opening a gate) (see Figure 12-12).**

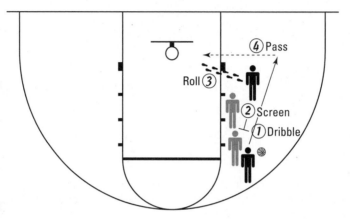

Figure 12-12:
The pick and roll requires a good screen and good timing.

4. **The ball handler delivers a pass to the screener, who's now moving toward the basket.**

The idea is for both defenders to follow the ball handler, leaving the screener an open lane to score.

Giving and going

The *give and go,* also referred to as *going backdoor,* is used against defenses that are guarding players closely and is intended to produce lay-ups. You can use the play anywhere on the court, although it works best while operating in a half-court offense. You execute the give and go between two players like this:

1. **The ball handler passes to his teammate.**

2. **After delivering the pass, he takes a couple steps toward the new ball handler, as though he's moving to set a screen or receive a return pass.**

3. **After those initial steps, he breaks sharply toward the basket.**

4. **The ball handler, who should be anticipating his teammate's move toward the basket, delivers a bounce pass to the cutting player (see Figure 12-13).**

He should be able to catch the pass in stride and go up for a basket.

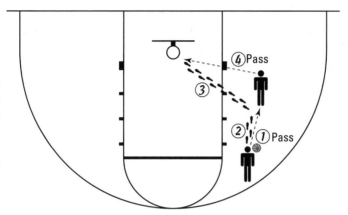

The give and go is perfect to use against aggressive, man-to-man defenses (see Chapter 13) whose players like to guard yours tightly, because a quick cut to the basket is tough to react to when the defender is playing close to his man. The play also works well against defenders who have a tendency to turn their backs to the ball or lose track of the ball handler, because they can't see when the pass has been made to a player cutting toward the basket.

Inbounding the ball

Getting the ball in bounds — safely — is a basic component of sound offensive play. When your team can't inbound the ball within the allotted five seconds and avoid a violation (see Chapter 3), you lose a critical possession and provide a big boost for the opposition.

The *box* and the *line* are the two basic formations for inbounding the ball and the ones you should rely on with young players. In this section, I present the box method when inbounding underneath your basket, and I show the line method when inbounding under the opponent's basket.

When inbounding the ball, keep these general tips in mind:

- ✔ **Pay attention to the tick tock:** The inbounder must develop an internal clock and know when he's approaching the five-second call.

- ✔ **Mix up your formations:** If you rely on the same formation every time, the defense will have a good idea of what's coming and will have a better chance of disrupting the play. Another option is to stick with the same formation and run several different plays from it so the opponent doesn't know what's coming.

✔ **Count on players with good passing skills:** The most effective inbounds plays are those that catch the defense off guard; to take full advantage of them, the inbounder must get the ball to an open player as soon as he becomes open. The slightest hesitation may be enough to allow the defense to recover.

You may face opposing coaches who employ tall players to guard your inbounds passer, which makes it more difficult to get the ball into play. Therefore, you should give all your players time in practice to inbound the ball and to handle the different responsibilities of various plays.

Under your basket

You can use the *box* inbounds play from under your basket to make guarding your players a little more difficult and (hopefully) free them up for open shots (see Figure 12-14). The following list shows how it works:

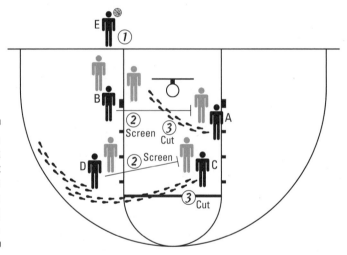

Figure 12-14:
The box alignment creates space when inbounding the ball.

1. **On Player E's command — he can call out a word or simply smack the ball with his hand — his teammates begin their moves.**

   As soon as the official hands the ball to the player, Player E needs to get his teammates on the court moving. He has only five seconds to inbound the ball, and the official begins his count as soon as the ball is handed over.

2. **Player B cuts across the lane to set a screen on the defender who's guarding Player A.**

   At the same time, Player D cuts across the lane to screen the defender who's covering Player C.

3. **Player C loops over the top and comes around to the other side of the lane.**

   At the same time, Player A cuts across the lane near the basket to receive a pass.

4. **If Player A isn't open, Player E can make a pass to Player C.**

Keep in mind the following points when inbounding the ball under your basket:

- ✔ **Look to score:** Teach your players to view the inbounds pass under your basket as a chance to attack and score, not just as a way to get the ball into play.

- ✔ **Utilize your top scorers:** At the advanced levels of play, take advantage of your top scorers by setting up plays for them.

- ✔ **Go long:** You can have a player serve as a safety valve for times when the inbounder has difficulty getting the ball into play. The player can run into the backcourt to receive a long pass.

Under your opponent's basket (or on a sideline)

The ability to make accurate passes is important to the success of your offense, and nowhere is it more crucial than when you're inbounding the ball under your opponent's basket. If you commit a turnover here, it usually results in a good scoring opportunity for the opposition. One popular inbounds play in this position is the *line* formation (see Figure 12-15). The following list shows the rundown of the line inbounds play under your opponent's basket. You can also modify this setup for a sideline inbounds:

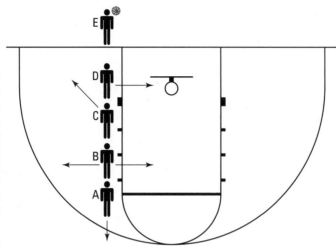

Figure 12-15: The line formation makes it difficult for the opponent to defend the inbounds pass.

1. **On Player E's command (or signal), the other players break into their moves.**

2. **Player A breaks for the other end of the floor.**

   If Player A's defender can't stick with him, Player E should deliver him a baseball pass (see the earlier section "Potent passing outlets") for a scoring opportunity. The pass must be thrown ahead of the player, who chases it down, to reduce the chances of it being stolen.

3. **Player D cuts across the lane, and Player C moves toward the corner.**

   If the inbounder passes the ball to Player C, that youngster must be ready to get rid of the ball quickly (a return pass to Player E as he steps onto the court, for instance) so that he doesn't get trapped by a double team in the corner (see Chapter 16).

4. **Player B chooses to move either to his left or right to look for a pass.**

When the inbounder is allowed to move on the baseline (after your opponent has scored a basket), that creates more opportunities for delivering a quality pass. Whenever kids have a chance to move with the ball, encourage them to do so. If they're standing still, they have fewer angles to work with to get the ball in play, which makes it easier for the defense to create a turnover or get a five-second call. (Be sure to check your league rules; see Chapters 2 and 3.)

Chapter 13

Coaching Defense 101

In This Chapter
▶ Dissecting your defensive options
▶ Focusing on the fundamentals of team defense

*W*hen youngsters play basketball, they love dribbling the ball and taking shots. Playing defense, on the other hand, is about as appealing as studying or doing their chores. As the coach, it's your responsibility to open up your youngsters' eyes to the importance of playing defense. Through your passion for teaching good defense — and making the learning process fun for the kids — your players will discover that it's just as satisfying to disrupt an opposing offense as it is to sink baskets or make great passes.

This chapter digs into what it takes to execute at the defensive end of the court. We introduce the most basic types of defenses, and we detail how you can use them. And because executing as a team is so important for good defense, we explain how to use double teams, go for loose balls, block shots, guard players on and off the ball, and communicate with teammates.

Identifying the Types of Defenses

One of the best indicators of a well-coached team is that its players not only execute at the offensive end of the floor, but also disrupt the opposition's offense. Even on days when your players' shots aren't falling, you can still pull out wins if your players form a sound defensive unit. Because your team spends roughly half of every game on defense, you need to find a defensive style that matches your overall coaching philosophy (see Chapter 2) and that melds best with your kids' abilities (see Chapters 5 and 8). If you coach at a more advanced level of play, the strengths and weaknesses of your opponent also should dictate some of your defensive decisions.

You can implement two basic styles of defense into your gameplan — man-to-man and zone. This section explains the styles in more depth.

Man-to-man defense: Stick to him like glue

Man-to-man is to defense what a lay-up is to offense: the most common and basic type. You should introduce man-to-man to your players first. In this defense, each player covers a specific offensive player assigned by you. A defender follows his player wherever he goes — if he has the ball or not. (Figure 13-1 shows an example of a team playing man-to-man defense.)

The man-to-man defender's goal is to stay between the offensive player and the basket. He shuffles and pivots, maintaining a distance just beyond a normal arm's reach from the opponent, with his hands up in the air to make it difficult for the opponent to pass or shoot (see Chapter 10). As soon as the offensive player picks up his dribble, the defender can move in closer to cut down his available passing angles.

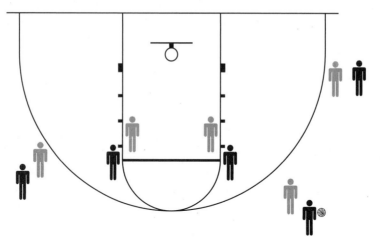

Figure 13-1: Each player guards one opponent in a man-to-man defense.

Man-to-man defense has several advantages, including the following:

✔ **The concept is simple.** This type of defense generally works best for beginning-level players, because the concept is pretty straightforward: Shadow the opposing player.

✔ **Each defender is accountable.** Man-to-man defense keeps players actively involved and focused on the game. When your team has a breakdown and an offensive player gets free, you can easily pinpoint what went wrong — in other words, who lost track of the player he was guarding.

- ✔ **It simplifies rebounding.** Boxing out (see Chapter 10) is easier from the man-to-man setup, because each defender has the player he's guarding in his sights. In a zone defense, defenders have to quickly scan their areas and choose the players they need to box out.

- ✔ **It showcases defensive strengths.** Much like talented artists enjoy displaying their paintings in galleries, good defensive basketball players savor the chance to put their skills to use, and playing man-to-man defense is the best forum for their art. Players who excel in defense can have a greater impact in the man-to-man format because they can be much more aggressive and take greater advantage of their quick hands and feet.

If your team is comprised of players who don't have an aggressive mindset or lack quickness, playing this type of defense can pose a lot of problems because they'll have trouble sticking to their players.

When teaching man-to-man defense, you can incorporate a couple different styles in your game plan, which we outline in the following list. Your best bet may be to find a comfortable level between these two styles; you can adjust accordingly based on the talent level of your opposition, the score of the game, and the time remaining in the game.

- ✔ **Aggressive:** An aggressive approach requires your youngsters to play a step or two closer than normal to their assigned players. By playing closer to the offensive players, your defenders give themselves a better chance to create turnovers. If you have many quick players, this style of defense will serve you well. You also can switch to this style when your team is trailing late in the game and you need a turnover, or when you want to catch a team off guard with some surprise pressure.

  The aggressive style works well against teams that handle the ball poorly or don't do a good job of protecting the ball. However, against more experienced teams, aggressive man-to-man D comes with greater risk, because players who dribble and pass efficiently can exploit it for easy baskets.

- ✔ **Passive:** In passive man-to-man defense, your youngsters play a few steps farther away from the offensive players so they have an extra cushion to work with. The cushion gives the defender a little extra time to react to cuts and makes it a little harder for a dribbler to drive to the basket.

  The passive style of play works against teams that don't shoot well from the outside (near or past the three-point line) or whose players are quicker than yours. Also, when your team has the lead late in a game, the passive style is effective because it reduces the likelihood of your players fouling or giving up easy baskets.

Zone defense: Protect your area

In a *zone defense,* each defender is responsible for covering and defending a certain area (zone) of the floor. When an offensive player enters a defender's area, the defender is accountable for guarding him. Players should move around the floor to defend their zones based on the location of the ball.

Zone defenses are complex schemes that coaches should save for older kids (ages 10 and up) because it's much easier for youngsters just learning the game to grasp man-to-man. Be sure to check your league's policy to find out what types of defenses it allows; many beginning-level programs allow only man-to-man defense so youngsters get a chance to become comfortable with the basics of the game before moving on to more advanced styles of play. (Check out Chapter 2 for more info on knowing your league's rules.)

You have many types of zones to choose from. Before you select a zone to teach, though, you need to understand the benefits of implementing the defense. The following list presents some of the advantages of the zone defense:

- ✔ **It provides protection.** Switching to a zone defense when you have players in foul trouble offers extra protection from additional fouls, because your defenders won't be quite as aggressive. (Most youth leagues allow unlimited fouls for kids; usually only at the advanced levels can players foul out of games.)

- ✔ **It forces outside shots.** Zone defenses make it difficult for offensive players to drive to the basket, because when players are properly positioned, there aren't a lot of open spaces available to attack.

- ✔ **It hides your players' weaknesses.** If several of your players aren't as quick as the offensive players, going to a zone can reduce the opportunities for opposing players to exploit that weakness.

- ✔ **It rests tired legs.** Although you want your players to hustle at all times, you may want to go to the zone defense for a couple of possessions here and there to allow them to catch their breath. In a zone, defenders don't have to work quite as hard as they do in man-to-man defense.

Depending on the team you're playing, using a zone defense can be ineffective, too. Here are some reasons why it may not be the right defense for your team:

- ✔ **Everyone must clearly understand it:** If each player doesn't completely understand his responsibilities on what areas of the floor he's responsible for defending, based on the position of the ball, frequent breakdowns will occur that the opponent can capitalize on.

✔ **Good shooters embrace zones:** The eyes of good shooters light up when they see defenses fall back into a zone. If your team faces an opponent that loves to take outside shots — and relies on long-range shots for the bulk of its scoring — you'll probably be better off applying more pressure with the man-to-man defense.

✔ **May affect team's aggressiveness:** Because zones are less aggressive, the attitude may carry over to the kids' play at the offensive end of the court and drain some of their aggressiveness.

Before you can implement a zone defense, you need to know the different types and the appropriate times to use particular zones. A numbering system labels most zones. The numbers in the label refer to the positioning of the players, beginning with those farthest away from the basket. The following sections provide a quick glance at the labeling system and the different types of zones you can teach and use.

2-3 zone

A *2-3 zone* features two defenders playing away from the basket (two guards, typically) and three positioned near the basket and the baseline (normally two forwards with a center in the middle; see Figure 13-2). This zone provides strong coverage in the lane, making it difficult to get off shots inside. This defense is good against teams that don't shoot the ball well from the outside. Teams that don't have reliable inside shooters also will struggle against this defense. And because one of its weak spots is the area near the free-throw line, if an opponent doesn't have a player who can attack that area, it won't enjoy much success.

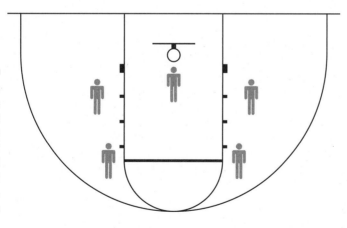

Figure 13-2:
The 2-3 zone makes it difficult to maneuver the ball inside the paint.

The 2-3 is an effective zone for trapping opposing players. *Trapping* refers to double teaming the player with the ball so that he can't dribble or find a passing lane. The two guards away from the basket can dictate the play of the offense by forcing the ball handler to pass to a teammate on the right or left side of the court, where you can execute the trap (see Chapter 16).

The 2-3 zone isn't as effective against teams with good outside shooters, who can usually find several openings along the perimeter to loft unguarded shots.

2-1-2 zone

A *2-1-2 zone* defense has two guards near the top of the key, a center in the post area, and two forwards outside the post area near the baseline (see Figure 13-3). If you're facing a team with strong inside players, the 2-1-2 zone is a good option, because when the ball is fed into the post, the forwards can slide over to provide support and clog up the lane so opponents can't find room to maneuver. Also, if you like to push the ball down the court quickly to create fast-break opportunities (see Chapter 15), you should try this defense, because one of the guards defending above the key can release after the opposition takes a shot.

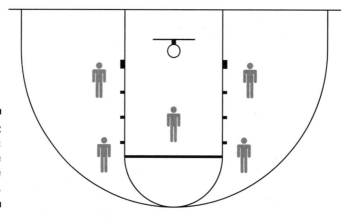

Figure 13-3:
The basic setup for the 2-1-2 zone defense.

The weakness of the 2-1-2 zone is the shooting opportunities it presents. Opponents can find open jump shots at the top of the key and along the baseline.

1-3-1 zone

The *1-3-1 zone* consists of a guard defending the area above the key; a guard and a forward on the wings, with the center between them around the free-throw line; and a forward down low in the post (see Figure 13-4). (Or, a forward and the center can be switched.) The key to setting this up is having your quickest player above the key and your two best rebounders nearest the basket (see Chapter 5 for evaluation tips). This defense sets up well against teams that like to attack from the outside or the high-post area, because the defenders positioned near the lane can cover shots from the perimeter *and* sag inside to provide support.

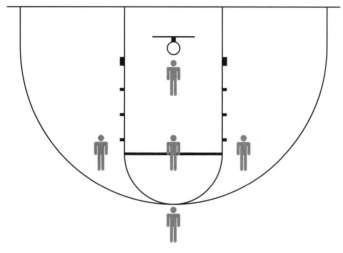

Figure 13-4:
The 1-3-1
zone
provides
strong
perimeter
coverage.

However, because you have only one player always near the basket, teams can exploit the low post and gain better position to rebound missed shots. Opponents also can attack the basket from the baseline.

1-2-2 zone

The *1-2-2 zone* has a guard above the key; a guard and a forward in the high post on the left and right; and a forward and center in the low post to the left and right of the basket (see Figure 13-5). If you want to apply pressure on your opponent's outside shooters, the 1-2-2 zone is a pretty good bet. The perimeter defender aggressively guards ball handlers when they venture near the top of the key; whenever the ball leaves the perimeter, he sags down near the lane to provide support. When the ball moves to the side, the defenders in the high-post area shift over to provide coverage; the player on the other side of the court can slide down into the lane to prevent passes coming into the middle of the lane.

The two defenders positioned along the baseline have the bulk of the responsibilities in this zone, because they must cover the most area. The 1-2-2 zone is effective against teams that shoot well from the outside, because the guard up top, along with the two players in the high post, can apply pressure to the perimeter and contest outside shots.

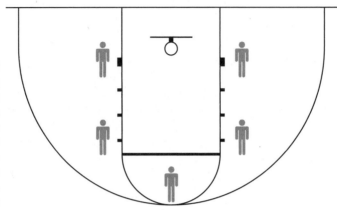

Figure 13-5:
The baseline defenders have many responsibilities in the 1-2-2 zone.

Against teams that have forwards who are efficient at hitting shots along the baseline, though, this zone isn't as effective. If your two baseline defenders don't react quickly on passes into the corners, your opponent can get off plenty of open medium-range shots. You also can leave a gap in the high-post area that's difficult to defend because of the emphasis on shutting down the perimeter shot.

3-2 zone

The *3-2 zone* defense consists of two guards and a forward positioned across the perimeter, while the other forward and center are down low defending the low-post area. This zone relies on quick, aggressive play from the three players up front, who must guard the perimeter, disrupt the passing lanes, and sag back to the lane to provide support when the ball enters the post area. The players in the low post must react quickly to balls passed down along the baseline; otherwise, the opponent will get open shots from medium range. The 3-2 works well against teams that don't shoot well from the outside and against teams that don't get back down the court quickly to defend on missed shots (because your perimeter players can hustle down the court).

The weakness of the 3-2 zone is down low, because you have only two defenders near the basket. Teams that have good ball handlers who pass the ball well can exploit this zone by feeding the ball down low to teammates, who can take advantage of the lack of post defense. Also, teams with quick ball handlers who can drive to the basket strong can exploit this setup, because the center of the lane is one of this defense's weakest areas.

2-2-1 zone

The *2-2-1 zone* features two guards on opposite sides of the key; two forwards outside the low post; and the center in the low-post area. Against teams that look to get the ball inside regularly, the 2-2-1 zone is good to employ because the forwards are positioned near the post and can quickly slide into the lane to double team opponents and rebound missed shots. You can generate fast breaks out of this defense pretty easily, and it sets up well for executing some half-court traps (see Chapter 16 for more on this strategy). The 2-2-1 zone is very similar to the 2-3 zone (such as in its weaknesses).

Combining zone and man-to-man defenses

You can combine different aspects of man-to-man and zone defenses and switch between them during games to take advantage of your team's strengths and the opposing team's weaknesses. In fact, the more defensive styles your team can play — and play well — the more effective you'll be at disrupting the opposition.

When a team calls timeout to set up a play, that's an opportune time to switch up your defense. For example, if you've been playing a 2-3 zone for several minutes, the opposing coach probably will set up a play for his team that's designed to be successful against that particular defense. So, if you switch to a man-to-man defense, you may prevent the team from producing a quality shot.

You also may want to mix the two types of defenses against certain teams — particularly against teams that have highly skilled players that you know your team has to contain. We present some combo Ds that are geared toward stopping good players in the sections that follow.

Combination defenses are a bit too advanced for younger players. Only teach them to your players if you're confident that they understand the basics of — and can play — both man-to-man and zone defenses.

Box-and-one

The *box-and-one* defense targets one player who can dominate a game on the perimeter. Four of your defenders play a zone defense by forming a box around the lane (see Figure 13-6) — with two players positioned near the free-throw line and two near the basket. The remaining defender plays man-to-man against the opponent's top scoring threat, shadowing him all over the court.

When choosing the player that you'll entrust with the one-on-one task, you want to keep matchups in mind. For example, if the opposing player is of average height but possesses quickness, you need a defender who's quick on his feet; otherwise, he probably won't be too successful at stopping his penetration. If the opponent's top gun is above average in height, you'll be better off choosing a defender who has a similar body type so that he can keep a hand in his face on shots and won't be at a disadvantage closer to the basket.

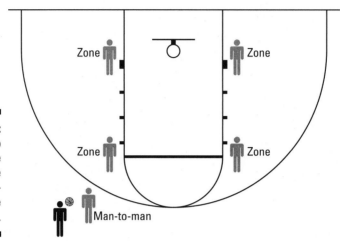

Figure 13-6:
The setup around the lane for the box-and-one defense.

Your remaining four players also should be focused on providing defensive support whenever the opponent's stud ventures near their coverage zones. If you have a player who excels defensively, the chances of this combination succeeding greatly increase because his teammates won't have to provide as much help.

Stay away from using the box-and-one defense against teams that count on points from several different players. You also may not want to single out one player on your team to assume such a big responsibility. Some kids may view the assignment as too daunting, while others may be so focused on not letting their teammates down that it detracts from their effectiveness on offense. Also, be careful how you present this defense to your team, because you risk offending some kids who are pretty proud of their defensive play and will question why they didn't get the assignment of tracking the opposition's best player.

Diamond-and-one

The *diamond-and-one* defense is simply a variation of the box-and-one. It's also ideal for stopping teams that rely on single players for the bulk of their offensive production. Four defenders form a diamond shape around the lane (see Figure 13-7). One player stands at the free-throw line, one moves to a position in front of the basket, and two go to the wings on each side. These four defenders play a zone defense; the remaining defender plays man-to-man against the opposition's best player. Because the two wing defenders are positioned a little farther out than they are in the box-and-one, this defense provides stronger coverage on the perimeter, with the drawback being that the opposition can exploit mid-post area.

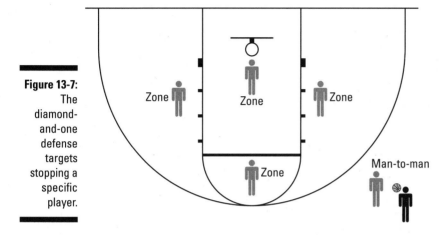

This defense isn't good to employ against strong passing teams because of its vulnerability in the middle of the diamond. If the team's top scorer distributes the ball well, he can deliver it to teammates for medium-range shots. Besides the gap in the middle of this defense, medium-range shots also are available along the baseline.

Teaching Good Team Defense

Executing at the defensive end of the court as a cohesive unit often is a difficult skill for teams to pick up and for coaches to teach. What makes playing team defense so challenging is that your players must react to a variety of situations and make split-second decisions. Also, when one defender misses an assignment or gets beat by an opposing player, your entire defense breaks down, which often leads to open shots from close range.

Yes, teaching good team defense puts your coaching skills to the test. Don't worry, though. We're confident that after you review the following sections, you'll have a strong foundation to piece together a stellar defensive unit. (For drills on individual defensive techniques, see Chapters 11 and 14.)

Oozing effort on the defensive end

A good defense starts with you. If you want your players to give you their best effort on the defensive end, make sure you emphasize the importance of effort and hustle. These attributes, more than skill and talent, define good defense, which gives every player the chance to contribute. Always applaud stellar plays that your defenders make, and do so as enthusiastically as you applaud made baskets.

Inform your players that each player on the team can make herself a strong defensive player who drives opponents crazy. Playing good defense doesn't require a big vertical jump or innate ability; it requires the willingness to work hard and adhere to basic defensive techniques. Every player can make significant contributions to the team without ever scoring a basket. If that doesn't fire up a young player — especially one without a lot of coordination or offensive ability (see Chapter 5) — what will?

The following advice — some of which focuses on you and some of which you can relay to your players — also helps your players give their best efforts on defense:

- **Neutralize strengths.** Focus on taking away the opponent's biggest strength and forcing the coach to resort to a second or third option. For example, if your opponent likes to attack on the fast break, advise your players to clamp down on outlet passes to slow down their movement across the court. If your opponent prefers walking the ball up the court, try implementing a full-court press to speed up the pace of play and get the offense out of its comfort zone (see Chapter 16).

- **Force the use of weak hands.** Advise your defenders to make offensive players dribble with their nondominant hands. For example, when a defender applies pressure to a ball handler who's bringing the ball across midcourt, he can force him to dribble with his left hand (if he's a right-hander) by taking away the angle to his right.

- **Avoid reaching in.** Sloppy defensive footwork and lazy technique result in your defenders reaching in to attempt steals. Reaching in leads to fouls and may allow ball handlers to dribble by your defenders because they've put themselves out of position by lunging in. (For tips on teaching the proper footwork, check out Chapter 10.)

- **Keep your feet untangled.** Ballet dancers and Vegas showgirls cross their feet — good defenders don't. Instruct your players to stick to shuffling and sliding their feet.

- **Keep your eyes everywhere.** You want your defenders focused on the players they're guarding, but you don't want them to lose sight of what else is going on.

- **Always hustle.** Players on the move make good things happen; youngsters who stay flat-footed become liabilities. After games and practices, recognize the kids who really hustled. Doing so is a great way to show that players don't have to score in double digits to be assets to the team.

- **Force lateral movement.** Teach your defenders to force ball handlers to move laterally toward the sidelines, where the offensive options are limited. This technique creates additional opportunities for trapping and double teaming (see Chapter 16).

✔ **Box out on every shot.** Whenever a shot goes up, each defender should locate an opponent and box her out (see Chapter 10). Boxing out cuts down on the second-chance points.

Communicating with teammates

Talking during class is a big no-no, which is why many kids love recess and turn to sports to interact with friends. Encourage this behavior — in terms of basketball communication, of course. On the basketball court, the more chatter you hear from your players, the better.

Here are some areas where you want your kids to exercise their vocal chords:

✔ **Recognize plays.** If a defender sees an offensive play unfolding, he should alert his teammates so they can prepare to make a stop.

✔ **Call out switches.** When a defender recognizes a screen, he should yell out "switch" so a teammate knows to pick up the free player (see Chapter 12 for more info on screens).

✔ **Warn teammates.** When a teammate doesn't see a screen coming, a defender should yell out "screen" to save him from crashing into the opponent.

✔ **Ask for help.** If a player gets by a defender and becomes a scoring threat, the defender must rely on his teammates for help. The defensive player should shout "help" to alert his teammates that a player is roaming free.

✔ **Turn defense into offense.** When a defender secures the ball, he can shout "break" or another code word to let his teammates know that they need to break for the other end of the court.

During defensive drills and scrimmages, make sure your players continually talk to each other and practice the communication from the previous list while the ball is in play. Practice makes communication second nature.

Dealing with screens

Teams use screens to break down the defense and create scoring opportunities for specific players. (Chapter 12 covers the skill in detail.) Determining the best defensive techniques for your team when it comes to dealing with pesky screens often is a process of trial and error. The following is a glance at two basic approaches:

✔ **Work through it:** This is the most basic answer to an opponent's screen. When the offense sets the screen, the defensive target simply tries to run around the player and does his best to keep up with the player he's guarding. If he loses that player and is at a big disadvantage, he calls out "help" to let his teammates know that they need to slide over and provide assistance (see the previous section). Remind your players that they can't push the screener; otherwise, they risk being called for a foul.

✔ **Switch:** If your team communicates well with each other, the switch technique is pretty effective in dealing with screens. When the screen is set, the defender simply calls out "switch." When he does this, he immediately takes over guarding the screener, and his teammate who was assigned to the screener guards the other offensive player.

The biggest disadvantage with switching is that it can create mismatches for your defense. For example, if you have a small guard who switches and finds himself covering a much taller forward or center, the opposition will look to get the ball inside to take advantage of the situation.

Guarding on and off the ball

Sticking with offensive players — whether they have the ball or are working to receive it — requires focus, good footwork, quickness, and, from time to time, a helping hand from teammates. If you spend plenty of practice time working on the following defensive principles, your opponents will have all sorts of problems creating and converting scoring opportunities (for more on practicing good footwork, see Chapter 10):

✔ **Maintain proper spacing.** Particularly at the beginning levels of play, youngsters may have difficulty judging how much space they should keep between themselves and the offensive players. During games, keep a close eye on spacing for the first few possessions, and make the appropriate adjustments by moving defenders closer or farther away — based on the opposing players' quickness and ball-handling abilities. (At the more advanced levels, the kids may be able to make these adjustments on their own.)

During practices, run one-on-one drills to allow players the chance to feel out how much space they need to have between them and the players they're guarding. Have some fun by telling the defenders you want them so close to the ball handlers that they can smell their breath.

✔ **Help whenever necessary.** Defense is a total team effort — especially when a player gets by a defender and becomes a scoring threat. When a defender yells "help," the defensive player closest to the ball handler should leave the player he's guarding and slide over to provide defensive support. All other players should quickly assess the situation and prepare to provide assistance to prevent a good scoring chance.

> ✔ **Focus on the feet.** Youngsters guarding players without the ball — most often in man-to-man defense — have a tendency to grab with their hands. Good footwork is the basis for good defensive play. Constantly remind your players to rely on shuffling their feet to gain the proper position to deny penetration.

Diving for loose balls

One of the trademarks of a good defensive team is the willingness of its players to hustle after every loose ball, regardless of the score. In tightly contested games, a victory may depend on which team chases down more loose balls. Every time your team beats an opponent to a loose ball, you gain one more possession that you otherwise wouldn't have had.

Securing loose balls comes down to hustle and which player wants it more. For example, if a ball comes loose on the court and two opposing players vie for it, the one who's willing to risk a floor burn from a dive usually winds up with it.

You can instill the importance of going after loose balls by recognizing players after games who showed real hustle. You can have an assistant or parent keep a tally of the number of loose balls your players grab and who gets them. After the game, you can glance at the stat sheet and applaud the hustle of your kids.

Deflecting passes

Kids who keep their hands in the passing lanes and make it difficult for opposing players to deliver passes, and deflect them when they do attempt them, are real assets to a team. Although pass deflections aren't as exciting as blocked shots, they're equally important when it comes to playing strong team defense. When you're recognizing players for hustling, rebounding, or any other area, be sure to praise the players who kept getting their hands on those passes. (Check out Chapter 10 for more on fundamentals.)

If you're coaching an advanced-level team, remind the kids to be aware of certain tendencies from the opposition. A lot of teams rely on a handful of set plays, so if your defenders recognize the plays and the habits certain players have, they'll increase their chances of deflecting passes.

Swatting shots

A blocked shot is one of the most exciting plays in basketball — unless it's your shot that's being swatted away! A *blocked shot* occurs when a defensive player deflects the ball during an offensive player's shot.

Players who can block shots are valuable pieces to your defensive puzzle, because they make it more difficult for opponents to score. Because most blocked shots occur closer to the basket, players in the paint may need to take shots from farther out or alter their normal shots to get the ball over a shot blocker's hands. The simple threat of a blocked shot can bolster your defense, because defenders cause opponents to become passive or alter their shots.

Although height is certainly an asset for blocking shots, it isn't a requirement. Your players should use sound defensive techniques: jumping up with an extended arm and aiming for the release point of the ball at the same time as the shooter leaves his feet, without running into his body, are essential techniques for denying shots.

Double teaming

The *double team* — where two players converge on a ball handler to play defense — is an aggressive tactic you can use to force errant passes or create turnovers. It works best on offensive players who have picked up their dribble, because their options are limited. (They can't dribble or move their pivot feet without being called for a violation; see Chapter 3.) You can also use a double team against players who are in position to score or to surround a player to prevent him from receiving the ball.

Keep the following tips in mind when it comes to teaching the art of the double team (see Chapter 14 for more on practicing the double team):

- ✔ **Make quick decisions.** If two players decide to double team an opponent, they need to make and act upon the decision quickly. If a player hesitates before leaving the player he's guarding, the double team has a pretty good chance of failing, because the hesitation gives the ball handler a little bit of extra time to get rid of the ball.

- ✔ **Refrain from reaching.** Young defenders often are tempted to swipe at the ball or grab for it when they have an opponent sandwiched in a double team. That tactic can give the ball handler a free pass out of trouble if a defender gets whistled for a reach-in foul.

> ✔ **Utilize the court as an extra defender.** The sidelines, baseline, and division line (when the ball is in the front court) can be your defenders' best friends, so be sure they use them whenever possible (see Chapter 3 for a layout of the basketball court). If your players can force the opposition toward places they can't go, they have a better chance of making the double team work.

Double teaming an excellent passer isn't wise because he'll likely spot an open teammate and make a good pass. Also, double teaming a player who's dribbling is a dangerous approach — especially if he's a good ball handler — because he may be able to dribble away from the defenders and drive to the basket or deliver a pass to an open teammate. (Check out Chapter 15 for details on how to teach your players to use the dribble and the pass to break out of double teams.)

Taking charges

A lot more goes into playing good team defense than simply guarding players and grabbing rebounds; the little things can help you gain possession of the ball, and taking a charge is one of them. A *charge* occurs when an offensive player displaces a set defender. A charge is as good as a steal, and fires up your teammates and fans! (For the scoop on teaching your kids how to take charges, flip to Chapter 10.)

Motivating kids to take charges can be challenging, because colliding with an opponent and hitting the floor isn't fun. Single out players after games who took charges. The extra attention can go a long way in motivating the kids. Who knows, a charge may decide the outcome of one of your games this season!

Defending cutters

Offensive players who don't have the ball rely on a variety of moves — called *cuts* — to lose their defenders and create openings receive passes and take shots. (Check out Chapter 12 for more info how your players can use cuts.) Your players' ability to defend cutters makes a big difference in the success of your defensive unit.

One of the keys for defending cutters is maintaining *inside position* — staying between your man and the ball. A good technique to teach youngsters is to work on beating a player to the spot. For example, if an opponent tries to cut from the sideline to the free-throw line, your defender can stay in good position and try to anticipate the pass; if he's quick enough, he can reach the spot first and disrupt the play.

The key is to teach your players to slightly bump the cutter off his desired route without being whistled for a foul. As the cutter moves toward the basket or ball, the defender contacts him with his inside arm at roughly a 45-degree angle. If he keeps his arm down to his side, he risks giving up good defensive position, and if he raises it up higher, he'll likely be called for a foul.

Chapter 14

Taking Your Drills to the Next Level

As your season moves along, your players ideally will progress in all different areas of the game. The kids will become pretty good at creating scoring chances on offense, and they'll play defense well enough to cause some problems for the opposition.

The key to continuing your players' learning and development is introducing challenging new drills that energize, inspire, and test your players. The drills you use for the first few weeks of the season won't be as effective — and certainly not as much fun — after your players grip certain fundamentals of the game. This chapter includes plenty of new drills that allow your players to work on both offensive and defensive skills. We introduce everything from screen setting and shooting drills to box out drills to help propel your team to exciting new levels of performance.

Working on Individual Drills

Players who consistently protect the basketball, deliver passes that find the hands of teammates, and put the ball in the basket when good scoring opportunities present themselves will create all sorts of trouble for the opposition. Additionally, if you have kids who are confident in their abilities to guard opponents — by limiting their penetration to the basket, making it difficult for them to get shots off, and controlling the majority of the rebounds — you'll have well-rounded players who enjoy plenty of success on the court.

This section presents a smorgasbord of individual drills that you can incorporate to help your kids raise their performance levels. These drills are fun, productive, and easy to implement. A bonus is that many have both offensive and defensive components. Although the focus may be on offense during a drill, your stand-in defenders can work on their techniques, too. (For more on teaching defense, head to Chapters 10 and 13.)

Dribbling drills

The better your players become at handling the ball — and fending off pesky opponents who try to force turnovers — the more chances your team will have to score points. This section presents a couple drills that will help your youngsters enhance their ball-handling skills.

Knockout

Knockout helps players practice dribbling the basketball without looking at it. Looking down is a crutch that many young players lean on when first starting in the game. Being able to dribble with their eyes spanning the court is a pretty handy skill for your players to have on game day, when they have to deal with intrusive defenders.

What you need: Your entire team. A basketball for each player. Cones to mark off the playing area.

How it works: Mark off a playing area about ¼ the size of the basketball court. Scatter the kids around the drill area so that you leave a few feet between each player.

1. **Begin the drill by having each player start dribbling his ball.**

2. **Players then start moving around the drill area trying to knock balls away from their teammates while maintaining possession of their own balls.**

3. **When a player loses his ball, he's knocked out of the drill.**

   The last player dribbling wins! If you don't have enough basketballs to go around, give half the kids balls to start with while the other half simply play defense. This is a good way to incorporate a defensive element into the drill — giving players practice guarding multiple ball handlers.

To minimize the standing-around time, you can set up another drill or perhaps a shooting station so kids who get knocked out can keep practicing while their teammates finish up this drill. You could even start this drill over in another area of the floor so kids who get knocked out can keep at it.

Coaching pointers: This drill puts a premium on being able to dribble without looking and with either hand. Encourage your kids to use their nondominant hands when possible so they can better skirt trouble and maintain possession of the ball. (The following drill continues the ambidextrous effort.)

Dueling dribblers

The *dueling dribblers* drill, which allows for some intense one-on-one ball handling work against a teammate, is effective for helping kids get comfortable dribbling with both hands. With this technique, they can protect the ball against aggressive defensive pressure.

What you need: Your entire team. One ball for every two players.

How it works: Break the team into pairs and give one player in each twosome a ball. Scatter the pairs around the floor so you leave ample room between each pair.

1. **On your whistle, have the players with the balls begin dribbling while their partners try to make a steal.**

   Allow the players to dribble in any direction they want, just like they can in a game.

2. **Run the drill for one minute.**

3. **If the defensive player makes a steal before the time expires, the roles reverse and he tries to keep control of the ball from his partner.**

   If time runs out before a steal is made, the defensive player takes over on offense. Either way, be sure to praise both the offensive player and the defensive player for their efforts.

Coaching pointers: Encourage aggressive defensive play during this drill to put a premium on good ball handling. Make sure your dribblers use both hands to move away from the defenders. Keep a close eye on the defensive players to make sure they remain in the proper defensive stance — on the balls of their feet, instead of trying to guard players flat-footed, which is a big no-no.

To upgrade the difficulty level, you can break the team into threesomes and have two defensive players going for a steal.

Passing drills

If you have several good shooters on your team, that's certainly good news. The bad news, though, is that if their teammates can't deliver the ball to them when they're open, your number of scoring chances will plummet. The following drills work to sharpen those all-important passing skills and put some sizzle in your team's "offensive" play.

Pressure passes

Players who can spot open teammates and deliver accurate passes, all while being pestered by aggressive defenders, make playing defense difficult for your opposition. The *pressure passes* drill helps your players stay cool under pressure and deliver accurate passes to teammates on the move.

What you need: Groups of three players. One ball for each group.

How it works: Break your team into groups of three, make two of them offensive players and one a defensive player, and move to one end of the court. One of the offensive players begins in the corner along the baseline and holds the ball (see Figure 14-1). His offensive partner begins above the key (at the top of the free-throw circle), with the defensive player between him and the basket.

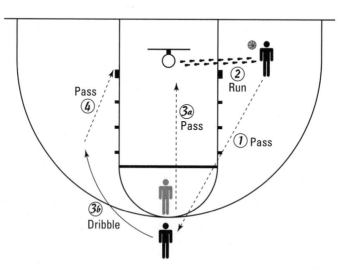

Figure 14-1:
The pressure-passes drill forces players to make accurate passes to teammates.

1. **On your whistle, the player with the ball delivers a chest pass to his partner.**

2. **After he delivers the pass, he cuts to the basket.**

   As soon as the other offensive player catches the ball, the defender begins guarding him closely, trying to deny another pass.

3. **If he can, the offensive player passes the ball to his cutting partner for a lay-up.**

   If a passing lane isn't available, the ball handler begins dribbling to his left or right until he can create an opening to pass the ball.

4. **Have the ball handler use pass fakes and attack the feet of the defender (step around him) until he can pass the ball to his partner.**

   From the point where the cutting player catches the return pass, he dribbles in for a lay-up.

Coaching pointers: You can run this drill on both sides of the basket and at each end of the court, as long as you alternate between groups at one end. This makes for very little standing-around time, because 12 kids can easily be involved in this drill at one time. Encourage defenders to attack the ball handlers and remain on the balls of their feet so they can make quick reactions and disrupt what the players are attempting to do.

Bull in the ring

The *bull in the ring* drill allows kids to work on their passing skills and gives defenders the opportunity to work on cutting down passing angles and trying for deflections and turnovers (see Chapter 13).

What you need: Three players. One ball.

How it works: Two offensive players begin about 15 feet from each other, with one defensive player in the middle. The object is for the two offensive players to pass the ball back and forth to one another — without dribbling — while the defensive player tries to deflect the ball or force an errant pass. The defender remains in the center until he can get his hands on the ball or force a bad pass.

Coaching pointers: You never want to embarrass a child, so if any defender is having trouble deflecting the ball, be sure to rotate him out so he isn't stuck in the middle for several minutes. Encourage the defenders to play aggressively and move their feet quickly between the offensive players.

Shooting drills

You can introduce a variety of shooting drills that will challenge your players to work on their accuracy, range, and — of course — the proper shooting technique (see Chapter 9). During games, your kids will find themselves in all types of shooting situations, and they should be prepared to shoot from different angles and distances while dealing with aggressive defenders. Practicing the drills in this section gets them ready to take — and make — myriad shots on game day.

Hand in the face

What player doesn't love to take uncontested shots? Unfortunately, your players won't get many open shots during games. They'll have to contend with defensive players' hands in their faces, stretching every which way to block the ball. The *hand in the face* drill helps kids practice getting off shots while being challenged by defenders.

What you need: Two players. One ball.

How it works: Position one player — the offensive player — along the baseline about 15 feet away from the basket; position the defensive player near the basket with a ball.

1. **On your whistle, the defender delivers a chest pass (see Chapter 9) to the shooter.**

2. **The defender follows the pass by running toward the shooter.**

3. **He stops a couple feet away and puts up his arms to distract the shooter, who takes the shot as the defender stops.**

    The defender shouldn't try to block the shot; he should simply play good defense and try to disrupt the shooter's attempt.

The next time through the drill, the defender should deliver a bounce pass so the shooter gets accustomed to handling different passes and taking shots after receiving them.

Coaching pointers: Watch the shooter's eyes to make sure they stay focused on the rim and not on the defender.

You can increase the difficulty of this drill by having the defender try to block the shot. You also can have the defender box out the shooter for a potential rebound (see Chapter 10). You can even incorporate decision making and driving skills by giving the player the option of using a shot fake and driving to the basket if he senses he can beat the defender (see Chapter 15).

Drive and pop

Players who have the ability to drive to the basket *and* to put the brakes on and put up medium-range shots present a lot of problems for defenders. This *drive and pop* drill enables your kids to work on these skills.

What you need: Three players. One ball.

How it works: One offensive player stands with the ball around the free-throw line, with the defensive player guarding her; the other offensive player stands near the three-point line (see Figure 14-2).

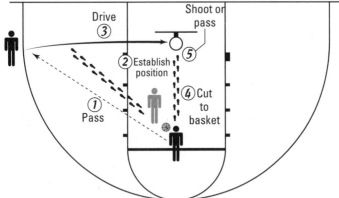

Figure 14-2: The offensive player can drive, pop, or pass in this drill to create scoring opportunities.

1. **On your whistle, the player with the ball delivers a bounce pass to her partner.**

2. **The defender runs to the baseline to establish good defensive position on the other player.**

3. **The player who receives the pass dribbles toward the defender.**

4. **The player who initially passed the ball pauses for a couple seconds after throwing it and then cuts toward the basket.**

5. **When the ball handler gets within a couple feet of the defender, she makes a decision between these three options:**

   - Jump straight in the air and take a jump shot.

   - Drive to the basket for a shot.

   - Deliver a pass to her partner who's cutting toward the basket.

Coaching pointers: If the offensive player stops her drive and pops a shot, make sure she goes straight up in the air when she takes off; if she's leaning forward, she risks bumping into the defender, which could result in a charging call (see Chapter 3 for more on rules violations).

You can modify this drill to increase the difficulty level for the shooter. For example, as the player is dribbling toward the defender, you can force her to make certain split-second decisions — just like she'll have to do during games — by yelling out "drive," "pass," or "shoot." You also can have the defender try to block the shot or swipe the ball to make it more challenging.

Peppering the Court with Team Drills

Team drills are important to use because they help build valuable chemistry — getting them used to the many different habits and styles of play their teammates display. This section presents a broad mixture of team drills that will help raise your players' offensive and defensive skills to new heights.

Finding and feeding the post

When your players (often guards; see Chapter 5) are handling the ball along the perimeter, they need to be able to recognize opportunities to deliver the ball into the post area. Because of the mass of players around the lane, post passes must be accurate passes. The *finding and feeding the post* drill helps your ball handlers recognize pass opportunities and make accurate post passes.

What you need: Six players. Two balls.

How it works: Position two offensive players on the perimeter to the right and left of the free-throw arc. Put an offensive and defensive player about a foot or so on the outside of each side of the lane (see Figure 14-3).

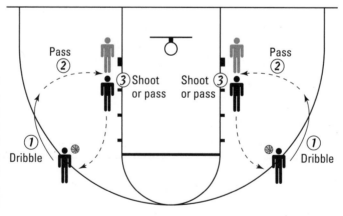

Figure 14-3:
Good inside play requires accurate passes into the post.

1. **On your whistle, the ball handlers on the perimeter start dribbling to the left or right to look for an open passing lane.**

   At the same time, the two offensive players in the post area should try to establish position to receive a pass, while the defenders should try to take away their position.

2. **When the ball handler finds an open passing lane, he makes the post pass.**

   Don't allow the perimeter players to cross the three-point line, where executing a post pass would be much easier.

3. **After receiving the pass, the post player can put up a shot or, if he's guarded very well, send a pass back out to his partner for a three-point shot.**

Coaching pointers: Making a good pass into the post is all about recognizing available angles. If the defender is taking away the *high side* (the area toward the middle of the lane), for instance, advise the ball handler to dribble toward the baseline to create a better passing lane (see Figure 14-4a). If the defender is positioned down low (see Figure 14-4b), advise the ball handler to move toward the top of the key to make the post pass. The perimeter player should always relocate himself after feeding the post so he'll be open on the return pass. If the youngster just passes the ball and stands still, he'll be easy to guard.

Figure 14-4:
Ball handlers must make adjustments to create openings for post passes.

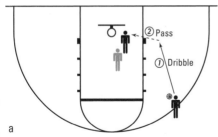
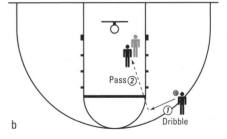

a   b

Chasing loose balls

Chasing down loose balls is all about hustle and heart. The more loose balls your players can get their hands on, the more chances you'll have to score. The *chasing loose balls* drill helps your kids practice battling on the floor.

What you need: Two players. One ball.

How it works: Position two players at midcourt a couple feet apart from each other, and stand between them with a ball.

1. **Roll the ball in a random direction.**

2. **As soon as you release the ball, the two players should take off after it and try to scoop it up.**

   You can have the player who gains possession attempt to drive to the basket and score, while the player who comes up empty-handed becomes the defender.

Coaching pointers: You really want to control this drill, because it's one of the most dangerous drills. Players at the advanced levels can become very competitive and could get hurt diving for the basketball. Make sure the kids don't commit fouls by pushing or elbowing to gain an unfair advantage. You can mix things up by rolling *and* bouncing balls so your players gain experience going after all types of loose balls.

Screening and switching

Screens are popular and — when done correctly — effective offensive weapons for getting teammates open shots. The *screening and switching* drill helps your players practice running screen plays. (Check out Chapter 12 for more about setting a legal screen.)

What you need: Three players. One ball.

How it works: Position one offensive player on the free-throw line with the ball. Place her offensive partner on the wing with a defensive player guarding her only a few feet away (check out Figure 14-5a).

Figure 14-5:
Setting screens is effective for eliminating defenders and creating chaos.

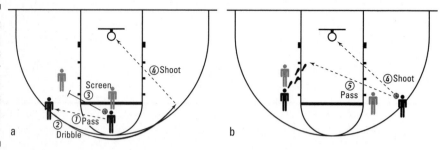

1. **On your whistle, the player with the ball passes to her partner.**

2. **As soon as she gains possession of the ball, the partner begins dribbling toward the former ball handler.**

3. **The partner sets a screen on the ball handler's defender (see Figure 14-5a).**

4. **If the screen is effective, the ball handler can cut in for a lay-up or take a medium-range jump shot.**

5. **If the defender avoids the screen and sticks with her player, the dribbler can pass the ball back to the screener for an open shot (see Figure 14-5b).**

Coaching pointers: Make sure the screener establishes a set position and doesn't move her feet as the defender approaches (a *moving screen*). A screen can succeed only if both players work together, so watch the ball handler, too; ensure that she runs as close to the screener as possible to eliminate the defender.

Breaking the trap

Teams that employ trapping defenses (see Chapter 16) want to create confusion and turnovers. Putting a team on the floor that can counteract this aggressive style of defense can turn the tables and create an advantage for your offense. The *breaking the trap* drill helps your players prepare for annoying trap defenses.

What you need: Five players. One ball. A stopwatch.

How it works: Choose two players for offense and three for defense. Put one offensive player behind the baseline and the other on the court. One defensive player should stand in front of the baseline player to disrupt his inbound pass. The other two defensive players should guard the offensive player who's trying to get open to receive a pass. On your whistle, the baseline player has five seconds to inbound the ball to his partner. The two offensive players must inbound the ball and reach halfcourt without turning it over within 10 seconds.

Coaching pointers: Make sure the offensive players keep their dribble until they're ready to pass the ball. A common mistake players make when under pressure is picking up their dribble, which allows defenders to swarm around them. As long as a player can use his dribble, he can take away some of the opponent's pressure advantage. The defenders should concentrate on trying to force the ball handler toward the sideline, which cuts down on his options.

One fun way to tweak this drill is for you and two assistant coaches (or parent helpers) to take on the defensive roles. You can pair up the kids and turn the drill into a fun competition to see which twosomes can advance the ball to halfcourt in the shortest amount of time.

Running the fast break

If your players can make accurate passes and dribble effectively up the court, they can create fast-break opportunities. And if you face a team that doesn't hustle back on defense, you can score some easy baskets. The *running the fast break* drill helps your players perfect their outlet passes and practice dribbling quickly up the court.

What you need: Four players. One ball.

How it works: Position one player at the top of the three-point arc with a ball and three players nearer the basket (see Figure 14-6). One player should be in the lane a few feet in front of the basket, and the other two players should be on each side of the lane even with the free-throw line.

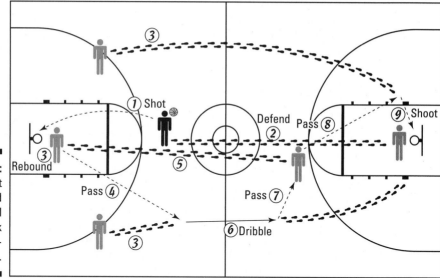

Figure 14-6: Good outlet passes and hustle fuel fast-break opportunities.

1. **On your whistle, the player with the ball launches a shot.**

2. **After shooting, he immediately retreats toward the other end of the court to play defense.**

3. **The player in the lane should rebound the ball.**

   During the rebound, the two players on the wing begin to break down the floor.

4. **The rebounder immediately looks to send an outlet pass to one of the streaking players.**

5. **After passing, he immediately runs up the middle of the court to join the break.**

6. **A wing player receives the outlet pass and dribbles across halfcourt.**

7. **He passes it back to the player in the middle (the rebounder) after he crosses halfcourt.**

8. **As the new ball handler approaches the free-throw line, he looks to distribute the ball to his left or right (the original wing players) so that either player can go in for a lay-up.**

9. **He passes the ball, and the new ball handler shoots a lay-up.**

   The defender tries to break up the play by deflecting the pass, blocking a shot, or creating a turnover.

Coaching pointers: Pay close attention to the outlet pass. You want the ball delivered out in front of the breaking player so he can catch the pass in stride. If he has to slow down or stop, the chances of the fast break succeeding are greatly diminished. Also, make sure the ball handler driving toward the basket doesn't hold onto the ball too long or charge into the defender.

Rebounding relays

Quick footwork is a necessity for boxing out opponents and grabbing rebounds. The *rebounding relays* drill keeps your kids' feet moving and gives them plenty of rebounding practice (see Chapter 10).

What you need: Six players. One ball. One coach.

How it works: Spread three offensive players about 20 feet from the basket and position three defensive players opposite them about five feet away. A coach stands under the basket with the ball (see Figure 14-7a).

Figure 14-7:
Good
rebounders
rely on their
box-out
skills.

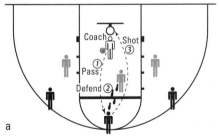

a

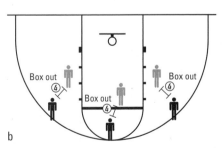

b

1. **The coach passes the ball to one of the offensive players.**

2. **The defensive player assigned to the new ball handler runs up to defend her.**

3. **The ball handler lofts a jump shot.**

4. **The player guarding her boxes her out.**

   The other defensive players also box out their opponents and attempt to secure the rebound (see Figure 14-7b). If the shot goes in, the ball is quickly recovered and passed back to the coach to keep the drill moving.

   If a defender grabs the rebound, she returns the ball to the coach. The players hustle back to their starting positions, and the coach makes a pass to another offensive player.

   If an offensive player grabs the rebound, the offense can work to get off another shot. Don't stop until the offense makes a basket or the defense gains possession of the ball.

Coaching pointers: Make sure the offensive players don't commit fouls in their efforts to snag rebounds. Rotate the threesomes so everyone gets a chance to play offense and defense.

This drill is perfect for fun competition. You can award points, such as one point for every defensive rebound and two points for every offensive rebound. Of course, be sure to award points for made baskets, too. You can play quick mini-games up to ten points.

Receiving and running

Because basketball is a fast-paced game, many of your drills should simulate game speed so the kids become comfortable handling the ball while on the move. The *receiving and running* drill helps enhance your players' hand-eye coordination so they can make plays while in motion.

What you need: Pairs of players. One ball for each pair.

How it works: Break up the kids into pairs and give each twosome a ball. Have as many pairs as you can start on the baseline, with the two players standing about 10 feet apart horizontally. On your whistle, they begin running down the floor, sending bounce passes back and forth as they go, stopping at the other baseline.

Coaching pointers: This is a difficult timing drill, but make sure that when the kids receive a pass, they quickly get rid of it. You don't want your players taking any more steps than they're allowed without dribbling or passing (a traveling violation; see Chapter 3).

Implementing Innovative Scrimmages

Playing a scrimmage is a great way to give your kids a taste of what playing in an actual game is like by allowing them to use their skills in a game-like setting. A *scrimmage* is when you split the team in half and have the halves play against each other. You can be creative and add some spice to your scrimmages by tweaking the rules. You can not only increase the fun, but also enhance the skill development of your players. The following list presents a few ways you can improvise on traditional scrimmages. Incorporate these ideas into your practices during the season:

- ✔ **Name the shooter:** When the offensive team brings the ball down the court, you signal which player you want to take the shot on that possession. This forces the kids to work hard at setting screens and making good passes to generate a good scoring opportunity for the selected individual, because the defenders will be focusing on him. You can make baskets made by this player worth more to serve as an incentive and to reward the offense's execution.

- ✔ **Nondominant hand:** During this scrimmage, allow right-handers to loft shots only with their left hands, and vice versa. This gives players practice in an area of their game that usually doesn't receive much attention. Another benefit is that players look to make passes to their teammates to get the closest shots possible, because many young players don't have the coordination yet to put up shots with their weaker hands.

- ✔ **No dribbling.** The offense has to generate points without dribbling the basketball. This drill really puts an emphasis on passing and cutting.

- ✔ **Reverse scoring:** Instead of rewarding long-range perimeter shots with the most points, mix up the scoring by awarding three points for shots made in the lane, two points for baskets made outside the lane but inside the three-point arc, and one point for shots made beyond the arc.

- ✔ **3 on 3:** This format is one of the best teachers because all the players are directly involved, from handling the ball and setting screens to shooting, defending, and rebounding. No one can stand around without really weakening the unit.

Be careful not to overuse scrimmages at the expense of drills focused more on skill development. For example, if kids have developed some bad habits shooting the ball, a scrimmage doesn't allow you to work on correcting them.

Having fun with innovative drills for older kids

When running practice drills with older (and perhaps slightly more experienced) kids, your job is a little more challenging because they may have been around the game longer. You don't want to run them through the same old tired drills all the time. You can make your personal stamp on the season by introducing the kids to drills that will have them talking to their friends about how cool your practices are. Here are a couple sample drills you can use with your team; if you prefer, you can simply review these drills to spark some ideas of your own:

✔ **Coach-player challenges:** Appealing to the kids' competitiveness is one of the best ways to get their attention and rev up their energy levels. For example, you can give each child one possession to go against you one-on-one to see if the player can score a basket. Or, you and an assistant coach can play two-on-two against two players, again giving the kids one chance to score. This option keeps the drill moving and eliminates some standing-around time. You also can run a five-minute scrimmage at the end of practice, pitting the kids against the coaches and some of the parents.

✔ **Elimination games:** Kids love putting their skills to the test against their teammates. No matter the skill, a child will enjoy the chance to claim that he was the best at performing a particular skill that day. For example, you can conduct a jump-shot competition (see Chapter 9) where each child takes one shot from a set distance on the floor. If a player sinks the shot, he remains in for the next round; if he misses, he's eliminated from the contest. The last player standing wins! Make sure you have a skill station where a player can go when eliminated so he doesn't have to stand on the sideline.

You can modify even the most basic drill — such as dribbling through pylons (see Chapter 11) — to meet the needs of older kids. For example, by timing the kids to see who can negotiate the course the fastest, you'll really get the competitive juices flowing and make the drill more game-like in nature because of its speed. You can also move the pylons all over the court so the kids must make cuts and turns in many different directions, just like they'll do when facing an opponent.

Part IV

Moving On to Advanced Basketball Strategies

The 5th Wave   By Rich Tennant

"Let's see – I'll need some children's aspirin for my players and some sedatives for their parents."

In this part . . .

As your players improve their skills — or if you're coaching an older, more advanced team — you need to step up your coaching game and introduce them to more advanced game strategies and techniques. This part shows you how to upgrade your team's offensive and defensive play with Coaching 201 chapters. We also include some advanced drills that will keep your kids' interest and spark their development.

Chapter 15

Coaching Offense 201

· ·

In This Chapter

▶ Calling your plays with hand signals

▶ Mixing up your offensive attack

▶ Exploiting different types of defenses

▶ Focusing on shot and pass fakes

· ·

As your season progresses, your players will pick up all sorts of offensive skills and will improve in many different offensive areas of the game, and you'll need to adjust your offensive approach to account for these advances. Of course, the teams you play will also improve their defensive skills. How effective your offense continues to be depends largely on how your players handle the improving defenses that play them.

Having knowledge of many different offensive skills and techniques, as well as having confidence in their ability to execute, makes your players tough for opposing defenses to stop. This chapter cracks open a more advanced playbook and reviews a wide range of offensive attacks that you can utilize to keep opposing defenses off-balance. We also show you how to attack different types of defenses. Finally, we cover an effective technique that advanced players of all ages love to use: the fake.

Communicating Plays during the Game

At the beginning levels of play, coaches on the floor can talk directly to their players and provide the necessary instruction and feedback to help them maneuver around the floor. One of the many unique aspects of coaching older players on game day, though — other than the fact that you have to stay on the sidelines — is that you can call for specific plays, both on offense and defense. On offense, you can use a signal to run a specific set play, and on defense, you can use a signal if you want your team to play a certain brand of defense. (Chapter 12 and the rest of this chapter cover offensive plays you can teach; for more information on coaching different types of defenses, flip to Chapters 13 and 16.)

Whatever method you use to communicate your set plays, be sure to use the same method during your practices. You can signal plays in a couple different manners:

- **You can use simple hand signals.** Basic numbers work well — for instance, holding up one finger, two fingers, and so on.

- **You can let your team give the plays fun names.** In more advanced leagues, you may want to have two names, such as a number and a name, to keep your opponent guessing.

- **You can use cards with a color or number on pasted on them that represents a specific play.** You or an assistant coach can hold up the cards for players to see.

Changing Your Offensive Approach

As your team's leader, you don't want to allow your players to fall into an offensive rut by going with the same offensive look every trip down the floor. Plus, doing so makes you predictable, and your opponent will know in advance what you're trying to do. At the advanced levels of play, you should mix things up on offense to keep opponents off-balance.

When introducing offensive sets, strategies, and plays, keep this in mind: the simpler, the better. You're much better off focusing on a handful of plays and helping the kids become proficient in those rather than overwhelming them with too much information. *Note:* You never want players passing up open, good shots just for the sake of running through a set play to its entirety.

Besides making your team more difficult to defend, incorporating different offensive sets into your attack keeps the game fun, fresh, and challenging for the kids because they won't have to be robotic in their execution. This section covers many new offensive approaches you can practice during the week and switch to during a game to achieve these ends.

The single low-post offense

To run a *single low-post offense,* you position your center in the low post, two forwards on the wings, and two guards above the perimeter at the top of the key (see Figure 15-1a). (Chapter 3 covers the floor setup, and Chapter 5 helps you evaluate players for positions.) From this setup, you can run many plays designed to get the ball into an advantageous scoring position in the low post.

For example, here's a simple play you can run from this setup: Player D moves down into the low post (see Figure 15-1b) and sets a screen on the defender guarding Player E as he comes across the lane. Player E loops around his screening teammate to receive a pass. If the defense doesn't react properly to this play, it can give you an easy path to the basket. At the very least, it can give you a mismatch if the forward who was guarding Player D switches over to guard your center. (For more on the basics of screening, refer to Chapter 12.)

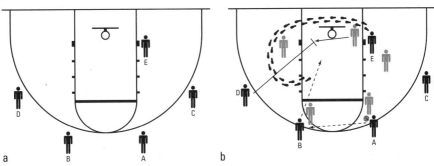

Figure 15-1: The players' positioning in the single low-post offense allows Player D to set a screen to free up Player E.

To get even more advanced, you can run a double screen to free Player E for a scoring opportunity (see Figure 15-2). Here's how you execute the double screen from the single low post:

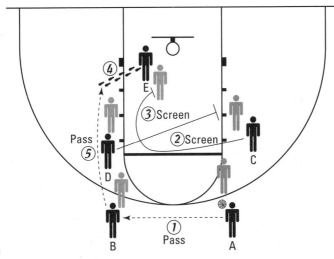

Figure 15-2: The double screen is an effective offensive technique in the low post.

1. **Player A sets the offense by passing around the perimeter to Player B.**

2. **While Player A is passing, Player D cuts across the lane and sets a screen on the defender guarding Player C.**

3. **Player C cuts around the screener and across the lane, at which point she loops down into the low-post area to screen the defender guarding Player E.**

4. **Player E uses the screen and steps out toward the sideline or curls into the lane to receive a pass from Player B.**

5. **Player B delivers a pass to Player E.**

The single high-post offense

In the *single high-post* alignment, the center plays a little farther away from the basket — near the free-throw line (see Figure 15-3a) — than he does in the single low-post offense (see the previous section).

Figure 15-3:
Your center plays closer to the free-throw line in the single high-post alignment, allowing for creative passing plays in the post.

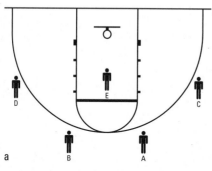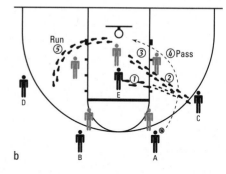

If you have a good passing team, you can use pick-and-rolls and back-door plays (which we cover in Chapter 12) from the single high-post setup to create good scoring chances.

In addition to the pick-and-rolls and back-door cuts, you can run this basic play out of the single high-post offense. It requires only a good cut from a forward and an accurate pass from a guard. Here's how you execute it:

1. **Player E moves across the lane as though she's setting a screen for Player C (see Figure 15-3b).**

   Player A controls the ball along the perimeter, while Players B and D keep their defenders away from the action on the other side of the court.

2. **Player C takes a couple steps toward Player E as though she plans to run her defender into the screen.**

3. **She then cuts hard toward the basket.**

4. **If Player C has her defender fooled and beaten, Player A delivers a pass — it may have to be a lob pass, depending on the angle available — to her for a close-range scoring chance.**

5. **If Player C remains well-covered, she runs through the lane and circles around Player D on the other wing.**

   At this point, Player A can pass the ball inside to Player E — an entry pass to the post — or send it over to Player B to reset the offense to enter the ball to player C.

The double-post offense

The *double-post offense* positions two players in the low-post area and three players along the perimeter. From this setup, you can run a basic screen in the low-post area to create a scoring opportunity. For example, using Figure 15-4a as a reference, Player D can cut across the lane and set a screen on the defender guarding Player E. Player E can then cut across the lane to the side of the ball handler to receive an entry pass. If the screen has created defensive confusion — an advantage for the offense — Player E can turn and shoot or drive to the basket.

Figure 15-4: The double-post offense can challenge defensive players who don't communicate well with one another.

a

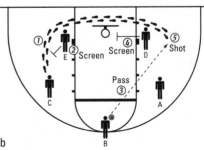

b

If you have some good outside shooters on your team, you can use the double-post alignment to create some open perimeter shots (see Chapter 5 for more on evaluating your players). You can use the following play to do this, for instance:

1. **Player C cuts toward the baseline.**

2. **At the same time, Player E moves away from the basket to set a screen on the defender guarding Player C (see Figure 15-4b).**

   Player C loops closely around the screen and continues across the lane.

3. **If the defensive players fail to communicate with one another and both stick with Player E, the ball handler can toss a pass to Player C for a lay-up.**

4. **If the defender sticks with Player C, or Player E's defender switches onto Player C, Player D sets a screen.**

   This is called a *double staggered screen.*

5. **Player C hustles to the wing or the three-point line and positions himself to receive a pass from the ball handler and loft a shot.**

Scoring off the fast break

If you coach an aggressive offense that pushes the ball up the court and continually looks to create advantages when you outnumber the opposition, you'll give your team many good fast-break scoring chances. The following sections look at how you can make the most of a couple fast-break situations against different defensive forces.

Fast-break opportunities often lead to lay-ups or other close-range shots (see Chapter 9). If your players can score with both hands near the basket, they'll be more difficult to guard. For instance, when a right-handed player is going up for a lay-up on the left side of the basket, have him use his left hand.

2-on-1 fast break

When your team has a 2-on-1 fast-break advantage, you want your players forcing the sole defender to commit to one direction. Practice the following sequence:

1. **The ball handler dribbles down the middle of the court while his teammate runs to the outside.**

2. **As the ball handler nears the free-throw line, he analyzes how the opponent is defending the fast break.**

If he's leaning toward the player without the ball, the ball handler should continue driving toward the basket and go in for a lay-up. If he intends to try to draw a charge by planting his feet in the middle of the lane, the ball handler should deliver a bounce pass (see Chapter 9) to his team-mate for a lay-up.

3-on-1 fast break

In the 3-on-1 fast-break opportunity, the additional scoring option should position himself on the other wing. To produce a basket out of this advantage, practice this sequence:

1. **The ball handler dribbles down the middle of the court while the two players on the wing stay on the outside.**

   Your players need to maintain good court balance so that they don't bunch together, which makes the defender's job easier. That simply means they should keep roughly the same amount of space between them as they move down the court.

2. **As the wing players reach the free-throw area — and they should arrive just a bit before the ball handler — they angle toward the basket.**

   If the defender maintains his position in the middle, the ball handler should deliver a bounce pass to either his left or right. If the defender moves to cover one of the wing players, the ball handler should continue on to the basket for a lay-up or deliver a bounce pass to the opposite wing player.

Attacking Opposing Defenses

You can greatly increase your team's chances of offensive success by recognizing the type of defense being played by the opposition and adjusting with offensive plays in your arsenal that have the best chance of producing points. Teaching your kids how to attack all defenses — while instilling in them the confidence that they can conquer any type of defense — paves the way to success and fun on game day and prepares them for their future in the game. This section gives you an overview of some offensive schemes you can teach to your players so they can strike opposing defenses.

Busting man-to-man defenses

The *man-to-man defense* is when each defender is responsible for covering a specific offensive player (for more, see Chapter 13). When facing man-to-man defenses, you can turn to a couple different modes of attack to bust through and score points: dribble penetration and set plays. Teach these advanced approaches to your team so that you can pose all sorts of problems for the opposition.

You should rely heavily on screens against man-to-man defenses. They help free players who are tightly guarded by stingy defenders. (For more on setting screens, see Chapter 12.)

Using dribble penetration

If you have excellent ball handlers who are difficult to defend (see Chapter 5 for team evaluation tips), you can create scoring opportunities for your team against the man-to-man defense. *Dribble penetration* refers to a player maneuvering the ball past a defender to weaken the interior of a defense and create an open shot for himself or a teammate.

This works as follows: As soon as the ball handler gets by his defender, other defenders are forced to adjust to account for the unguarded player. If they don't, the ball handler has an open shot. If another defender does slide over to offer support, the ball handler can pass to his teammate whom the helper left unguarded.

Relying on set plays

Relying on set plays is an effective way to attack man-to-man defenses because you can use strategies that the kids have become proficient at executing to break down the opposition. You want to have and use a handful of set plays that your kids are comfortable running — and have the confidence to execute, during the opening minute of a game *or* the final seconds of a tied game.

When designing set plays, make sure that you create a variety so that each player on your team has a chance to be the focal point of a play. Besides making all your kids feel like real parts of the team, this tactic also is a good strategic move.

Finding holes in zone defenses

A *zone defense* is where defensive players are responsible for covering areas of the floor, based on the location of the ball (see Chapter 13 for more). Coaches see zone defenses most often at the more advanced levels of play, because teaching zone responsibilities can be quite difficult. Check out this section for a quick preview of some of the most popular zone defenses and how you should attack them to put points on the scoreboard.

Attacking the 2-3 zone

The *2-3 zone* is one of the most popular zone defenses because three defenders can play in the low post and clog the lane, making it hard for offenses to score inside. Because of the nature of the 2-3, you must work hard with your players on making accurate passes to get off shots closer to the basket (for more on making good passes, see Chapter 9).

If you're team is going against a 2-3 zone defense, you can choose from many adjustments to help your team. Specifically, you can advise your players to

- ✔ **Maintain good spacing.** The closer your players are to one another, the easier they are for players in a zone to defend. Spread out your players so that the defense has to worry about covering more of the court.

- ✔ **Work the baseline.** Have your players run plays along the baseline — setting screens for their teammates or looking for openings themselves, for instance. With a lot of congestion down in the low post, the baseline offers many opportunities to set screens against the 2-3 zone.

- ✔ **Watch out for traps.** Make sure your ball handlers don't hold onto the ball too long, because this invites trouble in the form of double teams and traps (see the later section "Dealing with double teams").

- ✔ **Use skip passes.** A *skip pass* refers to a pass that goes from one side of the court to the other. Effective skip passes can catch a zone defense that over-commits itself to one side of the floor off-guard, and they're difficult to recover from.

Penetrating the 1-3-1 zone

Your best chance to beat the 1-3-1 zone defense is to attack in the corners and in the low post. And because only one player sits in the low-post area, that's a prime spot to target.

Here's a play you can use to create a scoring opportunity along the baseline; if everything works out in your favor, the play can lead to an easy lay-up. The play begins with two offensive players at the top of the key and two players in the low post on each side of the lane. The focal point of the play is on the wing (see Figure 15-5).

1. **When Player A gains control of the ball on the perimeter, Player D moves forward and sets a screen on the defender on the right wing.**

   At the onset of Step 1, Steps 2 and 3 happen simultaneously.

2. **Player E cuts across the lane and sets a screen on the defender in the low post.**

3. **Player C loops around both screens and the right baseline to the opposite baseline.**

4. **Player A delivers a pass to her along the baseline.**

   If she's open and has time, she can take a shot or drive the baseline.

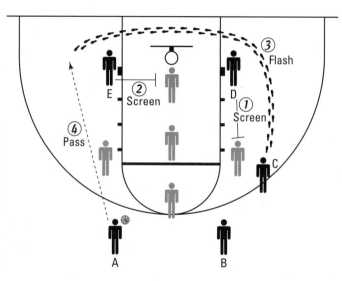

Figure 15-5:
Target the
baseline
areas when
attacking
the 1-3-1
zone
defense.

Dissecting the 1-2-2 zone

Because the 1-2-2 zone defense is designed to shut down perimeter shots (see Chapter 13), you want to target the opening that exists in the high-post area for passes and shots. Signal for your players to assume this formation: Your two guards are at the top of the key, with the center in the high-post area near the free-throw line. The two forwards are in the mid-post area on opposite sides of the lane (see Figure 15-6).

1. **Player A begins the play by passing the ball to Player E.**

2. **Player C sets a screen on the defender along the right wing.**

3. **Player D moves around the screen and into the high-post area.**

   Simultaneously, Player B moves down into the low-post area outside the lane.

4. **Player E passes the ball to Player D in the high-post area.**

5. **Player D turns and either takes a medium-range jump shot or sends a pass to Player B in the low-post area.**

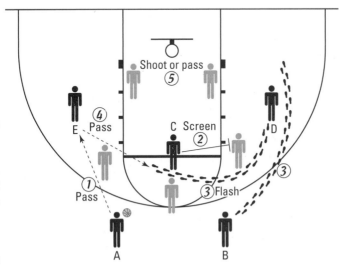

Figure 15-6:
The high-post area is a good spot to attack against the 1-2-2 zone defense.

Breaking full-court pressure

Advancing the ball past midcourt and into an offensive set can be a real nuisance against a good defensive team that uses full-court pressure (see Chapter 16). You can erase a lot of your headaches — and eliminate those aggravating ten-second calls (see Chapter 3) — by sticking to the following tips, which call for you to explain to your players to

✔ **Fill spots versus the press.** You should always have a player behind the ball (the safety or release player), someone on the middle of the floor, someone up the same side of the floor, and someone on the opposite side long down the floor.

✔ **Remember that ten seconds is a long time.** In the span of ten seconds, a lot can happen. Before working on breaking full-court pressure during practice, have the kids stand and count to ten. Sure, it sounds simplistic, but it helps reinforce that they have a lot of time to get the ball across halfcourt.

✔ **Remain calm.** When the pressure heats up, cooler heads should prevail. Presses prey on forcing ball handlers into making poor decisions in the heat of the moment.

✔ **Keep an eye on where you're going.** Remind your ball handlers to keep their eyes upcourt and on their teammates. When a player turns his back on his teammates, the opposition gains the advantage because he can't spot anyone who may be open to receive a pass.

✔ **Steer clear of the sidelines.** Opponents playing a full-court defense like to lure ball handlers to the sidelines, which serve as another defender. Your players should do what they can to stay in the middle of the court. If the sidelines are the only options available, remind your players to keep moving.

The following sections dig into some more specifics regarding going against full-court pressure (see Chapter 17 for a drill that works on this skill).

Inbounding the ball

Getting the ball into play against a full-court press often is the most difficult part of breaking it, because the defense has a chance to get set up and apply pressure where it really hurts. Stress the followings points with your players during practice so inbounding doesn't become problematic:

✔ **Don't be stationary:** After the opponent scores, the player inbounding the ball often can run the length of the baseline. Moving makes it difficult for the defenders to stay in position to disrupt the pass.

✔ **Raise your hands:** Encourage teammates who are open to raise their hands. With all the chaos going on, the player inbounding the ball may have trouble spotting open teammates.

✔ **Call timeout.** The inbounder can call timeout as a last resort. Assign the inbounder to be someone who can make quick decisions and who can know when to call out before the referee calls a five-second violation.

Using pass fakes can also help your inbounder free up some teammates for passes. And remind your kids that players receiving passes should always come to the pass to keep the defense from stepping in and stealing the ball.

Using an aggressive approach

Just because your opponent is forcing the action by pressuring your team doesn't mean your players need to become passive. You can match pressure with pressure by encouraging your players to explore safe passes that they can make farther down the court to create scoring advantages. By attacking the pressure — and hopefully generating some fast-break opportunities — you'll make your opponent think twice about resorting to full-court pressure.

The baseball pass (see Chapter 12) is a great press breaker, because your players can throw the ball over the top of the defenders and bypass the trouble. Plus, an accurate baseball pass can lead to an easy scoring opportunity.

Breaking half-court pressure

Opponents use half-court pressure for all sorts of reasons, ranging from the desire to break up a team's offensive rhythm to catching the ball handler off-guard and forcing a turnover. (For more on half-court pressure, see Chapter 16.)

During your practices, you can create drills that use extra defenders. These drills get the kids accustomed to dealing with half-court pressure and having fewer passing lanes to work with.

When your ball handler crosses halfcourt and has two defenders converge on him, the key is for the player not to panic and to maintain his dribble. As he sees the players approach, he should evaluate his passing options right away and get the ball to an open player as soon as he can. Also, it's important that his teammates come to his aid. When they see the pressure being applied, they shouldn't stand still and watch players converge on their teammate; instead, advise them to move toward the ball handler to shorten the length of his passing options.

Whenever your team does break free of traps, your players should immediately look to attack the basket for quality scoring chances.

Dealing with double teams

Opponents use *double teams* — two defenders guarding a single offensive player — to force ball handlers into turnovers or bad passes.

Double teams can be double trouble if you don't prepare your players to face them. The following list points out a do and a don't to teach your players so they can break double teams:

- **Don't try to dribble out of trouble:** Doing so usually leads to more problems, because as soon as the player puts the ball on the floor, he'll have two pairs of hands reaching in to take it.

- **Do find an open teammate:** Instruct your kids to make quick passes before the double team ever has a chance to establish itself. When a ball handler sees a double team coming, the teammate who's most likely to be open is the one whom the defender left to create the double team.

Your players should avoid making long, crosscourt passes when they get double teamed, because long passes are the ones that defenses feast on. They'll have the time to adjust and pick off the passes for easy transition baskets.

Adding Flair and Fanciness with Fakes

Faking is an important part of both shooting and passing at the more advanced levels of basketball. The better your players are at executing fakes, the more quality scoring chances they can create for themselves and their teammates. *Faking* simply means convincing the defender that you're going to do something that you have no intention of actually doing to gain an advantage. During your practices, be sure to devote some time to faking. This section looks at how you can teach your players to fake shots and passes.

Faking jump shots

A shot fake can create a weakness in the opposing defense that your ball handler can exploit. The shot fake's primary goal is to get the defender off his feet or out of position so that the offensive player can give himself a clearer look at the basket or an open path to drive through. The best shot fakes look exactly like the player is going to leave his feet and take a shot.

You want to teach your players to go through the exact same motions when using shot fakes as they do when executing actual jump shots. The player holds the ball in the proper position for taking a shot. He keeps his eyes focused on the basket to "sell" the defender that he plans to put up a shot. If he's looking at where he's going to pass the ball, the opponent isn't going to fall for the fake. Using his entire body, he rises up, bringing the ball up around head level, just like he would if he was actually planning on lofting a shot. The key to executing the fake is at the last possible second he keeps his pivot foot on the ground. If the defender goes for the fake and jumps in the air to block the shot, the ball handler has created an advantage and can dribble past him or pass to a teammate.

Faking passes

Executing a good pass fake is all about convincing the defender that you're really going to release the ball. Pass fakes are effective against teams that play aggressive defense and look to create many steals. By using the pass fake, your players can lure defenders into taking a couple steps out of position, in the direction that they force them to anticipate. This opens the door for your players to exploit the advantage.

Dribbling behind the back: Not for showboating

Dribbling behind the back — when done correctly and in the right situations (not to impress peers in the stands) — can be an effective maneuver. You should teach it only to older and more advanced players who have been around the game for several seasons. The best place to utilize a behind-the-back dribble is in the open court. The best time often is while bringing the ball up the court against a defender who's applying tight pressure, because the ball handler's body provides an extra layer of protection to prevent a steal. When the player is dribbling (say, with his right hand, for the sake of our example), and the defender pressures him on the side of the dribble, he can go behind his back to keep the ball out of the defender's reach. Here's how a player executes the behind-the-back dribble:

1. **The ball handler steps forward with his left foot and leans his body forward.**

   His body should be slightly in front of the ball.

2. **He dribbles the ball in his right hand at waist-level, or slightly below.**

   He dribbles slightly in front of his waist, and his left hand is at waist-level.

3. **He snaps his right wrist toward the ground and pushes the ball around his back.**

   The ball should make contact with the court behind his back.

4. **He catches the ball with his left palm and makes his next dribble with his left hand while moving forward.**

A pass fake requires the player to forcefully extend his arms out, as though he's releasing the ball. His head and eyes should be looking directly at the faking target he "wants" to pass to. But, as his arms stretch out, he holds onto the ball tightly so that it doesn't slip out when he abruptly stops his motion.

Your kids can get creative and spice up their pass fakes by calling out the teammate's name whom they want to fake to. This helps persuade the defender to be even more aggressive and increases the chances that he'll commit himself and create an opening for an attack.

Chapter 16

Coaching Defense 201

In This Chapter

▶ Zeroing in on proper zone positioning

▶ Putting on the defensive pressure

▶ Fending off fast breaks

*P*laying good defensive basketball requires a thorough understanding of the basics of the game. Playing *really* good defense, however — the kind of individual *and* team efforts that give the opposition little room to maneuver and few opportunities for quality shots — requires a broad range of skills and techniques and knowledge of the best ways to capitalize on them. And you, as the coach, must not only know how to teach these advanced techniques but also when the most opportune times are to have your players employ them on game day to rattle the opposition.

If you're coaching advanced-level kids, or overseeing teams involved in competitive leagues, this chapter is for you. We provide in-depth details on a variety of zone defenses that you can teach, explore the merits of full- and half-court pressure and other types of pressure defenses, and present the best approaches for defending fast breaks when your players are outnumbered. (For the basics of individual and team defense, see Chapters 10 and 13.)

Positioning Your Players for the Main Zone Defenses

Employing different types of zone defenses can make life pretty miserable for opposing teams — especially those who don't shoot the ball well from the outside or who are unfamiliar with how to attack them — which is what you want your players striving to achieve every time an opponent possesses the ball. The following sections explain the intricacies of the 2-3, the 1-2-2, and the 2-1-2 zone defenses. These are the most commonly used zones and will be the ones that your kids will derive the most benefits from using on game day. Regardless of the zone you want to call, the better your players understand where they should be on the court in relation to the ball, the tougher they'll make it for the opposition to score points.

During your practice drills (see Chapters 11, 14, and 17), monitor the communication between your players to ensure that plenty of talk takes place. If your kids are communicating with one another about defensive switches and assignments during practice — and not about their plans for after practice — the habit will carry over to game day and make your team's defense a lot tougher to score against.

2-3 zone defense

The *2-3 zone defense* is designed to protect the area around the basket. A good time to use this D is when the opponent is generating a lot of good scoring opportunities in close to the basket, or if it's not a real good shooting team from the perimeter. The following list explains how your players should position themselves based on the opposition's point of attack:

✔ **Ball on the wing:** When the ball goes to a player on the perimeter who isn't below the free-throw line, the guard nearest to him is responsible for coverage. He slides over to position himself between the ball handler and the basket (see Figure 16-1). The other guard should move to the free-throw line area. In the low-post area, the center should move forward a couple steps, and the forward farthest from the ball (Player C in Figure 16-1) shifts toward the lane while the other forward (Player E) doesn't stray and guards his territory.

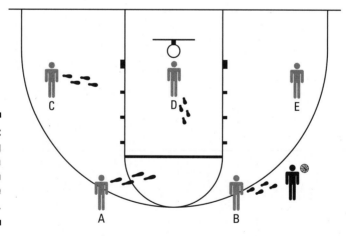

Figure 16-1:
Defending the ball on a wing with the 2-3 zone defense.

✔ **Ball in the corner:** Your forwards must be active when the ball goes into the corner by covering the opposing player quickly. You don't want to give an opponent an open jump shot or space to dribble along the baseline and penetrate or pass to a teammate. The forward closest to the ball handler should step out to defend (see Figure 16-2). The center should shift over to the side of the lane closest to the ball handler, and the other forward should step up into the lane. Both guards can shift to the ball handler's side of the court. The nearest guard should help take away the pass to the post or any flash from across the lane.

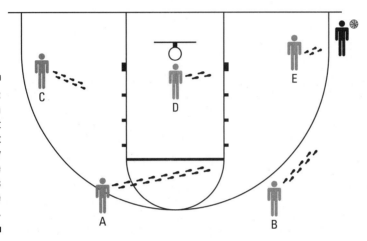

Figure 16-2:
Forwards in the 2-3 must react quickly when the ball moves to the corners.

When the opponent passes the ball into the corner, your team can take a more aggressive approach by trapping the player. To execute a *corner trap*, the forward steps out to cover the ball handler and the guard closest to him drops down to cut off the passing lanes (see Figure 16-3). The opposite forward shifts into the lane, and the other guard slides over about level with the free-throw line. The center is responsible for coverage in the middle of the lane to prevent an opposing player from cutting through and receiving a pass for a lay-up.

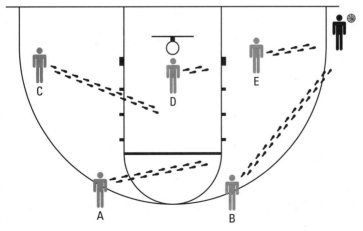

Figure 16-3:
Passes into the corner create trapping opportunities for the 2-3 defense.

✔ **Ball in the post:** When the ball enters the post area, your center moves up to defend the ball handler (see Figure 16-4). Your guards should drop down inside the three-point line, and both forwards should move toward the lane to protect the area vacated by the center.

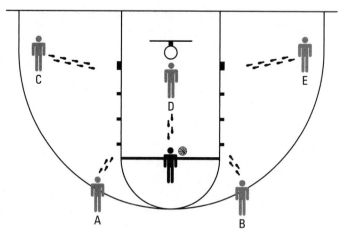

Figure 16-4:
The center must guard the player with the ball in the high-post area.

1-2-2 zone defense

When your team shifts to the *1-2-2 zone defense,* your players need to be based on the floor where the opposition has the ball. With this defense, you're applying pressure on the opponent's outside shooters. If you have a good defensive guard who is quick, this defense is good to disrupt the opposition's attack. The following list covers your players' positioning in the 1-2-2:

✔ **Ball on the wing:** When the ball moves to the left or right wing, your zone should shift in that direction. For example, if the ball goes to the defense's left (see Figure 16-5), the player at the top of the key drops down near the free-throw line. The defender nearest the ball handler steps out to guard him, maintaining his position between the ball handler and the basket. The defender's *mirror* — the player near the perimeter on the opposite side of the lane — drops down into the low-post area. The two players who occupied the low-post area each shift toward the direction of the ball handler.

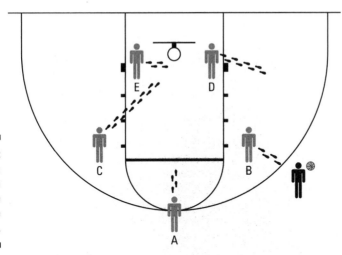

Figure 16-5:
Defending a
ball on a
wing in the
1-2-2 zone
defense.

✔ **Ball in the corner:** The players in the low post (Players D and E in
Figure 16-6) must cover the most territory to defend a ball in the corner.
The low-post player closest to the ball handler goes out to guard him,
and the other low-post player slides into the lane on that side of the
basket. As soon as the ball leaves the perimeter area, Player A sags
down around the free-throw line. Here, he's in a good position to steal
crosscourt passes that the ball handler attempts, as well as any passes
that aren't delivered with much force along the perimeter. Player C
angles into the lane to protect against penetration there.

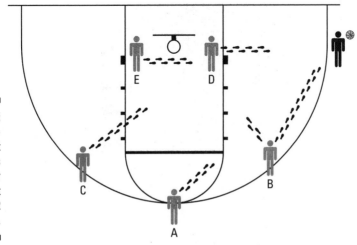

Figure 16-6:
The low-
post
defenders
must cover
a lot of court
in the 1-2-2
zone.

Player B has a couple different options when the ball moves to the corner in the 1-2-2 zone. He can assist Player D with his coverage by trapping the ball handler, or he can collapse closer to the lane to help prevent a pass into the high-post area. If the opposing player isn't efficient handling the ball, he'll probably want to assist with the trap to help create a turnover; if the player is pretty good handling the ball, he should opt to protect the lane and cut down on the passing options. Be sure to work with your players on each scenario during practice.

✔ **Ball in the post:** When the ball is in the post (see Figure 16-7), the guard at the top of the zone should slide down into the high-post area to deny any passes. If a pass still manages to reach a player in the post, the guard should maintain his positioning, and tries to slap the ball away or distract the high post player, and Players B and C should provide defensive support. The low-post players — D and E — must be aware of what's going on in the high post while covering the low post and corners, and be able to provide coverage in the lane so the ball handler can't just dribble straight to the basket.

Figure 16-7:
Your defenders must converge on the high-post area while still paying attention to the whole court.

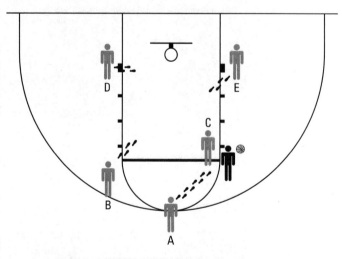

Defending the post area is one of the most challenging aspects of running the 1-2-2 zone, because opponents that have kids with good size who are also good shooters from medium range can exploit the high-post area and create easy scoring chances.

2-1-2 zone defense

The *2-1-2 zone defense* is designed to counteract a team's strong inside play and make it more difficult for low post players to get off quality shots. A good time to throw a 2-1-2 zone defense at an offense is when the team likes to pound the ball into the low post. Executing the 2-1-2 zone defense requires that your players shift their positions based on the following ball positions:

- ✔ **Ball on the wing:** When the ball moves to the wing, the defender closest to the ball handler (Player B in Figure 16-8) should move out to guard him. The other defender at the top of the key (Player A) slides down toward the free-throw line. Player C in the high-post area moves to the ball handler's side of the court, and Player D steps up to defend the area of the court that Player C vacated. Player E protects the area in the low post and along the baseline to prevent penetration.

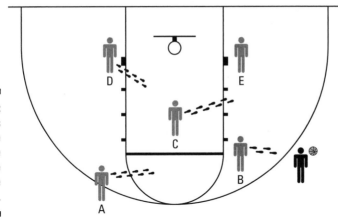

Figure 16-8:
Your players shift to the ball on the wing in the 2-1-2 zone defense.

- ✔ **Ball in the corner:** When the opponent swings the ball into the corner, the defender nearest the new ball handler should step out to guard him. The single defender in the post area drops down closer to the basket. The guard at the top of the zone on the ball handler's side of the court can either help his teammate in the corner with a trap or step into the post to cover the area vacated by Player C (see Figure 16-9). Player E in the low post slides over into the lane, while Player B angles toward the free-throw line.

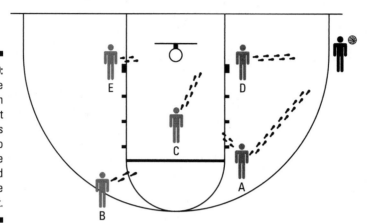

Figure 16-9:
The defender in the mid-post area moves down to cover the vacated area of the post.

✔ **Ball in the post:** When the ball moves into the high-post area, the defender on the perimeter nearest to the new ball handler who isn't covering the passer should drop down to the post to defend (see Figure 16-10). Player D in the low post slides into the lane to provide support, while Player C maintains his position in the mid-post area. Player E protects the baseline and the low-post area on his side of the lane.

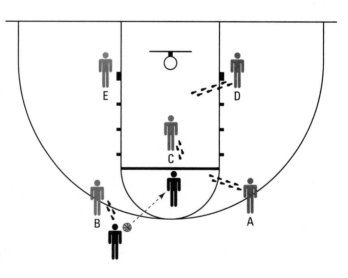

Figure 16-10:
The 2-1-2 zone defense works to shut down the opposition in the low-post area.

Applying Pressure with Your Whole Defensive Arsenal

Teaching your players how to play pressure defense can be one of the most enjoyable aspects of coaching youth basketball, because your kids will love the fast pace of play and raising the intensity level a few notches, and you'll love the results that come — namely, turnovers and more offensive possessions. Plus, your players will really like snagging the turnovers you can produce playing this defensive style. Nothing makes a coach happier than hard work, effort, and fun, and pressure defense allows you players to show all three. In this section, we introduce many types of pressure defense you can teach your players, from full-court pressure to inbounds pressure.

Remind your players that good pressure defense doesn't mean running all over the court to make haphazard steal attempts at balls they have no chance of reaching. Pressure defense is all about applying steady and controlled pressure all over the floor and being able to read and anticipate where the offense will pass the ball.

Suffocating with full-court pressure

Full-court pressure is used to create a turnover, whether it's a steal or forcing the opposition into a 10-second count, as well as to wear a team down so that it becomes tired and more prone to commit mistakes. As a coach, you can mix up your styles and have your team play different types of full-court pressure to keep your opponents off-balance. The two basic types of pressure — zone and man-to-man — offer plenty of variations. In this section, we take a look at a version you can use for each.

> ✔ **Zone press full-court pressure:** A *zone press* is when each player is responsible for an area of the court while applying pressure to the opposition. When the opposition is used to seeing your team's man-to-man pressure, using zone pressure is a good way to mix things up and catch the other team off guard. You set up the 1-3-1 zone press as you see in Figure 16-11:
>
>   1. Have one player stand near the opponent inbounding the ball, although not covering her or trying to prevent the pass onto the court.
>
>   2. Position one player around the midcourt area as the safety net. She'll attempt to prevent any long passes and deal with any players who break free down the court with the ball. Usually the best bet to handle this role is your center.

3. In this 1-3-1 zone press, your other guard and two forwards position themselves across the free-throw line area so that the width of the court is well covered.

4. When the opponent inbounds the ball, the player at the front of the press (Player A) and the next nearest defender (Player B) converge on the new ball handler to trap her. The other two closest defenders (Players C and D) take a couple steps toward the ball handler.

5. If the ball handler manages to dribble through the traps or pass to a teammate, Player C should rush over to provide support, and Player E should slide in that direction while angling backward.

Player E can't be too aggressive because she's the last line of defense. You never want the opponent to get behind your last line of defense for an easy basket.

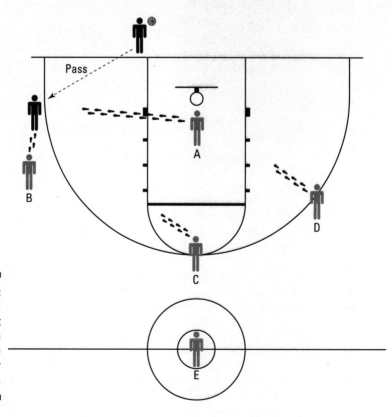

Figure 16-11:
The 1-3-1 full-court press can cause havoc for opponents.

✔ **Man-to-man full-court pressure:** With *man-to-man pressure,* each defender is responsible for applying pressure to the player he is guarding. So the defender on the ball handler plays close to him to make maneuvering the ball up the court as difficult as possible; while the other defenders guard their players just as closely to prevent them from getting open to receive passes. Executing this type of full-court pressure requires each defender to stick tightly to the player he's assigned to guard.

The most important duty is this: The player guarding the ball handler should take away the middle of the court and try to force the ball to the sidelines, because doing so opens the door for double-teaming (see Chapter 13) and cuts down on the ball handler's available passing lanes.

Remind your players that full-court pressure doesn't have to produce a turnover to be a success. Other benefits can result from organized pressure. For example, good full-court pressure can force opponents to use a lot of time getting the ball across halfcourt to set up their offense or cause the game to be sped up and force the offense into quick shots.

Trapping at halfcourt

The best defensive teams keep their opponents continually off-balance each time down the floor. In a word, they're unpredictable. Springing a half-court trap on a team is a great way to apply unexpected pressure and force a turnover. A *half-court trap* is when the defense attempts to surround the ball handler with two defenders after he crosses mid court to force him into a turnover. The half-court trap works best against teams whose guards don't handle the ball well dribbling or passing. It also works against inexperienced guards who probably aren't accustomed to dealing with a lot of pressure.

Half-court presses typically don't fair well against teams that have good ball handlers who are talented enough to dribble out of trouble or make accurate passes to teammates. These players, often guards, can generate scoring opportunities before your trap has a chance to become effective.

Here's a look at one type of half-court trap that you can use to ambush the opposition — the 2-1-2 zone trap:

1. **As the ball handler crosses halfcourt, the two guards nearest to him charge toward him for a double team (see Figure 16-12), ideally forcing him toward the sideline, if possible.**

   Another option is to have one defender meet the ball handler as he crosses halfcourt to try to force him to dribble toward the sideline. Meanwhile, your other guard rushes over toward the sideline to defend him; if he catches the ball handler off-guard, he can trap him along the sideline.

The key is to not let the opponent know the trap is coming. So, as the ball handler brings the ball down the floor, your players should set up like they would for the standard 2-1-2 zone defense (which we cover earlier in this chapter) with two players at the top of the perimeter, a player in the high post, and two players down in the low-post area.

2. **The defender in the middle of the zone should start angling toward the ball handler, while the defender farthest away in the low post steps up to fill the middle guy's area of the court.**

   This limits the number of passing options the ball handler has. The two players trapping the ball handler need to keep their hands active so that they don't allow him a passing lane to get the ball to a teammate.

3. **A lot of players panic when trapped, so your other defenders should watch the ball handler's eyes closely and be prepared to pounce on any passes in their area when they see him looking in their direction for a teammate to pass to.**

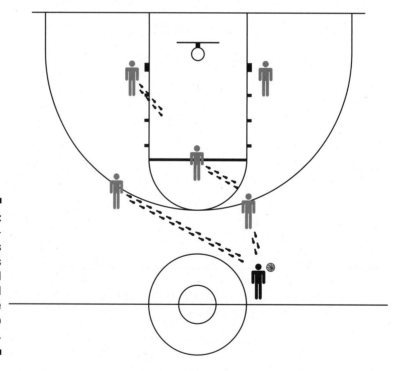

Figure 16-12:
Good half-court traps catch teams off-guard and pressure them into turnovers.

When trapping an opponent, your players need to stay close together (forming a "T" with their feet). If they leave a gap between their feet, the ball handler can step through to deliver a pass or dribble right on through (if he still has his dribble available; see Chapter 3 for more on the rules of the game).

Hoarding the inbounds pass

Many different times during the course of play, the offense will have to make an inbounds pass from the sidelines or baselines (see Chapter 15 for examples). The inbounds pass gives your defense a golden opportunity to set up and apply pressure to create turnovers. You have many ways to defend inbounds passes.

✔ You can employ a basic man-to-man defense, where four of your defenders cover the opposition's four players on the court. Your other defender doesn't cover the player inbounding the ball; he takes a spot near the mid-court area (see Figure 16-13) to protect against long passes and prevent players from driving to the basket uncontested.

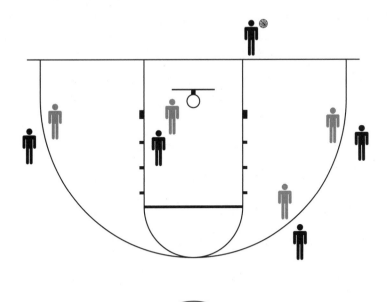

Figure 16-13:
Pressure makes inbounding the ball difficult for the opposition.

In the man-to-man inbounds defense, a defender's job is to stay between the player he's guarding and the inbounds passer. He can have his back turned to the passer, as long as he focuses on shadowing the player he's responsible for covering. This technique forces the inbounder to make a difficult lob pass over a defender's head, which creates a turnover opportunity. The mid-court defender also should keep a close eye on the action; if the inbounder throws an errant pass too far down the court, he should be ready to move forward and pounce.

✓ In the zone inbounds defense, each player is responsible for a specific area of the floor. This approach is good to use when defending near your basket. Because advanced-level teams like to use screens and picks to inbound the ball to create a quick scoring opportunity, a zone defense can counteract many of these plays because your players aren't caught up chasing a specific player around the court.

Defending Fast Breaks

No matter how efficient and suffocating your team's defense is, you'll face situations during a game when your players are outnumbered and at a serious disadvantage on defense. For the offense, this opportunity is called a *fast break*. If you teach your players how to respond when they're outnumbered, you can help minimize some of the damage. This section gives you the lowdown. (Chapter 15 covers how to handle the fast break on offense.)

Going against the 2-on-1

When faced with a 2-on-1 fast break approaching his basket, the defender is in a tough spot, but he can take a few different approaches that may help him get a big stop:

✓ He can stand his ground around the lane in hopes that the ball handler will run into him for a charge (see Chapter 10).

✓ He can attack the ball handler and force him to make a pass under pressure.

✓ He can foul the ball handler in the act of shooting to prevent an easy basket and force the player to earn points from the free-throw line. He can also foul the player before he goes into the act of shooting the ball. Doing so forces the team to inbound the ball, or sends the player to the free-throw line if your team is in the penalty (see Chapter 3).

✔ You can have the defender fake toward the ball handler and then retreat under the basket to guard the other offensive player heading to the basket, with the hope of forcing the ball handler to pick up his dribble. If the fake works, he's faced with having to sink a medium-range shot because his teammate is covered.

Surviving against the 3-on-1

Against experienced teams, the chances of stopping a 3-on-1 fast break are about as likely as winning the lottery. A player who finds herself in this unwanted position knows the odds are really stacked against her. Because the opposition is likely to score a basket, your defender has nothing to lose by being aggressive. You can instruct your players to go for a steal by guessing and lunging in the direction they think the ball handler will pass the ball. Your players can also foul the ball handler before she attempts a shot. Doing so forces the team to inbound the ball, or sends the player to the free-throw line if your team is in the penalty.

Or, if you're a more conservative coach, you can instruct a player to position herself around the free-throw line in hopes of drawing a charge or forcing an errant pass that results in a turnover. This has a chance to work if the ball handler is dribbling out of control or the kids are younger and more inexperienced.

Facing the 3-on-2

Defending a 3-on-2 fast break requires teamwork. Your two defenders must work together and communicate; otherwise, the result will be two points for the opposition. The following setup puts your players in a position to work together and succeed:

✔ **Player A:** When the opponent crosses halfcourt, one defender should position himself in the free-throw area. His primary job is to prevent the ball handler from having a clear path to the basket.

   As soon as the ball handler passes the ball to either wing, the top defender drops down into the lane to lend additional defensive support.

✔ **Player B:** The second defender positions himself around the middle of the lane. His primary job is to move in the direction of the pass to defend the wing player who receives the ball.

This player must not be overly aggressive so he doesn't allow the player to drive by him for an easy basket. He should do his best to force another pass, which is another chance for a turnover to take place. This drill is great to use during your practices, too. It helps the kids understand how to defend this type of break; with enough repetitions, chances are they'll become pretty good at denying their fair share of them.

The longer it takes the offense to put up a shot, the more time your other defenders have to join the action and eliminate the offense's advantage.

Ideally, you want the smaller player in the A position and the bigger player in the B position near the basket. This is where good communication plays a big role, with your players taking different responsibilities on the fly. Be sure to practice this setup many times. However, there isn't always time to be so precise with your set up. If your players don't have time to get aligned, they should simply put themselves in the best position possible and do their best. Remind them that any type of defense is better than no defense at all.

Chapter 17

Zoning In on Advanced Drills

. . . .

In This Chapter

▶ Implementing more challenging practice drills

▶ Understanding game clock situations and coaching based on them

. . . .

*Y*ou can be confident that your coaching is paying dividends if your kids are responding positively to your drills during practice, giving you positive feedback, and evolving as all-around basketball players. Now, more than ever, is an opportune time to capitalize on their progress by unveiling new, more challenging drills that may boost them to even higher levels of play. Or perhaps you've signed up to coach an older, more experienced team with players that know all the basics. In this chapter, we present advanced drills that cover many different facets of the game. By implementing these drills into your practices, you'll help your players continue learning and excelling, both offensively and defensively.

Upgrading Offensive and Defensive Drills

If you want to add some flair and excitement to your drills and put your players in situations that really challenge their offensive and defensive abilities, you've come to the right place. The drills that follow in this section are designed to push your players — who have already mastered many of basketball's more basic skills — to the next level. (If your players still need some work on basic skills, refer to the chapters of Parts III and IV.)

Passing: The over-the-top drill

How proficient your players are at passing the ball to open teammates often is the difference between an okay offense and one that's a real headache for opponents to defend. And if your players can make many different types of passes, you'll turn those headaches into migraines. One such pass is the long pass. Long, accurate passes can produce some easy lay-ups for your team and can bail out your offense when time is running out and you need to advance the ball quickly. This drill covers the basics.

What you need: Three players. One ball.

How it works: Position one offensive player on the baseline with the ball and put her partner at the free-throw line nearest the inbounder. Position the defender about five feet away from the player at the free-throw line.

1. **On your whistle, the offensive player at the free-throw line breaks for the basket down the court, and the player with the ball delivers a baseball pass (check out Chapter 12 for the proper technique).**

   The defender tries to intercept or deflect the pass so the offensive player can't get her hands on it.

2. **If the offensive player catches the pass, she should try to go in for a lay-up against the defender.**

   If the defender deflects the pass, the two players should vie for the loose ball. If the defender steals the pass, the drill ends.

Coaching pointers: If you're coaching kids who don't have a lot of strength yet, start the drill with the offensive players closer together. As for the technique, make sure the passer steps toward her target while releasing the ball for better accuracy and length.

To increase the difficulty of the drill, add a defender to cover the passer on the baseline. You also can incorporate more offensive players at the far end of the court for the ball handler to team with after receiving the pass, and defenders to guard them.

Ball handling: The half-court weave

Turnovers and off-target passes are unwelcome sights for coaches. If you help your players master ball-handling abilities — both dribbling and passing — your offensive productivity will flourish. The half-court weave features a heavy dose of fast-paced passing and dribbling, which is perfect for building a team that continually pushes the ball and attacks from all over the court.

The half-court weave is an ideal drill to use with teams of 12 players or less, because you can run the drill on each half of the court. When doing so, you leave only a few seconds of standing-around time before the players go back into action.

What you need: Groups of three players. One ball.

How it works: Player A begins at midcourt with the ball. Players B and C are flanked to the left and right of Player A (see Figure 17-1).

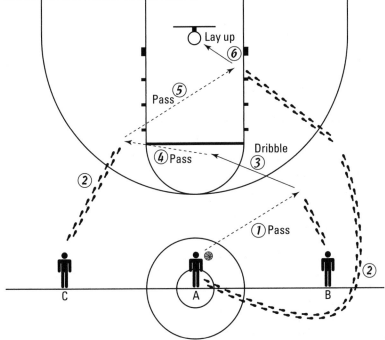

Figure 17-1:
The half-court weave features plenty of passing and dribbling action.

1. **To begin, Player A delivers a chest pass to Player B.**

   Chapter 9 explains the technique of the chest pass.

2. **After delivering the pass, Player A circles around Player B so that he's on the outside of him.**

   At this point, Player C begins moving toward the basket.

3. **Player B starts his dribble and angles toward the middle of the court, moving toward the basket.**

4. **Player B sends a bounce pass to Player C.**

5. **Player C catches the ball and delivers a bounce pass to Player A.**

6. **Player A goes in for a lay-up.**

7. **After taking the lay-up, Player A continues around to the other side of the court (see Figure 17-2), and Player C circles around to the opposite side of the court, too.**

8. **Player B grabs the rebound and sends a chest pass to Player C, who's heading back toward midcourt.**

9. **Player C delivers a crosscourt chest pass to Player A.**

10. **Player A catches the ball and makes a chest pass to the middle player in the next threesome.**

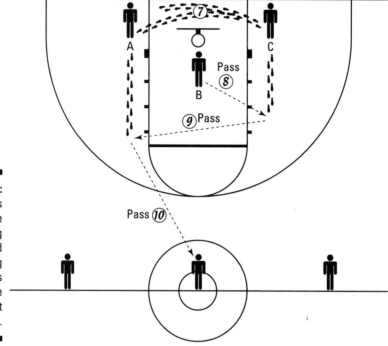

Figure 17-2:
Players
practice
passing
quickly and
making
sharp cuts
during the
half-court
weave.

Coaching pointers: You want to run this drill at top speed to simulate game action, which means you want your players moving down the floor and attacking at all times. During the fast-paced drill, make sure the players' heads are up so they can clearly see the court in front of them. If they're looking down at the ball during the drill, they limit their court vision, which takes away some of their effectiveness.

Rebounding: Tips and taps

Being a good rebounding team requires a total team effort. Each player on the floor has to give it his all to box out to gain control of the basketball. Tips and taps is a cool rebounding drill for kids ages 12 and older that allows you to involve all the players in a fun competition.

What you need: The entire team. Two basketballs.

How it works: Split the team in half and position each group in a single-file line at the free-throw stripe, one group on the right side of the basket and the other on the left. The first player in each group at the free-throw line should have a basketball.

1. **On your whistle, the first two players in line move forward and toss their basketballs off the backboard.**

   As soon as they toss the balls up, they run to the back of their lines and the next players move forward.

2. **The next player in each line runs forward, jumps up, and taps the ball back against the backboard while in the air, using both hands.**

3. **You run through the line a few times so all the players get several attempts at the tip.**

Coaching pointers: Encourage younger players to use both hands to tap the ball. You should also start them out closer to the basket to cut down on the difficulty. With older kids, you can increase the difficulty by allowing them to use only one hand. And you can easily make this drill a competition between the groups by seeing who can complete the most taps in a row.

A fun twist you can use is randomly calling out a player's name as he goes up for the ball. When the youngster hears his name, he must try to score a basket after grabbing the ball. Turn it into a fun competition by seeing which group can make five baskets first.

Shooting: Pillow pushes

Basketball is a contact sport, so players often get bumped, jostled, and fouled while taking shots. The ability to make shots despite contact creates opportunities for coveted three-point plays. The pillow pushes drill helps your players become more comfortable lofting shots while absorbing contact. You shouldn't have a hard time convincing kids to perform this drill, because kids love shooting the basketball as much as gamblers enjoy trips to Las Vegas!

What you need: One player. One coach. One pillow.

How it works: The player begins with the ball at the top of the key (see Chapter 3), and you (or an assistant) stand several feet in front of the basket with a pillow.

1. **On your whistle, the player dribbles into the lane and goes up for a lay-up.**

2. **When the player moves into the air, you gently bump him with the pillow to increase the difficulty of the shot.**

Coaching pointers: The kids enjoy the challenge of taking shots while you bump them with a pillow, but make sure you watch the players' eyes to keep them focused on the basket. The kids may have a tendency to watch you and the pillow instead of on the basket. Also, make sure you mix up where you bump the kids so they get used to contact on different parts of their bodies. This will better simulate the experience they'll have during games. You can also create contact as the youngsters shoot medium- and long-range jump shots to give them practice from all over the floor.

Fast breaks: Bounce passes on the run

Teams that can take advantage of fast-break opportunities give themselves many different scoring opportunities over the course of a game — often easy scoring chances. (For more on executing a basic fast break, run to Chapter 15.) And the ability to pass and catch the ball while moving at top speed can make your players really difficult to defend. The bounce passes on the run drill helps hone your players' hand-eye coordination — a key asset to have for fast breaks.

What you need: Two players. One assistant. One ball.

How it works: Position the two players about five feet away from the lane on opposite sides, and give one player the ball. Position the parent or assistant coach at the opposite end of the court in the middle of the lane.

1. **On your whistle, the player with the ball begins running down the court while dribbling, and his partner begins a full sprint.**

2. **After taking several steps, the ball handler delivers a bounce pass (see Chapter 9) to his partner while continuing his pace down the court.**

3. **The partner catches the ball on the run, dribbles until he reaches mid-court, and then delivers a bounce pass back to the original ball handler.**

4. **He catches the ball while running and dribbles toward the basket; when he approaches the coach in the lane, he makes a bounce pass back to his partner while trying to keep it away from the coach.**

   The coach can't move from his position, but he can wave his arms to distract the passer and attempt to knock away the pass.

5. **If the partner catches the pass, he goes in for a lay-up. If not, and the ball goes out of bounds, the drill starts over again.**

   If the coach gains possession, you start over as well. If the ball gets deflected, play continues and the players try to score on the coach.

Coaching pointers: Make sure the players don't commit traveling violations when they catch the ball on the run. Also, make sure the kids dribble with their heads up so they can see down court. You can encourage the players to make chest passes, too, as they move down the floor. This allows them to practice making and receiving both types of passes.

You can vary the drill and perhaps increase the difficulty by allowing the coach or parent assistant to move around, which presents the ball handler with a decision: Make a tough but good pass or take the ball in for a lay-up himself if he sees an opening.

Taking charges: Knock 'em down

Playing good team defense isn't just about deflecting passes and blocking shots. The most effective teams are those that have players who are willing — and understand how — to draw charges. The knock 'em down drill is perfect for helping your kids to practice taking charges — and it doesn't come with the bumps and bruises that can accompany a charge during a game. (Chapters 10 and 13 cover the basics of coaching defense in further detail.)

What you need: Four players. Three basketballs. One coach. One mat.

How it works: Position one player in the lane near the basket to serve as the defender, and place a large mat behind him. You stand behind the defensive player. Have three players stand around the free-throw arc, each with a basketball.

1. **You begin the drill by signaling which player you want to drive to the basket.**

2. **As the designated player moves toward the basket, the defender slides his feet into position to take a charge.**

   You can begin the drill at half speed so the kids get comfortable falling backward onto the mat.

3. **The offensive player contacts the defender, who falls backward onto the mat.**

4. **The defender gets up, grabs the basketball, and joins the other two players on the free-throw arc.**

   The offensive player assumes the defender's role. Repeat the drill several times so that all the players get a chance at both roles.

Coaching pointers: Before running this drill, you must go over the proper way to take charges so that your kids don't get injured (see Chapter 13). During the drill, make sure the kids fall down on their butts, not on their backs, shoulders, or heads. Also, make sure they don't extend their arms straight out to break their falls, which could lead to broken arms.

Managing the Game Clock

How well your team shoots, passes, and plays defense is important to its success on game day, but other areas are also important, even if they don't get a lot of attention. One very important area of the game that teams in competitive leagues must consider is time management. (At the beginning age levels, leagues rarely use game clocks. Plus, many of these leagues don't even keep score, because the emphasis is on teaching children the basics of the game.) This section takes a look at some different game situations that force you to pay attention to the clock. Also, we share some tips and drills that you can use to help your players become time-management wizards.

If you have the scoreboard clock available to you during your practices, make sure you use it. It gives the players the sense of a game situation.

Working the clock with a lead

Having a lead anytime during a game is advantageous, but it's particularly helpful in the closing minutes of a contest because your opponent will be desperate to score points and will be more likely to put up difficult shots to make it happen quickly. Every game and every situation is different, so you can't give your players any steadfast rules for holding a lead, but you can give them the following general tips to help them protect the leads that they've worked so hard to obtain:

- ✔ **Be patient and share to drain the seconds away.** When protecting a lead, you want your players working together to find the best shot available. You don't want to rush shots or take difficult ones, because that just helps the defense get the ball back quicker — a necessity for mounting a comeback.

- ✔ **Keep the ball in your guards' hands.** The players you have handling your team's guard responsibilities (for more on positioning players, check out Chapter 5) should have the ball in their hands as much as possible. Your guards are more than likely your team's best ball handlers. Having the ball in their hands limits the chances of turnovers.

You can run a ball-control scrimmage during practice to give your players some clock-draining experience. In this scrimmage, the catch is that you award bonus points based on how much time the offensive team can use before shooting. For example, you want to use drills that focus on ball possession rather than scoring. You can run a scrimmage where for every ten seconds that the offense hangs onto the ball without the defense getting its hands on it, they get one point.

Of course, when an easy lay-up opportunity presents itself early in a possession, you don't want your kids bypassing the shot just for the sake of running time off the clock. Tell your players that if an easy shot presents itself and is automatic for them, like a lay-up, then by all means take it.

Defending with the lead

The key to playing good defense when your team has the lead late in a game is to back off the aggression, because aggression can give the opposition easy points. For example, if you play an aggressive man-to-man style of defense, you need to pull back on the intensity just a bit. This has a couple of benefits:

✔ By being less aggressive, your players won't risk committing a foul and sending the opponent to the free-throw line to score easy points. Plus, the clock is stopped during free throws, which is exactly what the opponent wants — to score without draining time.

✔ Reining in your aggression decreases the chances of the opposition being able to get easy baskets off of back-door plays and so on. An aggressive defense means that your players are going for steals and hustling around the court, which may put them out of position at times.

You also don't want your players trying to block shots along the perimeter, because a three-point shot can suddenly turn into a four-point opportunity if the opposing player sinks the shot while being fouled.

Racing against time when trailing

When your team is trailing by a small margin in the closing minutes of a game, your players need to pick up the pace of play on offense to increase their chances of putting together a rally. Here are some strategies that your team can turn to when you're down and time is slipping away:

✔ **Push the ball up the floor.** This isn't the time for your players to walk the ball up the court. Have your players rush the ball up the court under control and get into your offense as quickly as possible. (For more on coaching set offenses, see Chapters 12 and 15.)

✔ **Take quick shots.** When trailing late, you don't have the luxury of waiting for a really good scoring opportunity because you'll burn up too much time in the process. In these situations, your players should loft shots more quickly. You don't want them taking ridiculous shots that have little chance of going in, but you also don't want them waiting to find perfect chances to score.

You can take the scrimmage we introduce in the "Working the clock with a lead" section and tweak it just a bit to focus on putting up shots at a quicker pace. For example, you can award a bonus point for shots made within the first 10 seconds of the shot clock.

✔ **Put up long-distance shots.** If your league has a three-point line, the comeback push is the time to take advantage of it. You don't need a degree in mathematics to know that sinking three-point shots will get your team back in the game quicker than laying in two-point shots. You can call a timeout and run some set plays to create opportunities for your best shooters to get open for three-point shots. (Chapters 7 and 15 cover timeout strategy.)

Fouling late in games

When your team is trailing in a game, a few things have to happen for a comeback to materialize: Your team must score points to make up the deficit (see the previous section), must keep the opposition from tallying points, and can't allow valuable seconds to tick off the clock.

One way teams can give themselves a chance is by purposely fouling opposing players. This is done so that the official calls a foul and the game clock stops. This strategic move can benefit your team several ways: If the player misses the free throws and your team grabs the rebound, you have the ball back in your hands to potentially score more points.

When you need your players to commit a foul to stop the clock, you don't want them being overly aggressive because you never want to put a player at risk of injury. Plus, by being too aggressive, they risk being whistled for an intentional foul. These result in the opposition receiving two free throws plus the ball back, which can smother your team's chances of putting together a rally. For example, when the opposition inbounds the ball, simply have the defender nearest to him grab his arm while swiping at the ball to get the official's attention.

Part V
Shooting for the Extra Points

"First of all, that's not a legal strategy, and secondly, Kevin, I can't believe you didn't notice what Travis shoved down your shorts."

In this part . . .

What your players do before they take the court impacts their ability to perform on it. In this part, we serve up some pre- and post-game nutritional tips to keep your players' energy running high, and we detail how you can help protect them from injuries that will smother the fun or derail their seasons.

And, wait, there's more! This part puts you in the bonus. If you're forced to deal with a problem parent, coach, or child, we have you covered in this part with some solutions. And if you have the opportunity to coach a more advanced travel team, we provide some helpful advice.

Chapter 18

Keeping Your Kids Healthy and Injury Free

● ●

In This Chapter

▶ Consuming the right foods for peak performance

▶ Stretching and cooling down to prevent injuries

▶ Treating common and severe injuries on the court

● ●

You're likely well aware that you'll devote most of your time this season to teaching kids the skills they need to excel at the offensive and defensive ends of the floor. You may not be quite as mindful of your other responsibilities, which include preventing, recognizing, and treating injuries; dealing with emergency situations; and telling your kids what types of foods and drinks they should consume before and after games.

Don't worry, you don't need to dash to your local library to check out a stack of books on sports medicine and nutrition. This chapter provides valuable information on the do's and don'ts of pre- and post-game nutrition and how to make sure your kids stay hydrated. It also explains what you need to know to reduce the chances of your players being injured. We cover warm-up stretches, detail the treatment of common injuries, and show you how to handle more serious cases if they arise.

Hoop Fuel: Eating Healthful

If your players don't eat the right foods and hydrate before and after they step on the court, they probably won't perform up to the best of their abilities. Although you can't sit in your players' kitchens to monitor what they put into their mouths, you can sit them (and their parents; see Chapter 4) down to discuss the importance of following good nutritional habits to maximize energy levels and performance. Although chatting about nutrition may not be as exciting as discussing jump shots, the topic can impact a child's health. You must do your part to undo the corruption caused by television commercials touting candy bars and sugar-coated cereals.

Here are the two main ingredients for fueling a child during practices and games — ingredients that get used up the longer an activity goes on:

- ✔ **Glucose:** Warning: You may now have a flashback to your middle school health class. You may recall learning back then that *glucose,* a sugar derived from carbohydrates, is an important muscle fuel. The bloodstream carries glucose to the working muscles, and the muscles store it in long chains called *glycogen.* With all the running, stopping, and starting that occurs in a basketball game, a child's glycogen stores become steadily depleted. The more carbohydrate fuel children lose during practice competition, the less energy they'll have to sink shots and guard opponents.

- ✔ **Fluids:** Kids lose fluids through perspiration, which is why water is such a vital ingredient to keep a child's body temperature from rising during exercise. The longer children play ball without replacing lost fluids, the less effective they'll be on the court, and the worse they'll feel.

When you talk to your players about good nutrition and hydration, zero in on how they affect the accuracy of their jump shots, their defense, or their ability to play at a top level throughout the entire game. Kids will be much more interested in what you're saying if they know that it relates to improved performance on the court. The following sections cover what should go into your players' young mouths before, during, and after practice and competition. Be sure to share this information with your players and their parents (during the preseason meeting; see Chapter 4).

What to eat pre-game

If your players show up for practices or games with nothing in their stomachs or with bellies full of burgers, fries, and soda consumed on the car ride over, their ability to perform and concentrate will suffer. Not to mention they may feel faint or sick! A nutritious pre-game meal clears the way for children to execute and concentrate at optimum levels. A youngster who eats a healthy meal — or at least a healthy snack — comprised of plenty of carbohydrates will have the muscle energy to play, play long, and play well.

Players should consume a pre-game meal two to three hours before the game. They shouldn't eat within an hour of game time because their bodies will spend the first half digesting their food, which will cut into their performance. The pre-game meal should consist of foods that derive most of their calories from carbohydrates, because carbs convert into energy quicker and more efficiently than other nutrients. For the most performance-enhancing punch, youngsters should opt for a combination of the following:

- ✔ Pastas
- ✔ Breads
- ✔ Chicken or fish
- ✔ Cereals
- ✔ Whole grains
- ✔ Fruits or vegetables

If the player and her parents don't want to eat a full meal before game time, they can settle on a healthy snack. Good pre-game snacks include

- ✔ Bagels
- ✔ Yogurt
- ✔ Dried or fresh fruit
- ✔ Energy bars or fruit granola bars
- ✔ Whole grain crackers with peanut butter or cheese

With older kids, encourage them to bring a piece of fruit, like a banana, to munch on at halftime to help fuel their energy in the second half.

If you notice that your players start to feel sluggish in the second half of games and their performance suffers, try a little experiment during practice. Ask them to consume some healthy snacks before a practice and see whether you notice a difference in their energy levels. If so, ask them to use that knowledge and feed their bodies those types of foods prior to games, too.

If your team has a morning game and your kids won't be able to get up early enough for a full pre-game meal, advise them to eat a nutritionally sound meal the night before. That meal should be a big serving of pasta with some vegetables, chicken, or fish. And even the night before a game, kids should steer clear of junk food that will rob them of much-needed energy.

What to eat post-game

What you say — and how you say it — after a game impacts your players' confidence and self-esteem (see Chapters 2 and 6). Similarly, what your players eat after a contest impacts their bodies and how they feel. Giving kids a tasty snack as a reward for a game well played is fun, but giving them junk food sends the wrong message (not to mention contradicts your pre-game advice). The following are some post-game eating tips for your players:

✔ **Keep concentrating on carbohydrates:** Kids shouldn't have the same concern about avoiding carbs that adults have. Foods rich in carbohydrates that also have protein value are beneficial for youngsters. Ideally, your players' post-game meals or snacks should look a lot like their pre-game meals. The only difference is that the portions should be a little bit smaller. One great post-game meal, for example, is turkey sandwiches, fresh fruit, and crackers with cheese.

✔ **The sooner the better:** The sooner your players dig into their post-game meals, the better. Foods packed with carbohydrates that kids consume within 30 minutes after a game or practice provide the most benefits for youngsters.

How to keep your players hydrated

You simply can't stress the importance of consuming plenty of the right kinds of fluids enough. While kids are running up and down the court exerting energy, their body temperatures rise. And the younger the children, the less they'll sweat because their sweat glands aren't completely developed yet. This makes hydration very important before and during the action.

The best form of hydration is water. How much water should kids consume? The amount will vary, because game conditions — such as playing in a hot, stuffy gym — should dictate whether your players need more water to remain sufficiently hydrated.

Water in a player's body is like money in the bank: You can't really have too much of either. Ideally, you want your kids drinking water with their pre-game meals, consuming water during pre-game warm-ups (see the following section), and taking sips from water bottles on the bench during games. When fluids aren't consumed before the activity, it's impossible for kids to replenish them after they take the court.

Here are some additional tips to quench your and your players' knowledge about fluids:

✔ **Talk specifics and don't let up.** Even though your young kids hear you telling them to drink water, they probably still aren't consuming enough. During a break in practice or a timeout in a game, tell your players to take five sips of water.

Kids should be sipping water from their water bottles while you talk to them during breaks in the action. Make sure each player's bottle is clearly marked with his name — doing so helps prevent the spread of germs by ensuring kids drink out of their own bottles.

✔ **Don't worry about too much water consumption.** Most kids drink water based on need. It's a voluntary habit, and thirst is the mechanism that tells them to drink.

✔ **Go with sports drinks.** Some kids prefer the tasty flavors of sports drinks rather than water. If that's the case, encourage them to consume these to get those valuable fluids in their systems.

✔ **Ask kids to keep drinking after the game.** After exerting themselves, kids need to consume fluids to replenish what they lost throughout the practice or game.

✔ **Involve the parents.** Ask the parents to remind their youngsters to sip from their water bottles on the rides to games and practices (Chapter 4 provides more advice on communicating with the parents).

✔ **Bring extra water.** Always have extra water on hand so your kids can refill their water bottles. You can even designate a couple parents each week to bring extra water.

Caffeinated beverages act as *diuretics,* which are substances that increase the production of urine and eliminate extra water from the body. These drinks do the exact opposite of what water does to keep kids hydrated.

Taking Steps to Avoid Basketball Injuries

Any youngster who steps onto the basketball court — regardless of his age, level of ability, or experience — can suffer an injury. Eliminating the threat of injuries during practices and games is impossible, but you *can* take steps to reduce the chances of injuries occurring and disrupting a child's season. A sound stretching regimen — performed before and after games and practices — not only enhances flexibility, but also provides added protection against unwanted aches and pains. This section gives the lowdown on how to create pre-game and post-game warm-up and cool-down sessions.

Stretching to warm up: What to remember

Maintaining and improving your players' flexibility is essential for not only preventing injuries, but also giving them a solid foundation of strength, balance, and coordination. Incorporating a variety of warm-up stretches is a key component for improving flexibility and preparing youngsters for the demands of basketball. Players who work on their flexibility can see dramatic improvements in their technique, which translates into more effective performances on the court.

Depending on the type of league you are coaching in, you may not have much time to squeeze in a complete warm-up if only a few minutes are allotted between games. If time is limited, modify your warm-up. Perhaps you can gather the team in a hallway for some stretches and light running in place to get loosened up. A few minutes of stretching is always better than none at all!

You should always begin your practices with the players warming up with a light exercise, such as a moderate-paced jog, before they stretch their muscles. Keep these additional points in mind when leading your team in stretching. And remember, a great way to boost kids' self-esteem is to rotate who leads the team warm-ups on game day. Make sure each child gets a chance.

✔ **Be consistent.** Always start practice and prepare for games with a warm-up. If your youngsters know that they'll be stretching at every practice, they'll recognize that warming up plays an important role in their development.

✔ **Keep it simple.** For young kids, the stretching period can be basic and quick. The goal is warm them up, introduce them to the concept, and get them in the habit of stretching before any activity.

✔ **Hit the key muscles.** Have your stretches cover all the major muscle groups that your kids will use. For basketball, you want to stretch the hamstrings, calves, arms, shoulders, and back. (Check out the next section for specific stretches to include in your warm-up.)

✔ **Focus on passive stretching.** Instead of bouncing, straining, or moving suddenly to reach a desired position, which can result in injury, your kids should focus on *passive stretching,* which stresses controlled movement. A player slowly moves to the desired position, just slightly beyond discomfort, while breathing in through the nose and exhaling through the mouth; holds that position for a short period of time; and then relaxes.

✔ **Be hands on.** During stretching exercises, go around for some one-on-one contact with all the kids. Most of them are probably unfamiliar with the concept of stretching. When a child is stretching out his hamstrings, for instance, you can place his hand on the back of his leg so that he feels the exact area that he's stretching.

✔ **Join in.** During practice, you'll run around on the court to teach skills, demonstrate techniques, and provide feedback, so join the kids (and your assistants) for stretching after the kids know how to perform the stretches correctly.

Constantly look for ways to turn basic exercises into fun-filled activities for the kids. For example, instead of having players run a boring lap around the court to get their hearts pumping, ask them to dribble a basketball while they jog. During the lap, you can yell out which hand you want them to dribble with and then shout "reverse" when you want them to change directions. Use your imagination to come up with all sorts of fun ways to liven up warm-ups. The following sections present some warm-up stretches you can try with your players to prevent injury and improve performance. You can complete a quality warm-up in five to ten minutes.

Including basic warm-up stretches

As a coach, you can customize the warm-up routine you use before practices and games to cater to your team's needs. In the following sections, we take a look at several different stretches you can use to prepare your youngsters' bodies for practices and games.

With youngsters who are just starting out in basketball, do sets of 10 repetitions, and have your players hold each stretch for a two-second count. You can slowly build from this base as the season unfolds and players become more limber, bumping up the number of repetitions and the holding length to around 10 seconds.

Hamstring stretch

To stretch his hamstrings — the muscles on the back of the thigh — the child sits down and assumes the hurdle position (see Figure 18-1) by extending her left leg fully and bending her right leg back in the opposite direction. While keeping her back straight, she slowly leans forward, bringing her chest toward her left knee and reaching with both hands toward her toes. (Make sure she isn't lunging for her toes. A player shouldn't feel any pain, just a slight tension in her muscles.) Depending on how much flexibility the child has, she either places her hands on the floor alongside her leg or holds her toes. She should hold the stretch for a couple seconds and then release. Have her repeat with the opposite leg.

You can modify this stretch by having the child bend her right leg in toward the groin, instead of bending it back behind her. This modification reduces the amount of strain placed on the knee joint.

Figure 18-1:
The hurdle position helps a player stretch out her hamstrings.

Quadriceps stretch

The quadriceps on the front of the thighs play a large part in many basketball activities — and they're easy to stretch! Have a player stand and grab his left foot or ankle and lift it behind his body (see Figure 18-2). He should press the top of his foot into his hand while pushing his hips slightly forward. He should keep his lower leg and foot directly behind his upper leg, without any twisting in or out. Make sure he stands up straight with his hips forward to feel the complete effect of the stretch. Repeat with the opposite leg.

Figure 18-2:
Kids can have fun balancing on one leg for this quadriceps stretch.

If a kid has trouble balancing on one leg for the quadriceps stretch, have him put his free hand on the shoulder of a stretching partner for balance. This stretch is a great exercise to work on a player's balance.

Groin stretch

To stretch his groin, a child can sit on the court and place the soles of his feet together with his knees off to the sides (see Figure 18-3). The child slowly presses forward, pushing his knees toward the floor until he feels a mild tension in his groin.

Figure 18-3:
Kids can take a seat on the court when performing the groin stretch.

Waist/lower-back stretch

The waist/lower-back stretch may make your kids think they're on an exercise infomercial. The child stands with her feet a bit beyond shoulder-width apart and arcs her left arm over her head to point to the right. She then leans down to her right while her right arm rests against her right knee (see Figure 18-4). After holding for two seconds, she can reverse to the other side, arcing her right arm over her head and pointing to the left. A player should perform several repetitions in each direction. This exercise also stretches the lats.

Figure 18-4:
Stretching the lower back helps kids make quick stops and starts on the court.

Upper-back stretch

To stretch the hard-to-access upper back, the youngster stretches both arms behind his back from the standing position. If possible, he clasps them together (see Figure 18-5) while puffing out his chest. Some kids may find it difficult to do this stretch alone, so you can pair up players to help each other. Have one player stand behind the other one and gently push the player's arms together behind his back. Make sure that the players never force anyone's arms together, but instead gradually work up to a greater stretch. This exercise also has the added benefit of stretching out the chest.

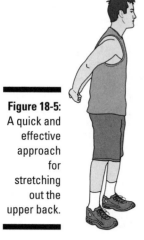

Figure 18-5:
A quick and effective approach for stretching out the upper back.

Calf stretch

From a standing position with her feet shoulder-width apart and her hands on her waist, the player rises onto the balls of both feet (see Figure 18-6). In a fluid motion, she slowly lowers herself back down toward the ground. She should stop just before her heels touch the ground and repeat the upward phase of the stretch. Have your players perform this exercise for ten reps.

Figure 18-6:
Players get on the balls of their feet for the calf stretch.

Hip stretch

The child plops down into the sitting position for the hip stretch. With his left leg flat and extended straight out and his toes pointing up (see Figure 18-7), he crosses his right leg over his left knee so that his right foot is flat on the ground. He places his right hand flat on the ground behind him and then extends his left arm out. To perform the stretch, he slowly turns his torso to the right to the point of mild tension so his left elbow crosses over his right knee. Repeat the stretch with the opposite legs and arms and a left torso turn.

Figure 18-7:
The hip stretch helps kids run at top speed all over the court.

Incorporating more advanced stretches

Just like when kids get older, you can introduce them to more-complex offensive and defensive skills and strategies, the same applies to the types of stretches you can use with them, too. As kids' bodies mature, you can use action-oriented stretches to help prepare their muscles for play. The following sections present some more-advanced, dynamic (motion-based) stretches (called *pylometrics*) you can institute with older players.

High knees

The high-knees stretch works the player's hips and shoulders and stretches her quadriceps, glutes, shoulders, and lower back. To perform the stretch, the child takes an exaggerated high step forward, lifting one knee as high as possible while simultaneously pushing up on the toes of her opposite foot (see Figure 18-8). She should swing the arm opposite her lifted leg up to chin level. Have your kids move down the court performing these movements and repeat on the way back.

Figure 18-8:
The high-knees stretch works the upper and lower parts of the body.

Running butt taps

Youngsters get a good stretch of their quadriceps and hip flexors with the running butt taps, a dynamic exercise. When the player begins running, he flexes his knees so that each time he lifts a foot off the ground, his heel comes all the way back and kicks his butt (see Figure 18-9). While kicking his own butt, the youngster should be leaning slightly forward, and his arms should swing close to his body. Starting from the baseline (see Chapter 3), have your kids complete 20 kicks total by the time they reach midcourt. If you don't have much room, you can have them do this exercise while running in place.

Figure 18-9:
Kids will get a kick out of performing this fun stretch.

Running carioca

Running carioca is a challenging exercise that focuses on stretching the player's abs, glutes, ankles, and hips. The youngster begins on the balls of her feet. Moving laterally, she twists her hips open and shut while crossing one leg in front of the other (see Figure 18-10). When she gets to the position you see in Figure 18-10, she brings her back leg across and crosses her lead leg behind the back leg. The player's shoulders should remain square through the entire drill.

Figure 18-10: The running carioca challenges older players and gets all their parts moving.

Properly cooling down

Although the warm-up usually gets most of the attention, post-practice and post-game cool-downs are also important for your players' health. Get your youngsters in the habit of going through the cool-down process you design every time they participate in a practice or game. Performing some of the light stretches that you used for warm-ups gives players the following benefits:

- ✔ Prevents the tightening of the muscles that accompany exercise
- ✔ Reduces soreness
- ✔ Aids circulation
- ✔ Helps clear waste products from the muscles

Addressing Injuries on the Court

How you address and handle injuries that happen during practices and games impacts how your kids will feel about the sport in the future and may even factor in to a decision on whether to continue on with you this season. Hauling a first-aid kit around may seem like more trouble than it's worth, but you'll be thankful you have it when you have to deal with an injury. Being prepared is better than simply hoping nothing bad happens. (For the rundown of everything that you should include in your kit, check out Chapter 6.)

Some leagues issue first-aid kits to their coaches, and some leave it up to them. (For information on getting to know your league, see Chapter 2.) Many facilities keep a first-aid kit on hand so you can use it if you don't have one or if you don't have a particular item in your own kit. Just make sure you know where the kit is kept or where to go to request it. To help you win the trust of your players and parents and to prepare you for the minor and the worst, this section points out how to treat common basketball injuries and how to handle first-aid situations.

Whenever a player suffers an injury that you provide treatment for, write down exactly what you did, regardless of how minor it is, and always inform the child's parents. In a practice planner or a separate log book, write down the nature of the injury, how it happened, and what treatment you provided. Do so the same day, while the event is still fresh in your mind. We live in a litigious society, so having an accurate account of injury situations helps protect you in a court of law.

Treating common basketball injuries

Most injuries you encounter on the basketball court will be "minor" bumps, bruises, and cuts and twisted ankles. These injuries may seem minor to you, but they'll be pretty major to a child who suddenly can't put weight on a twisted ankle or who sees blood. By acting quickly and administering the proper treatment for routine injuries, all while comforting the youngster, you can help a player bounce back and return to action as a fearless baler in no time. The following sections show you how.

Cuts and scrapes

Kids can suffer skinned knees when diving for balls or suffer cuts from opposing players' fingers, among many other minor injuries. Cuts and scrapes can produce major tears with young players, but you can treat them quickly and effectively with the materials in your first-aid kit. (Having a first-aid kit nearby is important; check out Chapter 6.) Keep the following system in mind when treating cuts and scrapes:

1. **Put on latex gloves.**

   When one of your players suffers a cut or has an open wound, immediately put on a pair of latex gloves or use some other type of blood barrier to limit your contact with the blood.

2. **Apply direct pressure.**

   If you have a bleeding situation, grab some clean dressing and try to stop the bleeding by applying direct pressure to the wound. If you have trouble stopping the bleeding, elevate the child's injured area above her heart while maintaining pressure.

3. **Clean the wound.**

   After you stop the bleeding, you should clean the wound. You can use pre-moistened towelettes to clean minor cuts and scrapes, or you can use over-the-counter alcohol swabs or antibiotic creams.

4. **Cover the wound.**

   Use a bandage or a piece of sterile gauze to cover the cut, and be sure to secure the covering tightly in place — particularly if the child wants (and is able) to continue playing.

5. **Discard the trash.**

   Place your gloves and any other cleaning materials that you used in a sealed bag, and place the bag in the trash.

Twists, sprains, and strains

Basketball requires that players make a lot of sudden stops, starts, and turns, sometimes while coming into contact with other players. These movements — and some of the collisions that accompany them — can result in twists, strains, and sprains. Most of these types of injuries involve the ankles, knees, hands, and fingers.

When a player strains a muscle, or sprains or twists a body part, keep in mind the RICE method for treatment:

1. **R**est: Immediately move the child to the sideline so that she can rest the injury. If she has twisted her ankle, for example, have an assistant coach or a parent help you carry her off the court so that she doesn't put any additional pressure on the injured area.

2. **I**ce: Apply an ice pack to the injured area. The coldness helps reduce the swelling and pain. Don't apply the ice directly to the skin. Wrap an ice bag in a towel and then place the bag on the injured area. Apply the ice for approximately 20 minutes, and then remove for 20 minutes. Continue with the ice on and off every 20 minutes for the next few hours.

3. Compress: Compress the injured area by using athletic tape or another type of material to hold the ice pack in place.

4. Elevate: Have the child elevate the injured area above her heart level to prevent blood from pooling in the area.

After any swelling, discoloration, or pain subsides, you can allow the youngster to return to the action. If any of these symptoms remain for more than a couple days, a physician should examine the player before you allow her back on the court. Never let a child return to action before her injury has completely healed; if you do, you put her at greater risk of re-injuring the area and missing even more time.

Other common but painful injuries

At the more competitive levels of basketball, the players are bigger, faster, and stronger. With this added physical prowess comes a greater chance of more serious injuries occurring. Here's a look at some of these injuries and how you should respond:

- ✔ **Concussion:** A *concussion* is a jarring injury to the head, face, or jaw that results in a disturbance of the brain. These injuries can be mild or severe. Mild concussions may require up to a week for recovery; a physician must set the timetable for return. Severe concussions require at least four weeks of recovery; a head-injury specialist must give permission to return. Symptoms include a brief loss of consciousness, headache, grogginess, confusion, glassy-eyed look, amnesia, disturbed balance, or slight dizziness.

  After a blow to the head, immediate care includes having the child rest on the sidelines with an adult to provide careful observation. If you or the adult see any evidence of something more serious — such as prolonged unconsciousness, change in the size of his pupils, or convulsions — take an immediate trip by ambulance to a hospital.

- ✔ **Injury to the eyeball:** A direct injury to the eyeball is an immediate medical emergency. Symptoms include extreme pain, loss of vision, hazy vision, double vision, change in vision colors, or obvious cuts or scrapes to the eye. Put on your latex gloves and apply a sterile eye patch or piece of gauze to the eye along with a bag of soft, crushed ice. Immediately have the youngster taken to an emergency facility. (See the following section for more on handling emergency situations.)

- ✔ **Poked in eye:** When a youngster gets poked in the eye, first examine his eye. If the youngster isn't in significant pain and you see minimal redness and no discharge or bleeding, simply clean the area with cool water and allow the athlete to rest for awhile. If you see any type of discharge or blood, get the child to a doctor immediately.

✔ **Shin splints:** *Shin splints* are painful injuries that occur on the lower shin — it feels like the front of your lower leg is burning — and can require a lengthy healing process. They primarily are caused by the weight pounding down on the player's shin. Other factors that can contribute are muscle weakness, poor flexibility, improper warm-up and cool-down exercises, and improper footwear. The four stages associated with shin splints are

- Pain after activity

- Pain before and after activity that doesn't affect performance

- Pain before, during, and after activity that adversely affects performance

- Constant pain that prohibits activity

✔ **Wind knocked out:** A youngster who gets the wind knocked out of him for the first time will likely start to panic when he has trouble breathing. Comfort him and have him take short, quick breaths. Ask him to pant like a puppy until he can resume breathing normally. You two can share a laugh about it later!

✔ **Tooth knocked out:** If a child has a tooth knocked out by an errant elbow or other incident, retrieve the tooth and place it in a sterile gauze pad with some saline added. Have the child immediately taken to a dentist (with the tooth along for the ride, of course).

✔ **Nosebleed:** When a player gets a bloody nose, slide on your latex gloves, grab some gauze to absorb the blood, and gently squeeze his nostrils together to try to stop the bleeding. If the bleeding doesn't stop after a couple minutes, get him to a doctor, because the injury could be more serious, such as a nasal fracture.

Handling emergency/first-aid situations

You devote countless hours during the season to working on offensive and defensive fundamentals. However, fast breaks and rebounds aren't life-and-death situations. You also need to find time to go over how you'll handle emergency situations. How you respond — and how quickly — can make the difference in saving a youngster's life. The following list presents some pointers to keep in mind:

✔ **Assess the situation.** You must be prepared for any type of injury, including unconsciousness. The acronym *COACH* is a handy reminder of how to respond in an emergency situation:

- **C:** Determine whether the child is *conscious*.

- **O:** Is the child breathing and getting *oxygen?*

Look at his lip color, feel his chest, or put your cheek next to his nose to see whether he's breathing. Feel for a pulse in his neck or wrist. If he has a pulse but isn't breathing, begin mouth-to-mouth resuscitation, but don't use chest compressions. If he isn't breathing and you can't find a pulse, initiate CPR and have someone call for immediate medical assistance. With young children, be especially careful not to press down on the lowest portion of the breastbone; doing so could injure the internal organs.

A coach should never provide any treatment that he isn't trained to do, because that can make the child's situation worse.

If the answer to the first two questions is *yes,* move on.

- **A:** *Ask* the youngster where he's hurt.

- **C:** *Control* the painful area.

- **H:** What type of *help* is required?

  Decide whether you need to call for immediate medical assistance and have the child taken to the hospital.

✔ **Know where you're playing.** Be aware of the name of the facility where you're playing or practicing, as well as the address. If you have to call 911, you'll want to provide as much accurate information as possible to ensure a quick response.

✔ **Have medical forms handy.** Medical personnel will benefit, as will the child, if you have the medical forms we discuss in Chapter 4. The form tells if a child is allergic to any type of medication, for example. Always carry the forms in your first-aid kit and have the kit easily accessible.

✔ **Provide first aid.** While awaiting the arrival of medical personnel, provide the first-aid care that you're trained to perform.

Proceed cautiously when dealing with any type of injury — particularly if the injury involves the head, neck, or spine. Never attempt to move a player who's lying on the ground with such an injury because you may cause further damage.

✔ **Alert the child's parents.** If the child's parents aren't in attendance, have one of your assistants call and let them know what's going on. Your foremost responsibility is caring for the child, so designate someone else to make that initial call to the parents.

✔ **Comfort the child.** If the child is conscious, comfort him by talking in a calm and relaxed voice. Tell him that he'll be okay and that medical help is on the way.

We encourage you to take a CPR class before the season begins. You can receive CPR and first-aid training from the American Red Cross or another nationally recognized organization.

Chapter 19

Challenges Every Coach Faces

• •

In This Chapter

▶ Solving parent problems

▶ Addressing issues with opposing and assistant coaches

▶ Handling problems with your own players

▶ Silencing bad spectator behavior

• •

Coaching a youth basketball team involves many fun activities that you're probably aware of, like designing practices and teaching skills, and some bad ones that may not be so obvious — and definitely aren't any fun — such as dealing with disruptive parents or other spectators, opposing coaches, and players. Hopefully, the times you must discipline a youngster or have a discussion with a parent regarding inappropriate comments will be few and far between. If a situation arises, this chapter is right there to give you the scoop on solving these issues so they don't spoil your players' season.

Dealing with Problematic Parents

Coaching youth basketball comes with many challenges, including some that pop up away from the court. Unfortunately, parents often present some of these challenges, many of which are unexpected for new coaches. Taking the time to conduct a preseason parents' meeting (see Chapter 4) helps lay the ground rules for the season, but sometimes the meeting isn't enough of a deterrent. Outlining your expectations for parental behavior doesn't guarantee that parents will be models of good sportsmanship all season long.

You must be prepared to step forward at the first hint of parental trouble. Turning your back on a problematic situation sends a message that bad behavior is acceptable and everything you talked about during your preseason meeting was meaningless. Dealing with problems swiftly lets the other team parents know that if they step out of line, you'll deal with them accordingly. The entire team of parents will appreciate your commitment to ensuring that the kids' experience won't be marred. Bottom line: Don't let a problem cast an ominous shadow over the team and your season. The following sections take a look at some of the more common problems that parents may pose and what approaches work best for handling them.

Why-doesn't-he-play-more parents

The most common complaint coaches hear from parents is that their youngsters aren't receiving the proper amount of playing time. Parents want the best for their kids, and when they sign them up for a basketball program, they want to see them out on the court dribbling, shooting, and defending rather than watching from the bench. That's why some parents track their kids' playing time more closely than their stocks and bonds.

Many of these parents have ridiculously unrealistic expectations of their kids' basketball abilities. As soon as parents see their child sitting on the bench, they begin worrying that you're compromising his athletic future and jeopardizing his basketball scholarship to a prestigious university.

Furthermore, some parents view their child's status on the team as a reflection of their parenting skills or their own athletic skills — a distorted thought indeed. They think if their child is skilled at sinking jump shots or grabbing rebounds — and he receives more playing time because of those skills — they must be doing a good parenting job. In their eyes, their child's playing time becomes a status symbol as they sit among the other parents in the stands.

If you have to deal with why-doesn't-he-play-more parents, keep the following points in mind to help calm the brewing storm:

- ✔ **Point to your league policy.** If your league has a policy on equal playing time, and you explain this policy to all the parents during your preseason meeting (see Chapter 4), you have more than enough ammunition to explain why you're rotating the kids in and out of the lineup. Let upset parents know that you enjoy coaching their child and you'd love to provide more playing time for him, but in fairness to the entire team and in your obligation to your league's rules, your job is to look out for the best interests of every youngster.

- ✔ **Remind them about your coaching philosophy.** Remind upset parents about your coaching philosophy (stated during the preseason meeting) that every child receives an equal amount of playing time. Also, if you hand out playing time based on practice attendance and not on ability, remind them and then work with them on solutions to ensure their child arrives on time. (See Chapter 2 for info on molding your philosophy.)

✔ **Track every child's playing time.** If parents question whether you're equally distributing playing time, you can refer to your minute-tracking sheet to show them that you (or an assistant coach) carefully monitor the playing time of each child. Written documentation of the measures you take to make the season fair is usually enough to quiet your critics.

Distributing playing time becomes even trickier — yes, that's hard to imagine — at the more advanced levels of play. At these levels, you give out minutes based on ability. For parents, seeing or hearing that their child isn't good enough to be on the court full time — or at least as much as the neighbor's kid — can be pretty tough. Be open with the parents and share your thoughts on how they can help practice with their youngster at home, if he's interested. For example, if the child is struggling with his jump shot, a few minutes each day at home, under the supervision of mom or dad, working on their release may be all it takes to get back on track and challenge for more playing time.

Perpetually late parents

One of the biggest headaches you're likely to deal with is a child who continually arrives late for practice or disrupts your playing-time rotation by showing up in the middle of games. Punishing a youngster for the tardiness of his parents is a touchy area and poses some tricky challenges for you. (As we discuss in Chapter 4, you should address the importance of punctuality at your preseason parents' meeting; however, sometimes that isn't enough.)

Some parents may not realize what a disruption their late arrival causes for everyone. If a parent is repeatedly tardy, have a brief conversation with him to discuss the necessity of preventing tardiness, and how it could negatively affect the child and take away from his enjoyment of and participation in the sport. The following are a few things you may want to mention:

✔ **Tardiness takes away teaching time.** Kids who aren't at practice on time miss your instruction and valuable participation time in drills.

✔ **Tardiness minimizes skill development.** Because many of the skills you'll teach follow a natural progression and build on each other, tardiness puts you and the child in a tough spot. When a child misses valuable instruction time, the situation compromises his development and limits his practice with particular skills.

✔ **Practice attendance equals playing time.** Remind parents that you'll distribute playing time in games based on practice attendance. The kids who regularly show up for practices deserve the bulk of the playing time on game day. Of course, use your best discretion if a child misses practice and has a good reason why. Certainly, a family emergency involving someone's health qualifies as a reasonable excuse and shouldn't detract from the child's playing time; while others, such as attending a friend's birthday party, isn't acceptable.

Be willing to explore solutions to fix a tardiness or absence problem. It could be as simple as having a teammate's parent drive from nearby to pick up the youngster and bring him to practice.

Win-at-all-costs parents

Naturally, parents want to see their kids excel on the court, and many want their kids to bring home shiny first-place trophies. This often stems from parents trying to live their lives through their children. Unfortunately, some parents place unrealistic expectations on their children — and you — to perform at exceedingly high levels and win tons of games, because maybe they were never able to enjoy athletic success growing up and to them their child's athletic pursuits represent another chance to do so. This state of mind forces a child to deal with skyrocketing expectations and the pressure to win, which is out of his control.

Win-at-all-costs parents, blinded by visions of championships, do whatever they can to ensure that their child's team wins, and that their youngster looks good in the process. They shout remarks at officials to intimidate them and get favorable calls, and they criticize opposing coaches when their child's team is losing. And yes, they even throw criticism your way.

As a coach, you have to make sure that your kids don't lose sight of what's really important: having fun, developing skills, learning the game, and displaying good sportsmanship. You must ensure that overly competitive parents don't get out of control and ruin the experience for everyone. Here are some points to keep in mind to handle these parents:

- ✔ **Recognize the warning signs.** You or an assistant should pay attention to parents' comments and reactions during games or what they say to their kids afterward. If they're counterproductive to what you're trying to teach, you must address them. Groans when your team misses a shot or when a call goes in the other team's favor are clear signals that the parents' behavior is headed in the wrong direction. Keeping an eye for these reactions can also give you some insight into what type of environment the child is living in at home, and perhaps hearing more positive words of encouragement from you during practices and games can counteract a lot of the negativity the child is forced to endure daily.

- ✔ **Understand that there may be a target on your back.** When you deal with win-at-all-costs parents, you should recognize that you're their biggest target for criticism. They may critique every decision you make, from your starting lineup to your substitution patterns, and offer unsolicited advice — even more so after a loss!

Although you don't have control over what parents say at home, you do have control over what's said while you're coaching at practice or games. Look at the basketball court as a classroom where you teach the kids the game and life lessons. Don't allow outside influences to disrupt the messages that you want to send.

 Give the parents a brief and friendly talk before your next game or practice to remind them that winning isn't the most important factor (see Chapter 2 for more on your coaching philosophy). Explain that they need to keep their emotions in check and that you'd hate to see a child embarrassed because of his parents' behavior. If the behavior continues, they start to become disruptive parents. Head to the later "Disruptive parents" section for the lowdown on how to take action from here.

Babysitting-service parents

Parents juggle chaotic schedules when it comes to their children, work, and all their extracurricular activities. Some parents, in efforts to manage their time, look at basketball practices and games as a convenient babysitting service. They can swing by, drop off their children, and knock off some errands while the kids are under your care. Mom or dad simply may not have the luxury of being able to hang out courtside during practices. But, ideally, you want the parents to be, at least to some extent, part of the practice regimen, providing positive support and encouragement for the entire team. As for game day, strongly encourage all the parents to attend. Doing so is important for children to have positive support and encouragement from their loved ones, because it makes sinking those shots and grabbing those rebounds that much more special and meaningful.

Share with parents before and during the season that it's important to attend practices, because parents who regularly show up gain valuable insight into the skill development of their children. Having parents at practice also reinforces your coaching philosophies and strategies because they'll get to see how you interact with their kids on a regular basis.

 One of the best ways to get parents to stick around for practice is to include them in some of your drills, which we discuss in Chapter 6. When babysitting-service parents get to see how involved the other parents are with their children, they may want to start hanging around to be a part of the action. Just make sure that you retain control of the practice and don't allow it to veer off course by well-meaning parents who begin throwing out their own ideas for how to run the drill or execute a skill. Explain beforehand that you welcome their involvement, but to leave the teaching and instructing to you so that the players aren't overwhelmed.

A parent's presence at practice is important for several other reasons, too. Here are some more examples:

- When the kids sink shots from the perimeter during practice, being able to see their parents smiling is the type of moment that sticks in their heads — and gives them confidence that they can do it again the next time down the floor.

- When they know their parents will be there, kids look forward to returning to practice to go at it and gain parental approval.

- Parents who attend practice can see how their kids interact with other kids and listen to and follow coaching instructions. If they don't like what they see, they can take the appropriate action. If they're impressed, they can pile on the praise!

Disruptive parents

The majority of your parents will provide positive support and encouragement to their kids and their teammates. Unfortunately, parents who display disruptive behaviors at youth basketball events have become increasingly common. Insults, cursing, ranting, and raving — along with violent outbreaks — appear far too often. Why some parents behave irresponsibly and irrationally is perplexing, and the answer probably involves a bunch of factors that are completely out of your control. But what *is* in your control is your ability to keep negative behavior from embarrassing the children, disrupting the game or practice, and impacting everyone's enjoyment of the sport.

How do you approach a disruptive parent? Although we hope you never have to deal with these unpleasant situations, in the following sections we provide you with some strategies in the event that you do. And because you're only human and such disruptions can test your patience, we also advise you on what not to do.

What to do

The following list presents some approaches you can use to help keep parents' tempers in check and the game/practice moving along without any unnecessary disruptions:

- **Meet with the offending parent a day after the game.** Arrange to speak with the offending parent the following day. Giving the individual 24 hours to cool down often gives him a different perspective than if you talk soon after the game when emotions can still be high. If it was a relatively minor comment, but one that still needs to be corrected, you can chat in private to make sure it doesn't happen again. Try something along the lines of, "I know your son got fouled on that jump shot and the official missed the call, but not all the calls will go our way this season. Please remember that I need you and the other parents to set an example of good sportsmanship. I know it's difficult, but please don't let it happen again."

✔ **Maintain calm behavior.** Keeping calm is the key to defusing a tense situation between you and an upset parent. Setting a civil tone right from the start is a critical building block for a productive discussion that won't spiral out of control. Never surrender to frustration and raise your voice or lose control of your emotions; as soon as you allow that to happen, you lose the respect of the other parents.

✔ **Provide a friendly reminder.** Many times, parents may not even realize that they're behaving inappropriately. A firm but friendly reminder to keep their emotions in check often is all that's needed.

✔ **Remove parents from the facility only as a last resort.** Removal is an extreme step to take. Go this route if it's the only option left to ensure the well-being of the young participants and the spectators. Being thrown out is embarrassing not only for the parent, but also for the child whose game is being interrupted by mom or dad's removal.

✔ **Know your league's options.** An increasing number of basketball leagues around the country are instituting parent sportsmanship programs — both voluntary and mandatory — to give parents a clear understanding of their roles and responsibilities. You may want to recommend that your league adopt a program so that all the parents can work together to help ensure that you meet the best interests of the kids. (For more on getting familiar with your league, head to Chapter 2.)

What not to do

Sometimes, as frustration levels mount, you may be tempted to try all sorts of ill-advised tactics to rid yourself of a parental problem. We advise you to steer clear of the following methods for handling disruptive parents:

✔ **Don't get defensive.** Some parents may use a meeting that you set up to discuss a problem as an opportunity to bombard you with accusations, complaints, and other negative comments. No matter how frustrated or upset you get, resist the urge to fire back in defense of your coaching abilities; doing so only inflames an already tense situation.

✔ **Don't embarrass the parent.** Being the parent of a young player isn't easy. Parents, because they want the best for their youngsters, may react without thinking to certain situations. For instance, if they see their child get fouled hard and the official doesn't blow the whistle, keeping their displeasure to themselves can be extremely difficult. When you hear a comment shouted from the stands, try just looking over your shoulder at the offending parent rather than saying something that everyone can hear. The brief eye contact lets the parent know that shouting in that manner is unacceptable.

✔ **Don't direct frustration with a parent toward his child.** No matter how poorly behaved a parent is, never take out your frustration on the child. The youngsters on your team have no control over how their parents behave, so don't trim down their playing time, shift their positions, or take any other drastic measures to rein in the emotional outbursts of their parents. Chances are the youngster is already embarrassed by his parents' actions. Continue coaching the children and applauding their efforts; hopefully, your chats with the parents will sink in and change their behavior.

✔ **Don't resort to physical threats or violence to make your point.** No matter the situation, violence (or the threat of it) is never the answer to solve a problem. If you encounter a volatile situation that jeopardizes the safety and well-being of the kids or spectators, contact the authorities immediately.

Some league policies stipulate that the coach contact the league director when problems arise, and the director deals with them accordingly. Be sure you know your league's policies, but never hesitate to call the police if the situation gets out of control.

Putting a Muzzle on Problematic Coaches

Chances are good that if your coaching career spans multiple seasons, you'll encounter a coach who just doesn't get the point of youth basketball. Situations can happen on the opposing bench or even on your bench with an assistant coach. Although you're more likely to see rude and offensive behavior in the more advanced levels, when the competition becomes more intense, it also occurs at the beginning levels.

The best way to combat inappropriate behavior from an opposing coach is to maintain a level head and a calm demeanor. These situations test how well you can adhere to your coaching philosophy (which we discuss in Chapter 2). The following sections show some types of offensive coaches you may run into and give some tips for maintaining your composure.

Your top priority at all times is protecting the best interests of your players. Your kids take their cues from you and how you act when tensions rise and the blood pressure escalates.

Opposing coaches who encourage unsafe play

Ensuring the safety of your players is always one of your top priorities. Sure, some minor bumps and bruises are part of the game. However, if your team is going against a coach whose players use unsafe methods that put your team's safety in jeopardy, you have to take immediate action. Never hesitate to address a safety issue, which could involve players using excessive force when fouling or pushing a player from behind when he's going for a lay-up. Seeing unnecessary force being used on the court is pretty obvious to spot — such as players being knocked to the ground while attempting shots. The following list presents some steps you can take:

✔ **Speak with an official.** Address your concerns in a respectable manner and express the reasons for why you think your players are being put at unnecessary risk. Be clear that you're concerned about the welfare of all the kids and not about how the official is calling the game. One of an official's most important responsibilities is to ensure the safety of all the players, so work with him — not against him.

✔ **Pull your kids off the court.** If you feel the tone and nature of the game haven't changed after speaking with an official, your only recourse is removing your team from the court. Chances are, you'll never encounter a situation this bad, but if you do, take action immediately. Continuing with the game just for the sake of finishing it, risking an injury to your players, just isn't worth it.

✔ **Speak with the league director.** Have him watch a game with this particular team to make his own opinion. If he agrees with you, he can definitely put a stop to the improper methods this coach is using.

Don't confront the opposing coach. Always use an official as your intermediary. Heading over to the other bench just creates the potential for more conflict to develop. Your approach can also antagonize the other coach, who may feel threatened, as if you're questioning his coaching techniques in front of everyone. He may react negatively and view the situation as a ploy to affect his team's play — particularly if his team is ahead.

Opposing coaches who are poor sports

We hope that all the coaches in your league will take after you and exhibit model behavior instead of acting like they're coaching in the NBA. Nonetheless, you need to know how to deal with unsportsmanlike coaches in case they get out of hand. What are some examples of unsportsmanlike behavior? A coach questioning every call that goes against his team; making comments to spectators in the stands about the official or the opposing team; and making comments for all to hear belittling your players while going on about how his players are so much better. Here are a few tips to keep in mind for handling yourself and your team:

✔ **Stay calm.** Opposing coaches who exhibit unsportsmanlike behavior will challenge your patience and test your poise. No matter what, avoid retaliating and remain a model of good behavior for your team.

✔ **Tell your players to ignore the coach's behavior and turn it into a valuable lesson.** Kids can see and hear what's going on, so use the situation to your advantage. Point out to your team that the coach's antics are unacceptable, and challenge them to rise above this type of behavior and play hard while being good sports. Ask them to forget about his shouting and stick to how they've been taught to play the game.

✔ **Alert the league director.** When an opposing coach behaves inappropriately, be sure to make the league director aware of the situation so that she can take steps to prevent this type of behavior from occurring again.

Handling your dissenting assistants

Assistant coaches are valuable assets to a youth basketball team, fulfilling a number of roles and responsibilities. But anytime you bring in another person to help out, you run the risk that he may stray from what's best for the players — in other words, stray from your coaching philosophy. (As we discuss in Chapter 4, you need to exercise great caution and do some research before enlisting help.)

What are some of the problems that your assistant coaches may pose? The following list takes a look at some of the more common issues:

✔ **He wants his child on the court more.** Perhaps your assistant had ulterior motives from the start, grabbing the role to get his child on the court more or to ensure that he gets to play a particular position.

✔ **He causes distractions on game day.** Even the nicest and quietest assistants can turn into lunatics who want to scream instructions to the players as soon as the game tips off.

✔ **He's a poor teacher.** You don't want to teach your youngsters the wrong ways to perform skills or, worst of all, unsafe techniques that can put everyone at unnecessary risk. You may have some great, well-meaning parents who volunteered to assist, but if their knowledge of basketball is limited or skewed, they can cause many problems on your team. Have the assistant follow your lead while teaching each skill. This way he sees exactly how you want skills taught.

✔ **His philosophy conflicts with yours.** During your preseason meeting with the parents, you should stress that winning takes a backseat to skill development and fun. Even if the parent you choose as an assistant nods his head in agreement, you may learn that he won't be on board with those views when the games start.

Keep an eye out — especially during your first few practices — to closely monitor how your assistants interact with and teach the kids. If they're not getting the job done to your standards or adhering to your philosophies, have a private, one-on-one talk with them right away. During the chat, reinforce your goals for this season. Usually, this chat is enough to get assistants back on the right track. If it isn't and problems continue, or the coaches simply don't agree with your vision or opinions, let them know that it's in the team's best interest that they surrender their duties.

Taking Care of Discipline Problems on Your Team

Teaching kids how to execute on offense and how to break an opposing defense are some of the many areas of the game that you know will challenge your coaching skills. Making sure the kids listen to your instructions, respect your authority, and abide by your team rules, however, can pose a whole new set of challenges that you may not have been aware of — or prepared for — when you volunteered for your post.

Because you're dealing with kids, you'll probably have to discipline a child who steps over the line at some point during the season. Your first responsibility is to uncover what is bothering the child, and then work to fix it. Many times, children act out for the same types of reasons because they're frustrated at their lack of progress or because they feel like you, your assistants, their teammates, or their parents don't value their contributions.

When dealing with problematic players, you always hold the trump card: playing time. Withholding playing time is a great equalizer, attitude adjuster, personality changer, and attention getter, all rolled up into one. Kids don't enjoy having their fannies stuck on the bench while their friends are out on the court. Taking away playing time is no different than a parent taking away television, computer games, or treats from a child at home. Use it as needed to get the results you want. For more advice on dealing with kids who give you problems, check out the following sections. (Chapter 5 goes into detail about how to deal with many types of young people — a valuable asset to have for the upcoming season.)

Disciplining players: Some general advice

When dealing with behavioral problems among your players, keep the following guidelines in mind for how you should handle the situations:

- **Make the punishment fit the crime.** The punishment you dispense must match the team rule that was broken. When determining punishment, allow yourself flexibility based on the severity of the problem. Every situation is different and must be dealt with accordingly.

  For example, a child forgetting her water bottle at practice doesn't merit losing playing time in the next game. A youngster who swears at an official, however, deserves to spend the next game on the bench.

  When handing out punishment, let the rest of the team know why you're disciplining that youngster — for example, why she won't be available for the first half of the next game. This reinforces that you won't tolerate bad behavior, reducing the chances of others making the same mistake.

- **Follow through with your punishment.** When you tell players how they'll be punished for their misbehavior, be sure to follow through with it — no matter how much you hate doing so. You want to maintain your authority and respect with the team.

- **Subject all players to the same discipline.** One of the most disastrous moves you can make is to play favorites by punishing some kids for infractions and not others. A youngster's advanced ability to shoot the basketball doesn't mean that a separate set of rules apply to her. Elevating certain players above others is a terrible precedent to set, because it sabotages team chemistry and creates friction.

- **Forgive and forget.** After the discipline with the child is complete, sweep the situation to the side and move on. Don't hold a grudge or treat the child differently than you did before the problem occurred. Forgive, forget, and focus on making sure the youngster feels like a valued member of the team. Right away, recognize when he does something well to reassure him that you've forgotten the past problems.

Now that you have some advice on what to do when handing out discipline, be sure to heed the following advice on what not to do:

- **Avoid laps.** When a child misbehaves, sending her on a lap or two around the court may be really tempting, but refrain from doing so. If children relate conditioning and running with punishment, they may develop a negative outlook on this aspect of the sport, which becomes especially important at the more advanced levels of play.

Instead of sending players on laps, send them to the sidelines. Watching teammates play from the sidelines is no fun, making it a pretty effective form of punishment. You also can have them round up all the basketballs and pylons at the end of practice as punishment.

✔ **Don't discipline for playing mistakes.** Never discipline kids who make mistakes in practices or games — such as failing to guard an opposing player or box out an opponent on a rebound. Mistakes are simply part of playing basketball.

If one of your players intentionally tries to injure another player or displays unsportsmanlike conduct toward the opposing team or a referee, immediately remove her from the game. This type of behavior may warrant further disciplinary action, depending on the severity of the action, her intent, and other factors that led up to the incident.

Child who refuses to listen to instructions

You may have kids on your team who think that they know everything there is to know about basketball. These youngsters may tune out your teachings and instructions and do their own thing. Inattentiveness can be especially troublesome if these players employ incorrect techniques during drills.

If a child isn't performing a skill correctly, and you suspect that the reason is because she wasn't paying attention to your instruction, ask the child — it's okay to do so in front of the team in a non-threatening and non-embarrassing manner — why she isn't executing the skill like you just demonstrated. Maybe she didn't understand your instructions, and out of frustration, she tried performing the skill the way she thought it should be done. Of course, use your discretion on how you want to confront the child based on her personality and how she has responded to interaction with you throughout the season.

If the child has no good excuse, or you actually saw her purposely ignoring your instructions, sit her down and have her watch how the rest of the team practices what you've told them to do. After a few minutes, ask her if she's ready to return to play and willing to listen. A non-listener should be much more receptive to your instruction after spending time on the sidelines watching her teammates having fun.

Child who's disruptive when you're talking

Some of your kids may be more talkative than television newscasters. Unfortunately, kids who are more interested in talking than in listening to what you have to say can be major distractions to the team — even if they are entertaining and funny. If the other players only hear bits and pieces of your instructions, it compromises your effectiveness as a coach.

How do you quiet the vocal cords of kids whose mouths seem to be constantly moving? At the first sign of a problem, don't embarrass the child; simply remind the whole team that when you're speaking, everyone needs to remain quiet and pay attention. If that approach fails, you may have to call the player out in front of his teammates. For example, you can say something like, "Evan, please be quiet while I'm addressing the team. It's important that everyone hears what I'm going over. If you have a comment or question, please wait until I'm done to speak up." You can also ask players to repeat what you just said. Often, this is enough to grab their attention because they know that you are holding everyone accountable for what you are teaching them.

Employing the three-strike technique

Addressing discipline problems at the first sign of trouble, before they escalate and cause further disruption, is crucial for maintaining team order — and your sanity. The *three-strike technique* works well for disciplining players in a timely and fair fashion. This approach is firm but gives youngsters a little room to maneuver so they don't ruin their seasons the first time they cross the line. (Informing the parents of the disciplinary procedures you'll follow throughout the season is a good idea; Chapter 4 covers the preseason meeting, a perfect time to do this.) The following sections show how the three-strike technique works.

Strike one! Issue a verbal warning

The first time a child displays unacceptable behavior calls for a verbal warning. The warning puts him on notice that you're not pleased with his behavior, and if it happens again, he'll face harsher punishment. Some examples of behaviors that merit a strike one warning include unsportsmanlike conduct, such as refusing to shake the hand of an opposing player following a loss, or pouting when he is removed from the game for a teammate.

You may have to deliver the warning in public depending on when the unacceptable behavior occurs. If it happens after the game, you can pull the child aside and talk to him in private. If it happens during the game, a one-on-one talk on the bench, in which others may be in earshot, may be enough. Just keep your voice low and keep the child's attention on what you're telling him he did that isn't acceptable.

If the child acts out in the same manner again, this action warrants a strike two measure, because it's clear that the child is challenging you (check out the next section). Be prepared; never allow a child to trample your authority.

When you have to reprimand a child, be sure to let his parents know about it. Let them know that you want their child to be a part of this team and that he won't face repercussions the rest of the season if he behaves appropriately. Relay exactly what you said to the child in his verbal warning so that his parents can reinforce what you said at home. Reinforcement by parents makes the child aware of the seriousness of his behavior, and conveys that he must make immediate improvement to continue playing on the team.

Strike two! Discipline the player

When a child knows that you'll enforce a stricter measure of punishment if he repeats a behavior, he often won't do it again. Of course, kids are kids, and some can't break their bad habits or simply want to put you to the test to see if you're really serious about punishing them. If a player continues to disobey your instructions, you have to bump up the severity of the punishment in order to derail the behavior before it becomes a major distraction.

Taking away some of his playing time in the next game sends a strong message that if he doesn't stop this behavior immediately, he won't get back on the court. If you're coaching young kids, have them pick up all the loose basketballs and pylons after practice. At the advanced levels of play, if the problem is with a starter, replace him in the starting line-up.

When doling out the strike two punishment, let the player know in clear and specific terms that if he misbehaves any more, he'll jeopardize his future with the team.

Strike three! Remove the player from the team (at least for now)

Rarely do youngsters venture into strike three territory. With this three-tiered approach to punishment, and with coveted playing time at stake, most bad behavior takes a dramatic turn for the better before kids ever reach this point. In the rare event that a child simply refuses to adhere to your instructions, you may have to remove him from the team. You have a responsibility to meet the needs of all the kids on your team, so you can't allow the behavior of one child to ruin the season for everyone. You never want to banish a child, though sometimes it's unavoidable.

Before making the decision to remove the child, meet with the league director — and parents — to inform them of what has transpired so far. Perhaps you can all reach a solution that doesn't require such a drastic measure.

In order to give the child every opportunity to make amends, you can allow him to return to the team — if he's willing to apologize to you and the team and he promises to display good behavior. Kids can definitely turn over a new leaf; maybe a few days away from the team has made the player realize how much he truly loves playing basketball and being with his teammates at practice. Upon his dismissal, if he knows that you've left the door cracked open for his return as long as he offers an apology for his previous indiscretions, everything may work out in the end.

Snuffing Out Problematic Spectators

You have a responsibility to the kids on both teams, and to all the peaceful spectators, to ensure that negative comments from the stands don't infringe on people's enjoyment of the game. On game day, many people will pack the stands. Some will be familiar faces — the moms and dads and brothers and sisters of your players. Maybe some aunts and uncles and even grandparents will come, armed with their cameras and video recorders. Perhaps coaches who just finished games or who will be taking the court in the next game also will take a seat to watch. With such a mix of people on hand, there's a possibility that disruptive behavior will occur.

When you (or an assistant coach) hear inappropriate comments made by spectators — other than from the moms and dads of your players, whom you've established relationships with — get the attention of the league director or the person in charge at the facility. He or she will take the appropriate action from that point. You can also send an assistant coach to get the director so you don't surrender valuable time with your players.

Because you don't know the individual making the inappropriate comments, you don't want to make matters worse by confronting him or her. Doing so increases the chances of the situation becoming volatile. Instead, rely on the league director to speak with the offending individual or, if necessary, have that person removed from the stands.

During your preseason parents' meeting (see Chapter 4), encourage parents to avoid confronting unruly spectators during the season. What could be more embarrassing for the child than to see a parent arguing with someone in the stands? Ask them to alert the league director who can take the appropriate action.

Chapter 20

Coaching a Travel Team

Some experienced young basketball players will start to develop real talent and real passion for playing the game. These youngsters will crave opportunities to participate at more competitive levels. The same goes for many coaches who gain experience; they'll want to seek chances to work with kids at more advanced stages. What these players and coaches seek is the world of travel (and all-star) teams. Coaching an advanced team can provide plenty of challenges for you, because the players are more skilled, the games are more intense, and your game-day strategy (see Chapter 7) is more vital.

If you think you're ready to coach a travel team, this chapter is for you. Here we give you the secrets to putting together and conducting a tryout for the team — one of the most important components of coaching a travel team. We outline what you should keep your eye on when evaluating players and give you the scoop on breaking bad news to kids who don't make the team. After the season gets underway, you may encounter issues that you haven't considered before, such as preventing burnout, dealing with travel accommodations, and even handling curfews. This chapter also shows you how to handle these unique issues. Good luck!

Defining a Travel Team

Travel teams are for skilled youngsters who want to focus on basketball as their main sport and want to play against top-level competition on a regular basis. The travel-team environment is vastly different from that of the regular youth league programs we cover in the rest of this book. For instance:

- ✔ The games are highly competitive, and teams face opponents from different communities, cities, or, in some cases, states.

- ✔ Being part of a travel team requires more time commitment on the part of everyone. A typical week involves a couple practices, and the weekends are filled with travel and tournament competition.

- ✔ Travel-team seasons typically run longer than recreational seasons, and they usually entail a larger financial commitment from parents. The money covers tournament entry fees and travel and hotel expenses.

Before volunteering to coach a travel team, make sure you get answers to all your questions about league type, age group, and travel ahead of time. You don't want to find yourself overwhelmed by the demands (and time away from your family) if the job turns out to be much more than you anticipated. The following sections provide a bit more detail about what a travel team is.

What age groups are travel teams appropriate for?

Because of the enormous time commitment, most experts recommend that kids under 12 shouldn't be involved with travel teams. That's a general guideline, because kids mature at different rates — both emotionally and physically. Some 11-year-olds may be better equipped to handle the travel-team experience than some 13-year-olds, for example.

Even with youngsters who reach their teenage years and are involved in travel teams, the experience shouldn't dominate their lives to such an extent that they don't have the time or energy to participate in other sports or school activities.

Youngsters on a travel team must have a real desire and motivation to play more frequently. If their interest and motivation is suspect, they should stick with the recreational style of basketball we cover in the rest of this book. As long as you focus on the best interests of all the kids, the recreational and the travel-team experiences can be richly rewarding for all involved.

How much travel is typically involved?

The travel associated with all star teams varies from community to community. One travel team may have enough competition in the surrounding area, limiting its travel time to a few minutes on local highways or city streets; another team may have to pack its suitcases for overnight stays more often than a flight attendant. Depending on the program in your area, you may get a say in how much traveling you do to get to tournaments. The age and skill level of the players also dictates the travel schedule.

Assembling Your Travel Team

Putting together a travel team is a challenging process that involves several steps: You have to put together and conduct a tryout; watch and evaluate potential players; and break the news — both good and bad — to the youngsters about whether they made the team. Although the process is challenging, you can do it. This section helps make sure the process runs smoothly and achieves its goal: finding you a talented and cohesive team.

Holding a tryout (not a beauty pageant)

A well-planned and executed tryout reflects your good coaching skills, impresses parents and other onlookers, and makes choosing the players who are best suited to play on your team that much easier. You can't hold a successful tryout by winging it. Heed the pointers in the following sections to hold a tryout that allows you to select the best players for your team.

Planning the tryout

When hosting a tryout, make sure parents and youngsters are aware of it. Contact your weekly community newspapers, which should be happy to run your tryout announcement at no cost. The same goes for other media outlets, such as radio stations, daily newspapers, and public access television stations in your area. Local recreation agencies and schools also are great places to distribute flyers about the tryout. In most cases, the team you're coaching will be part of a parks and recreation program, so you can arrange court time for tryouts by contacting the recreation director.

Starting the tryout on the right foot

The kids and their parents will be nervous before the tryout begins. To ease everyone's nerves, start the tryout with a good first impression. Basketball is fun to play, and the tryout process shouldn't be life or death. Even though coveted spots on the team are at stake, don't make the tryout process feel any more stressful than it already is. The bottom line: Everyone should know that they're special players, but that only a certain number can be chosen to fill out the roster.

These simple steps lighten the atmosphere and help you run a smooth tryout:

1. **Greet everyone with a warm smile and a friendly hello.**

2. **Introduce yourself and any assistants who are helping out.**

   Doing so puts a name with a face and helps make the kids more comfortable with you and your staff. Following your introductions, you can thank the parents for bringing their child to the tryout, and politely ask them to remain in the stands to watch so you can ensure that there are no distractions on the floor.

3. **Explain how you've structured the tryout (see the following section).**

   Telling kids what to expect will help ease their stress, calm their nerves, and allow them to perform to the best of their abilities.

4. **Run the kids through a series of stretches to adequately prepare their bodies to participate in the tryout.**

   Even though you won't see some of these kids again, you need to ensure the safety and well-being of every child under your watch. Approach the tryout the same way you would an ordinary practice (see Chapter 18).

Don't choose prospective players to lead the stretches. Even if you're familiar with a player and know that he would do a great job, singling him out sends the wrong message to the others. Some kids and parents may think that you're already playing favorites and that certain kids have made the team before the tryout even begins.

Running a well-structured and effective tryout

A well-structured tryout is limited to one hour for kids ages 12 and under. For older kids, you can bump it up to 1½ to 2 hours. If you need to hold multiple short sessions to effectively evaluate a great number of kids, that's fine. The more times you can see a youngster play and evaluate his skills, the better handle you'll get on his abilities. Plus, a talented youngster who's highly skilled may have a bad day, so getting another look at him during a second session will give you a better gauge of his abilities.

To make the best use of your time, keep the following points in mind:

- **Simulate game situations.** Put players in situations that closely mirror game conditions to see how they respond. For example, timed sprints down the court and trying to determine how quickly a youngster can dribble the ball through a series of cones aren't great evaluation tools.

  An alternative to dribbling through cones is to pair the kids up, with one youngster on offense and the other on defense. Have the offensive player dribble the length of the floor while the defender tries to make that action as difficult as possible. This drill gives you a good sense of how kids will handle the ball with defenders in their faces, and how they'll put pressure on opposing players. (For some other drills you can use during the tryout, head to Chapters 11, 14, and 17.)

✔ **Play mini-games.** Observing players in two-on-two or three-on-three games provides a wealth of information on their abilities. They get to handle the ball more often than in a five-on-five game. They'll face other situations more often as well, such as defending a player driving to the basket or delivering a pass to a teammate who's cutting toward the hoop.

✔ **Limit the stations.** Using *stations* — a spot reserved for free-throw shooting or bounce passing, for instance — is fine; just be sure you don't load the floor with too many of them. If you run a dozen stations simultaneously, you can't effectively evaluate all the players.

Because the purpose of the tryout is to evaluate the kids' skills, both social and basketball, you don't want to get too caught up in coaching. You can sprinkle your tryout with a *few* coaching pointers if you notice improper technique; this way, you can observe how the kids react to instruction, feedback, and even constructive criticism.

After the tryout, be sure to thank the players for following your instructions and giving their best effort, and thank the parents for getting the kids to the tryout on time and adjusting their busy schedules to accommodate their kids.

Evaluating during the tryout

As the kids run up and down the court performing their skills, your job — and that of any assistants — is to keep close tabs on their performances to determine who deserves the chance to play on your team. During your evaluation, utilize the following suggestions:

✔ **Use assistants.** Particularly if you have a large turnout, having a few more sets of eyes is helpful. If you have several adults helping you out, make sure that they get a chance to see all the kids; otherwise, their evaluations won't be as accurate and comprehensive as they can be.

If you're taking the place of a coach who handled the team last season, or you know another travel-team coach, ask for his advice or see whether he can come out to give you his input. A former coach has valuable experience on what type of kids it takes to play and compete at this level.

✔ **Put together a list of skills.** Make a list of the skills you want to check out, such as dribbling, passing, shooting, team play, rebounding, attitude, and defending. Hand out the list to your assistants, and keep one for yourself.

✔ **Develop a rating system.** You can use a basic method where evaluators rate kids on a three-point scale. A 3 means that the player performs the skill above average; a 2 means he's average at the skill; and a 1 means he's below average. The less complex your rating system, the greater the chance that you'll identify the best players.

✔ **Hand out rosters.** Create a roster with the kids' names or tryout numbers on it, along with clearly marked categories to rate the kids. Leave space for additional comments, which can be useful when trying to decide between two players who finish the tryout with similar scores.

Selecting the most fitting players

Evaluating how a youngster handles and shoots the ball, as well as how she performs at the defensive end of the floor — pure basketball skills — is obviously important. However, other areas that you may not have given a lot of thought to deserve your attention, too, such as the following:

✔ **Teamwork:** Assessing how players work with their teammates is crucial. A great ball handler is an asset to your team if she looks for open teammates, but she's a liability if she's reluctant to give up the ball. A highly skilled player must also be a team player in order to fit into the framework of your squad.

✔ **Demeanor:** Does the player get noticeably upset when a teammate fails to deliver an accurate pass to her? Does she get visibly frustrated when teammates don't handle her passes efficiently? You want players on your team who are supportive rather than negative toward their teammates.

✔ **Level of competitiveness:** Don't neglect the mental side of the game. Monitor which kids are the real competitors. For example, when a player has a shot blocked, does she become tentative and reluctant to shoot again, or does she remain aggressive and continue taking the ball to the basket? Likewise, is she a good sport who plays within the rules, or does she resort to less-than-ideal tactics when things aren't going her way?

After you take into consideration all this feedback, you need to make a decision. Meet with your assistant coaches immediately following the tryout so everyone can share their observations while the session is fresh in your minds. Your first priority is to put a starting lineup on the floor, so discuss who's best-suited to handle each position. After that, focus on building depth at each position, because having several centers won't do you much good if you don't have players you can count on at the other positions.

Although the assistants' evaluations are helpful, as the head coach you have the final say. Don't just count on an evaluation score to determine a child's fate. Rely on your instincts and gut feelings, too, about whether the child is a good fit for your team.

Breaking the good and bad news

One of the best parts of coaching a travel team is seeing the huge smiles on the kids' faces when you let them know that they've made the team. Of course, one of the worst aspects of the job is telling the other kids that they didn't make it. Here are some pointers to keep in mind when breaking both the good and the bad news:

- ✔ **Notify each player face to face.** In fairness to every kid who sweated and gave it his all, you should personally let every child know whether he made it. The youngster gave the tryout his best, and he deserves to hear in person your evaluation of his play. If a large number of players tried out and having one-on-one conversations in person isn't feasible, deliver the news over the phone at the very least.

- ✔ **Make your decisions in a timely manner.** Think about how it drives you crazy waiting to hear a prospective employer's decision after you go through a job interview. The kids feel the same way after the tryout, so don't drag out the process.

- ✔ **Spell out playing-time specifics.** When giving the good news, clearly explain to the kids and their parents that you determine playing time by ability. Some parents may be under the impression that your decision means their child will start every game or have plenty of playing time thrown his way. Make sure everyone understands that this level is much different from the recreational level. Also, remind them when practices and games will be played to ensure that the youngsters, as well as the parents, can handle the schedule demands.

- ✔ **Sprinkle encouraging words throughout any conversation.** You never want a child to regret that he tried out because he didn't make the team. Sure, he'll feel disappointment, but what you say and how you say it will determine whether the disappointment lingers for a couple days or drags on for months. You want the child to use this experience as motivation to work on his skills so he returns a stronger player the next time tryouts are held. Make sure you encourage the player to try out again next time.

Informing a child that he didn't make the team can crush his confidence and self-esteem, so do everything you can to minimize his disappointment. Let the youngster and his parents know what areas of his game impressed you, and identify the areas that they can devote more time to. Offer recommendations for improvement, and encourage him to try out again next season. Even if the reason he failed to make the team is a touchy area — because of poor sportsmanship, for instance — you need to address the issue so it doesn't keep him from participating again next season.

Hitting the Road

Coaching a travel team involves more than figuring out who you should start at center or whether you should employ a zone defense in your next game. You have plenty of other issues to deal with — especially away from the court — that directly impact your team's (and the parents') experience. These issues include safety, other off-the-court issues, and travel arrangements. This section highlights these areas and prepares you for the road ahead.

Addressing safety issues off the court

What happens on the court is just one of your major responsibilities when coaching a travel team; you also have to monitor and control what takes place away from it. Taking your team to an out-of-town tournament that requires an overnight stay is an enormous responsibility. You have to ensure the safety of every child on the court, on the road, and at the location where the team stays overnight. You're accountable for all the kids at all times.

Implement a buddy system — each child is assigned a partner that he must keep track of at all times — to ensure that no youngster wanders off out of sight. Strictly enforce that no player is ever to leave the premises for any reason and that doing so will result in being banned from the team for the remainder of the season (see Chapter 19 for more disciplinary actions).

Handling other off-court issues

When you take a team of kids — and their parents — to an out-of-town tournament, the potential for problems exists. Along with "organizer" and "protector," the title of coach requires that you assume the role of "cop." Some of the issues you may have to deal with on the road include

- ✔ **Enforcing curfews:** Someone has to be the bad guy when it comes to enforcing curfews, and this job falls on your shoulders. To perform at their best on the court, the kids need to stick to the established curfew. The ages of your kids and the starting time of your next game should dictate the curfew you set.

- ✔ **Allowing extracurricular activities:** Competing in tournaments in different locations may provide opportunities for sightseeing and other extracurricular activities away from the court. The season isn't just about basketball. Visiting new locales can be a culturally enriching experience and something the kids will remember and benefit from long after their basketball careers are over.

You must consider several factors when determining what activities your players can do. You don't want them to be so exhausted that they can't give you their best effort. Before departing for an event, go over the tournament schedule with the players and their parents and let them know whether they have time for extracurricular activities.

Choosing destinations

As the head coach, you have the final say on everything from who starts in the next game to how long the kids will practice. You also make the call on which tournaments the team will participate in. After you determine where the team will compete, arrangements need to be made to get the players and parents there.

Try to appoint a travel team coordinator to assist with these responsibilities. Check to see if any of the parents has an interest in handling this duty, because it can be a time-consuming task. You also need to meet with the parents to determine who's willing to drive, or if you need to rent a van or bus to keep the kids together.

Surviving the Travel Team Season

Because a typical travel team schedule features more practices and games than youngsters are accustomed to, they often take a little time to adjust. Besides the extra amount of time spent on the court, they have other adjustments to make, too, such as getting used to traveling to play, battling teammates for playing time, and playing against more advanced competition. You can do your part to ease the transition by helping prevent burnout and involving every player on the team — not just the superstars. The following sections are here to show you the way.

Avoiding burnout

Some travel team seasons stretch on for several months, which increases the chance of players suffering burnout. *Burnout* occurs when a player grows tired of the game, and it typically involves a combination of physical and emotional exhaustion. When you subject young kids to a heavy practice and game schedule that they aren't accustomed to, they're susceptible to burnout, no matter how much they love the game.

Here are some tips to consider to keep your travel team fresh and energized:

- ✔ **Spice up your practices.** The more variety you introduce into your practices, the less likely the kids are to become drained from participating. (See Chapter 6 for more practice tips you can use for any type of team.)

- ✔ **Downplay the importance of winning.** The pressure to win can be a heavy burden on a travel team; eventually, it can sap your kids' energy and cripple their enthusiasm — major signs of burnout. Even though the travel team is a more competitive level of play, don't lose sight of the fun factor. When you put the emphasis on fun and team improvement and then winning, kids will be more likely to perform and stay interested. Keep statistics — such as hustle plays or free-throw percentage — that you can show the kids to let them know they're improving in different areas of the game.

- ✔ **Know when to cut down the court time.** If you know you're going to play a lot of games in a short time span, ease back on the practice schedule leading up to those games.

If you notice that a player seems burned out, have a private chat with him to see if there's anything you can do to re-energize his enthusiasm for the game. Keep in mind that if he's burning out, other players may be, too. You may need to scale back the schedule a bit to give the players more breaks so they come to the court refreshed.

Keeping everyone involved

Even though you need to give the bulk of the playing time to the best players at this level, you can't forget that every child — whether she's the team's leading scorer, best rebounder, or the least talented of the group — has an important role. After all, you handpicked each child to be on the team for a reason, right? Make sure all your players are fully aware of that, too.

Encourage each player to take an active role in all areas of the game, whether she's on the court or not. Your encouragement will enhance the player's experience and further instill that she's a valuable member of the team. For example, when players are on the bench during games, ask them to cheer on and support their teammates. Also, encourage them to monitor the action on the court closely.

Part VI
The Part of Tens

The 5th Wave   By Rich Tennant

"We covered the basics today—dribbling the ball, tying our shoelaces, and why I have hair growing out of my nose."

In this part . . .

You can get by on the Xs and Os and basics of coaching, but many dedicated volunteers are looking for more to make their seasons as fun and productive as possible. If you want to know what to say to your players before the game and how to remain realistic while working with your kids, this part is for you. You can incorporate these suggestions into your coaching or review them to ignite some ideas of your own.

Chapter 21

Ten (Or So) Things to Say to Your Team before the Game

*W*hat you say to your players before tip-off — and how you say it — can have a big impact on how they play the game. You want your players to be stress-free and excited for their day on the court. This chapter gives you the scoop on what to say to your team before a game to set the tone for a fun day of basketball. (For more on the game-day responsibilities you have, head to Chapter 7.)

One of the worst discussions you can have with kids before a game is talking about the opponent's win-loss record. Concentrating on records sends the unwanted signal that winning is the most important thing to you. Instead, try to steer conversations to other areas, such as those in this chapter.

Being Nervous Is a Good Thing

Adults get nervous before asking someone out on a date, making a presentation to the boss, going on a job interview, and so on, because they care about what will happen. Young basketball players — especially at the more advanced levels — experience jitters before a game because they want to do well, too (or maybe just don't want to be embarrassed).

Let your players know that having sweaty palms or butterflies in their stomachs is perfectly normal and actually preferred. Nervousness is a good sign that they care about the game. Tell them that even pros get nervous before games! Remind the kids to take a few deep breaths to calm their nerves and relax and simply focus on performing the basic skills well (see Chapters 9 and 10).

Win or Lose, I Support You All the Same

No matter if a child scores in double digits and your team wins or if he fails to sink a basket and you lose, he should always receive the same treatment from you: support and positive reinforcement. And the child should know before the game that he'll get this. Remind the kids that doing their best and having fun is what you value by taking some of the focus away from the game. Steer the focus of the pre-game meeting to areas of the game that are important but have nothing to do with the scoreboard. Topics such as how you're looking forward to watching the kids be good sports and how they'll hustle on every play and for every loose ball are ideal pre-game conversation pieces.

You can send a positive message to your own child (or ask the parents to do so) before he steps on the court by asking where he wants to go afterward — the arcade, the movies, out for some pizza, and so on. Make it clear that, win or lose, good performance or bad, your support will never waver.

Mistakes Are Okay

If you let your players know that even the best basketball players make mistakes and that you accept mistakes as part of the game, you'll enable them to take the court more relaxed. Chances are, they'll play more effectively because they won't fear failure or your reaction to it.

If you take your team (or child) on a field trip to see a basketball game or watch a game on television with your child, take advantage of the opportunity to point out professional (or at least advanced) miscues. Actually seeing them helps kids clearly understand that mistakes happen all the time at all levels of play. Make sure that you also point out how the player responds to his mistakes — using only good examples, of course! When kids see that older players don't hang their heads or pout, they become better equipped to move past their own miscues.

Be a Supportive Teammate

Kids who have the support of their coach and teammates will perform better on the court and will be more motivated to excel. Talk to your players about the roles they can play in setting a positive tone for the team. When players hear teammates applauding and see them giving high-fives, they'll be much more likely to adopt positive behaviors as well. This also keeps the kids on the bench into the game so that as soon as they step on the court, they're ready to play. Plus, having your starters provide encouragement for the reserves builds team cohesion.

With an older team, you can even confide in one player to deliver some positive reinforcement during pre-game warm-ups (see Chapter 7) to a teammate who's struggling. Sometimes, when a player hears uplifting comments from a teammate, he feels more at ease and draws extra motivation from the support. A talk from a teammate may have a bigger impact than a speech from you.

Be a Good Sport

Remind your players before the game about the importance of good sportsmanship. They should hold their heads up and be respectful whether the team wins or loses, or whether they have a great day or a sub-par day. If a child has one of those days where every shot she takes bounces off the rim, she'll be frustrated and may feel like venting. You don't want to see her pouting or using any type of profanity. Also, let your youngsters know that you want them to show respect toward opponents and officials.

During One of My Games, I . . .

By sharing some stories from your childhood basketball experiences, you help your kids remain calm, relaxed, and in the right frame of mind before the game begins. You can help a child see that she's just playing a game that she should enjoy. If you can laugh at yourself and joke about what happened during your playing days, a child can laugh with you, and she'll be less likely to take herself so seriously when she makes a turnover.

Talk about Your Pals on the Other Team

Ask your players if they know any of the kids on the other team. Doing so shifts the focus away from winning and losing and puts their minds on talking about their friends. If you're coaching an advanced-level team, you can also ask about the opponent's tendencies. Maybe some of your players are familiar with the opposition, and if they tend to drive to the basket or prefer to loft jump shots, for example. If you played the team earlier in the season, discuss the positive aspects of your team's play that day to help put them in a positive frame of mind.

I'm Excited to Watch You in Action

Kids want to play well to make their parents and coaches proud, so when you tell them that you have confidence in them and are eager to watch them perform, you give their self-esteem a big boost. Specifically, you can talk to players about skills they worked on in practice the past week and improved upon. Talk about how you're excited to see their work pay off in the game and exclaim that you're proud of their effort.

Tell Me What You're Looking Forward To

A great pre-game conversation piece is asking what the players are looking forward to most about the game. Be prepared, because you may be surprised by what tumbles out of their mouths! Maybe certain players are excited because their grandmas are coming to the game today; others may be eager about going over to a friend's house for a sleepover.

You should prepare yourself for the chance that a player may say something that sends out a warning signal. For example, a player may mention how good your opponent is. His comment may provide you with some insight about how the entire team is feeling. Utilize this information to ease not only the child's concerns, but also his teammates'. Make it a priority to defuse the tension and refocus your players on just doing their best and having fun, not on winning and losing.

Also, look back at your past comments, instructions, and discussions. Perhaps you instilled this thought in their heads by talking too much about winning and losing. Always be ready to evaluate your coaching style and make changes! (Head to Chapter 8 for more on changing your coaching style.)

Chapter 22

Ten Ways to Stay Realistic When Coaching Children

Amid all the excitement that surrounds coaching a youth basketball team, coaches can easily lose sight of what's best for the kids. Namely, that they should be having fun and learning skills in a safe and stress-free setting. Remaining levelheaded and maintaining realistic expectations for your players is important. When you achieve a balance in your coaching approach between having fun and striving to be competitive, your kids will learn the necessary skills and have an enjoyable experience. In this chapter, we present methods that you can rely on to help keep everything in perspective this season. (For more on crafting your coaching philosophy, head to Chapter 2.)

Step Back in Time

For some of you, many birthdays have elapsed since you last participated in youth basketball, or in any type of youth sports program for that matter. Still, do your best to shake off the cobwebs and reflect on your playing days. Think of what made stepping on the court fun for you. The things that put a smile on your face back then — being with friends, learning some cool skills, and playing for a fun and caring coach — should work just as well for your players today. Focus on these things and scale back the focus on winning, competing, and living for basketball.

Focus on Fun instead of Wins

If you focus on fun and making sure the players have plenty of it — and don't waver from this philosophy at any point — you'll oversee a season that your kids will remember fondly. If you get too caught up in wins and losses, you may forget what coaching kids is all about and begin adopting unrealistic expectations. Keep close track of your players' smiles and laughter, and forget about the number of games you win and lose.

Put Yourself in Their Small Shoes

When you're planning a practice (see Chapter 6), running a drill (see Chapters 11, 14, and 17), providing instruction, or giving feedback, remember your audience! Just because a child has a number on her jersey and maybe even a name on her back doesn't mean that she should be treated like a miniature professional.

These kids are playing a game. Put yourself in their size-4 shoes: How would you want to be treated by a coach? How much would you want to run? Practice? How many reps in that drill would you want to do? Interact with them accordingly.

Keep the Goals Reasonable

One of the most rewarding aspects of coaching a youth basketball team is seeing the kids learn and develop skills while achieving goals in the process — both personal and team-oriented. Of course, the key to making this happen is keeping the goals reasonable. If the goals you and the kids set are too far-fetched and unreachable, they'll set up the kids for a big dose of disappointment.

Use the first few practices of the season to gauge the kids' skills and abilities, and then set some short-term goals they can — excuse the pun — shoot for. (For more on goal setting, check out Chapter 8.)

Ditch the "Star Builder" Mindset

Your job should revolve around teaching the kids skills in a fun and safe environment, not helping them catch the eye of college or high school coaches. The problem is, you may encounter some parents who actually believe that's your job! (For more on dealing with parent problems, flip to Chapter 19.) Keep in mind that the youth program you're coaching in isn't a springboard to a college scholarship or the NBA; your role is to enhance the kids' skills and foster a love for the game.

Don't Arrive with Preconceived Ideas

When you take on the job of coaching a youth basketball team, don't come on the floor with any predetermined notions on the talent level of your squad. Begin the season with an open mind — much like a painter approaches a blank canvas — so you can keep everything in perspective. After you have the chance to evaluate the skill level of all your kids, you'll be able to plan practices that meet their needs (see Chapter 6). For more on evaluating your players, head to Chapter 5.

Poll Your Players

To help keep your practice sessions focused on the right things and to maintain happy attitudes throughout the year, have informal chats with the kids during your practices. Ask them questions to get a sense of what they're looking for out of their experience on your team. Hearing about desires and concerns directly from players helps ensure that you take care of their needs instead of focusing on your own.

The best time to chat with kids is before or after practices rather than on a typical game day, when they may be nervous. You can ask players what they would do to make practices more fun if they were the coach; what areas of the game they want to work on more; and if the season is everything they had hoped it would be (if not, ask a follow-up question to determine why not — and then plan on correcting the situation).

Don't Copy What You See on Television

Although watching professional and college basketball is fun because the players are highly skilled and the coaches are intense, you don't want to adopt any of the coaches' behaviors when you coach (and your players may not want to copy all the pro players' behaviors, either). Many college and professional coaches pace the sidelines, shout instructions, call plays, and dispute calls. Much of this behavior has no place in youth basketball.

A coach's job at a high level depends on how his or her team performs, so you can understand if he or she gets a little heated. You, on the other hand, don't need to apply that kind of pressure to the young kids you coach or to yourself. The kids didn't sign up to be yelled at or criticized. They're in the program to learn and have fun, and it's your job to fulfill those wishes.

Understand Your Motivations

Coaching youth basketball isn't about what you want out of the experience; it's strictly about what the youngsters want. A youth coach can lose sight of that after he or she becomes wrapped up in planning practices (see Chapter 6) and coaching in games (see Chapter 7). We hope you volunteered for all the right reasons — you want to help kids have fun learning and playing the game in a safe, pressure-free setting — and not because you want to win a shiny first-place trophy or coach your kid all the way to college.

Realize Kids Begin at Different Levels

The chances are pretty good that you'll see a wide disparity in the skill level of your players. You have to be ready to meet the needs of every youngster, whether a player is a great outside shooter or has difficulty getting the ball to the rim. During your practices, you can tweak drills — without the kids even being aware of it — to accommodate a variety of skill levels.

For example, if you're doing a shooting drill where you're passing the ball to each player before he shoots, you can make some minor adjustments based on each player's ability. For the highly-skilled player, you can make the pass a little more challenging to handle; for the lesser-skilled player, you can deliver an accurate pass that allows him to put all his focus on taking the shot. To meet the needs of every player, the smallest changes can make the biggest difference. (For more drills you can run during practice, refer to Chapters 11, 14, and 17.)

Index

NESS, CAREERS & PERSONAL FINANCE

0-7645-9847-3

0-7645-2431-3

Also available:

- Business Plans Kit For Dummies
  0-7645-9794-9
- Economics For Dummies
  0-7645-5726-2
- Grant Writing For Dummies
  0-7645-8416-2
- Home Buying For Dummies
  0-7645-5331-3
- Managing For Dummies
  0-7645-1771-6
- Marketing For Dummies
  0-7645-5600-2

- Personal Finance For Dummies
  0-7645-2590-5*
- Resumes For Dummies
  0-7645-5471-9
- Selling For Dummies
  0-7645-5363-1
- Six Sigma For Dummies
  0-7645-6798-5
- Small Business Kit For Dummies
  0-7645-5984-2
- Starting an eBay Business For Dummies
  0-7645-6924-4
- Your Dream Career For Dummies
  0-7645-9795-7

ME & BUSINESS COMPUTER BASICS

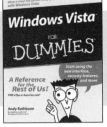

0-470-05432-8

0-471-75421-8

Also available:

- Cleaning Windows Vista For Dummies
  0-471-78293-9
- Excel 2007 For Dummies
  0-470-03737-7
- Mac OS X Tiger For Dummies
  0-7645-7675-5
- MacBook For Dummies
  0-470-04859-X
- Macs For Dummies
  0-470-04849-2
- Office 2007 For Dummies
  0-470-00923-3

- Outlook 2007 For Dummies
  0-470-03830-6
- PCs For Dummies
  0-7645-8958-X
- Salesforce.com For Dummies
  0-470-04893-X
- Upgrading & Fixing Laptops For Dummies
  0-7645-8959-8
- Word 2007 For Dummies
  0-470-03658-3
- Quicken 2007 For Dummies
  0-470-04600-7

D, HOME, GARDEN, HOBBIES, MUSIC & PETS

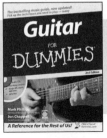

0-7645-8404-9

0-7645-9904-6

Also available:

- Candy Making For Dummies
  0-7645-9734-5
- Card Games For Dummies
  0-7645-9910-0
- Crocheting For Dummies
  0-7645-4151-X
- Dog Training For Dummies
  0-7645-8418-9
- Healthy Carb Cookbook For Dummies
  0-7645-8476-6
- Home Maintenance For Dummies
  0-7645-5215-5

- Horses For Dummies
  0-7645-9797-3
- Jewelry Making & Beading For Dummies
  0-7645-2571-9
- Orchids For Dummies
  0-7645-6759-4
- Puppies For Dummies
  0-7645-5255-4
- Rock Guitar For Dummies
  0-7645-5356-9
- Sewing For Dummies
  0-7645-6847-7
- Singing For Dummies
  0-7645-2475-5

ERNET & DIGITAL MEDIA

0-470-04529-9

0-470-04894-8

Also available:

- Blogging For Dummies
  0-471-77084-1
- Digital Photography For Dummies
  0-7645-9802-3
- Digital Photography All-in-One Desk Reference For Dummies
  0-470-03743-1
- Digital SLR Cameras and Photography For Dummies
  0-7645-9803-1
- eBay Business All-in-One Desk Reference For Dummies
  0-7645-8438-3
- HDTV For Dummies
  0-470-09673-X

- Home Entertainment PCs For Dummies
  0-470-05523-5
- MySpace For Dummies
  0-470-09529-6
- Search Engine Optimization For Dummies
  0-471-97998-8
- Skype For Dummies
  0-470-04891-3
- The Internet For Dummies
  0-7645-8996-2
- Wiring Your Digital Home For Dummies
  0-471-91830-X

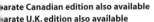

arate Canadian edition also available
arate U.K. edition also available

ble wherever books are sold. For more information or to order direct: U.S. customers visit www.dummies.com or call 1-877-762-2974.
ustomers visit www.wileyeurope.com or call 0800 243407. Canadian customers visit www.wiley.ca or call 1-800-567-4797.

SPORTS, FITNESS, PARENTING, RELIGION & SPIRITUALITY

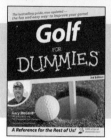

0-471-76871-5

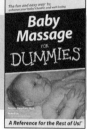

0-7645-7841-3

Also available:
- Catholicism For Dummies
  0-7645-5391-7
- Exercise Balls For Dummies
  0-7645-5623-1
- Fitness For Dummies
  0-7645-7851-0
- Football For Dummies
  0-7645-3936-1
- Judaism For Dummies
  0-7645-5299-6
- Potty Training For Dummies
  0-7645-5417-4
- Buddhism For Dummies
  0-7645-5359-3

- Pregnancy For Dummies
  0-7645-4483-7 †
- Ten Minute Tone-Ups For Dummi
  0-7645-7207-5
- NASCAR For Dummies
  0-7645-7681-X
- Religion For Dummies
  0-7645-5264-3
- Soccer For Dummies ·
  0-7645-5229-5
- Women in the Bible For Dummies
  0-7645-8475-8

TRAVEL

0-7645-7749-2

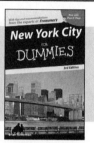

0-7645-6945-7

Also available:
- Alaska For Dummies
  0-7645-7746-8
- Cruise Vacations For Dummies
  0-7645-6941-4
- England For Dummies
  0-7645-4276-1
- Europe For Dummies
  0-7645-7529-5
- Germany For Dummies
  0-7645-7823-5
- Hawaii For Dummies
  0-7645-7402-7

- Italy For Dummies
  0-7645-7386-1
- Las Vegas For Dummies
  0-7645-7382-9
- London For Dummies
  0-7645-4277-X
- Paris For Dummies
  0-7645-7630-5
- RV Vacations For Dummies
  0-7645-4442-X
- Walt Disney World & Orlando
  For Dummies
  0-7645-9660-8

GRAPHICS, DESIGN & WEB DEVELOPMENT

0-7645-8815-X

0-7645-9571-7

Also available:
- 3D Game Animation For Dummies
  0-7645-8789-7
- AutoCAD 2006 For Dummies
  0-7645-8925-3
- Building a Web Site For Dummies
  0-7645-7144-3
- Creating Web Pages For Dummies
  0-470-08030-2
- Creating Web Pages All-in-One Desk
  Reference For Dummies
  0-7645-4345-8
- Dreamweaver 8 For Dummies
  0-7645-9649-7

- InDesign CS2 For Dummies
  0-7645-9572-5
- Macromedia Flash 8 For Dummies
  0-7645-9691-8
- Photoshop CS2 and Digital
  Photography For Dummies
  0-7645-9580-6
- Photoshop Elements 4 For Dumm
  0-471-77483-9
- Syndicating Web Sites with RSS Fe
  For Dummies
  0-7645-8848-6
- Yahoo! SiteBuilder For Dummies
  0-7645-9800-7

NETWORKING, SECURITY, PROGRAMMING & DATABASES

0-7645-7728-X

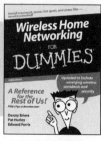

0-471-74940-0

Also available:
- Access 2007 For Dummies
  0-470-04612-0
- ASP.NET 2 For Dummies
  0-7645-7907-X
- C# 2005 For Dummies
  0-7645-9704-3
- Hacking For Dummies
  0-470-05235-X
- Hacking Wireless Networks
  For Dummies
  0-7645-9730-2
- Java For Dummies
  0-470-08716-1

- Microsoft SQL Server 2005 For Dum
  0-7645-7755-7
- Networking All-in-One Desk Refer
  For Dummies
  0-7645-9939-9
- Preventing Identity Theft For Dumm
  0-7645-7336-5
- Telecom For Dummies
  0-471-77085-X
- Visual Studio 2005 All-in-One Desk
  Reference For Dummies
  0-7645-9775-2
- XML For Dummies
  0-7645-8845-1